"The Target Is Destroyed"

"The Target Is Destroyed"

What Really Happened to Flight 007 and What America Knew About It

Seymour M. Hersh

VINTAGE BOOKS

A Division of Random House

NEW YORK

First Vintage Books Edition, September 1987

Copyright © 1986, 1987 by Seymour M. Hersh

All rights reserved under International and Pan-American
Copyright Conventions. Published in the United States
by Random House, Inc., New York, and simultaneously
in Canada by Random House of Canada Limited,
Toronto. Originally published, in hardcover,
by Random House, Inc., in 1986.

Library of Congress Cataloging-in-Publication Data
Hersh, Seymour M.
    "The target is destroyed."
    Includes index.
    1. Korean Air Lines Incident, 1983.
I. Title.
[E183.8.S65H46   1987]   909'.096454   87-40074
ISBN 0-394-75527-8 (pbk.)

Design by Robert Bull Design

Manufactured in the United States of America

10   9   8   7   6   5   4   3

*For Elizabeth,
Matthew, Melissa, and Joshua*

Contents

Preface to the Vintage Edition

In June 1986, three months before this book was scheduled to be published, William J. Casey, director of the Central Intelligence Agency, telephoned to warn me I faced criminal prosecution if the book contained intelligence data. He knew nothing "specific" about my investigation of the Korean Air Lines shootdown, Casey added, but wanted me to understand as a "matter of fairness" that he had been given to understand that the book contained secret SIGINT (signals intelligence) information. If so, he said, it would violate federal law, although he did not specify which law or how it could be invoked. There was nothing avuncular in his message—he and I had tangled in the past. "I'm apprising you," he continued, "that there is this damn law and we have to take it seriously. . . . We have to consider using the law under appropriate circumstances." Casey left me with the distinct impression that the Justice Department would fully investigate and prosecute me—unless I chose to make my manuscript available to his office for review prior to publication.

I've had dozens of mythical conversations with Casey since then, in which I've sternly told the CIA director that his telephone call to me was intimidating and obviously was meant to be, and as such was an outrageous and unwarranted interference in my First Amendment rights as a journalist. If the government chose, so my fantasy confrontation went, Casey and the Justice Department could prosecute—but not until publication. There could be no prior restraint without any showing of a threat to national security and Casey, by acknowledging that he did not know what was in my book, had not begun to meet that legal standard. He and the president had to understand, I imagined myself saying, that the First Amendment had yet to be rescinded, despite their best efforts.

In fact, the CIA director's call shook me up—I was at work that summer on other national security stories for the Washington bureau of the New York *Times*—and I said none of the above. What I did say, lamely, was that I thought he and the American government would be pleased with one basic finding of the book, that the Korean airliner was not a spy plane. Casey responded coldly that "our SIGINT capabilities are more important that any charges we sent a spy plane." He was absolutely correct, of course, and his tough-mindedness and confidence added to the threat. The head of the CIA was making no attempt to negotiate; he just assumed that he could telephone a senior Washington journalist and threaten him at will.

The National Security Agency, as I understood, has

been and continues to be a sacrosanct institution in America, one whose highly secret intelligence output is considered above reproach—and above political tampering. I already had been warned by friends in the intelligence community that Lieutenant General William E. Odom, the NSA director, had been angered by my two-year investigation into the shootdown and by the fact that I obviously had gotten some officials to talk. One senior Pentagon intelligence official and close Odom colleague had gone so far as to warn retired colleagues not to speak to me on the grounds that my my book posed a national security threat. That kind of activity was quickly reported to me and I understood it as old-fashioned hardball—standard operating procedure and part of the game as it's played in Washington. Casey's telephone call was an escalation.

A few months earlier Casey and Vice Admiral John M. Poindexter, the president's national security advisor, had similarly threatened to invoke federal law, citing a 1950 statute that makes it illegal to publish classified communications intelligence, in a largely successful attempt to limit reporting by the Washington *Post* and other newspapers into the case of Ronald Pelton, a former NSA official who subsequently was convicted of selling highly secret communications intelligence to the Soviet Union. And now the Reagan administration, apparently relying on the same statute, was suggesting that my as yet unpublished book was an appropriate subject for legal action. My Washington attorneys, Michael Nussbaum and Kate Martin, added to my fear by concluding, on the basis of Casey's

warning to me, that my office and home were subject
to a court-approved Federal Bureau of Investigation
search warrant. I spent half the night going through
files and removing any clues as to my sources inside the
American communications intelligence network. In
more than twenty years of often hard confrontation
with government authorities stemming from my reporting on national security subjects, I had never been
urged by my attorneys to anticipate a possible FBI
search of my files. Chilling doesn't begin to describe
my feelings as I read through my office files, realizing
that both I and those officials who spoke on a confidential basis to me would have been in big trouble if the
government had executed a search warrant and seized
my papers.

The anger did come, but not that first day—and
certainly not in my brief conversation with William
Casey. Like most citizens confronted with the power
of the federal government, my first instinct had been
to blink. It was suddenly much easier to understand
how men such as Casey, who have both a major Cabi-
net-level position and a personal relationship with the
president, can accumulate so much authority. Only an
exceptional State Department or Pentagon official
would dare to risk his career by opposing him. It had
happened very rarely, if at all.

Casey, at my suggestion, then relayed his concerns—and his threat—in telephone calls to Robert D.
Loomis, my editor, and Robert L. Bernstein, chairman
and chief executive officer of Random House. A similar call from Casey to Bob Woodward of the Washington *Post*, who was then at work on a book on the CIA,
also became known.

Loomis already had been mystified—and troubled—by a call a day or so before from a man identifying himself as an NSA employee, who requested a set of galleys, saying that the agency needed an advance copy before deciding whether to purchase copies of the book for its libraries. No one at the publishing house could recall a similar request (and reporters were subsequently unable to find the NSA employee at the telephone number he left). In the view of Random House, as explained by Loomis to Casey, *"The Target Is Destroyed"* contained no information that was obtained from classified government documents nor had any of the information provided to me explicitly been described by my sources as classified. Casey dismissed that view, telling Loomis that federal law says that *nothing* about communications intelligence may be published.

Appropriately, Loomis and Bernstein were concerned by the high-level attention and retained outside counsel to advise them on how best to proceed. There was inevitable tension between author and publisher. My fear was that Random House would back down and submit the manuscript for yet another legal review, delaying publication and perhaps leading to extensive revisions.

The most important aspect of the Flight 007 book, we understood, was its uncovering of the government's willingness to manipulate communications intelligence about the shootdown for short-range political purposes. I had done as much as I could, as Loomis and Bernstein knew, to protect the real secrets. My manuscript had been read earlier in the summer by five current and former American intelligence officers, including men in the NSA who had served at the time of the shootdown. These men, all known inside the intelligence community for their personal integrity, had made some recommendations for deletions that, in all cases save one, I acceded to. None of the deletions affected the basic events surrounding the shootdown. There was undoubtedly material that the government might claim was classified, but none of it—as my readers attested—would do anything to threaten ongoing NSA intelligence activities. And there always was the possibility, the kind of possibility that makes journalism so rewarding, that the book's main point—about the importance of untainted intelligence—could diminish the administration's insistence on distorting information to score propaganda points against the Soviet Union.

My confidence in the administration's handling of intelligence, and in the integrity of those at the top, including Casey, was so low that I would never have discussed any potential problems with any of the officials then running the various intelligence agencies. The situation had been different in previous administrations, going back to the Lyndon B. Johnson presidency, in which I had always known one or two key officials whose advice on what to print and not to print I could trust.

We rallied. There was no other option. A key factor, in retrospect, was Casey's misstatement of the law. The statute in question, which has yet to be tested in the courts, had been enacted in 1950, at the height of the Cold War, and explicitly bars the publication of classified data about communications intelligence. The legislation, however, says nothing about unclassified information. Random House subsequently made public Casey's telephone threats and Bernstein publicly criticized the CIA director, telling newsmen that "It is clear that the transparent approach by the NSA 'book buyer' and Mr. Casey's follow-up calls are linked. It is especially disturbing," Bernstein said, "that Mr. Casey, who is an attorney and head of one of the most powerful agencies in government, would call our editor and exaggerate the reach of the law that he said he must uphold. . . . I think it is unwise and even improper for the head of the CIA, or any other government official, to express concern about a manuscript that he has not read, particularly if the book involves the agency for which that official is responsible. The implication of such a call has to be that the official either wants to censor the book or ultimately stop it, and no law gives him the power to do that. Indeed, the Constitution forbids it. No responsible publisher or author wants to violate the law, but it is impossible to make the government an editor of a manuscript about the government.

"We find it difficult," Bernstein concluded, "to take this series of calls from the NSA and Casey as anything other than a desire to stop publication of this book."

The administration backed off. "*The Target Is Destroyed*" was published without incident in September, and the Administration chose to make no formal response to the book's assertion that communications intelligence had been manipulated by senior officials for anti-Soviet propaganda purposes. The NSA's General Odom was furious over the book and reportedly sought an investigation, but William Casey—as the subsequent Iran-*contra* scandal made clear—had other fish to fry. So did the Justice Department.

The publication of *"The Target Is Destroyed"* clearly diminished the zeal of those public interest groups that had been insisting Flight 007 was an American or South Korean spy plane deliberately sent over the Soviet Union. Most authorities now agree that something went wrong inside the cockpit of the airliner—precisely what will never be known—and it is the direct result of those unknown series of errors that endures as the most provocative aspect of the incident: the two superpowers, each relying on untruths, began a frightening war of words because an airliner got off course. There is a parallel between the Reagan administration's manipulation of the intelligence involving the shootdown and its attempt three years later to prevent a full account of those manipulations from being published: an essential lack of confidence and trust in the democratic system and the American way that ultimately led administration foreign-policy makers to secrecy, distortion, covert wars, and attempted censorship. William Casey acted in the Korean shootdown before all the facts were in; he was operating not as a sophisticated intelligence officer but as a political crony of a harshly anti-communist president. His approach in attempting to censor this book was consistent, telephoning me and my publisher and editor before having any knowledge of the book's contents. In the end, the Reagan men became, as did Richard Nixon and his colleagues a generation earlier, the victims of their policy. But if they failed to change the system, they came much closer than they should have.

—Seymour M. Hersh
May 1987

Introduction

This book began because of the courage of a senior military intelligence officer who, while being interviewed late in 1984 on the shootdown of Flight 007, decided to tell what he thought was the real story: the abuse of communications intelligence. Aided by that first account, I was able to locate others who had knowledge of the event through their work for the National Security Agency and in Air Force and Navy communications intelligence and found them willing to talk. Senior officials of the Japanese government also agreed to tell their story.

One of the inherent difficulties of interviewing such men and women is their nonexistence in the normal day-to-day world of journalism. Theirs is a world closed to outsiders, even to family members. Those who chose to talk to me did so out of a conviction that political abuse of communications intelligence has become a reality in the Reagan administration, and a belief that to protest to their superiors about it would be futile and damaging to their careers. Some of those interviewed did retire from intelligence service shortly after the events described in this book. In a few cases, the mishandling of Flight 007 played a role in their decision to get out.

I am aware that those who talked risked much. Many, despite more than twenty-five years of public service, had never spoken to a journalist before. Their act of faith in helping to tell this story is one that now has to be shared by the reader. This is a book whose key allegations hinge on unnamed sources. It is a book replete with mysterious "government officials" and "intelligence analysts." Where feasible, I have cited names and places. I have tried to be specific in as many ways as possible to make up for the lack of named sources, and I have also tried to verify and double-check information to the best of my ability. I only hope that I have done justice to those who put so much faith in me.

—Seymour M. Hersh
Washington, D.C.

BOOK I

The Scene

1

The First Shootdown

The multibillion-dollar American intelligence system had perhaps never worked better than it did on April 20, 1978.

Korean Air Lines Flight 902 from Paris to Seoul via the polar route had somehow become lost and was flying on a heading directly toward the Soviet Union, with ninety-seven passengers and a crew of thirteen aboard. The Soviet Air Defense Force was intently tracking the aircraft by radar and had been doing so for more than an hour. Its jet interceptors, always on alert, were scrambled as the airliner flew into Soviet airspace. Precisely what happened next is murky. One or two Soviet supersonic interceptors, Sukhoi SU-15s, known as Flagons to American military men, closely approached the aircraft, either did or did not make a warning signal, and then, with or without notice, one of them shot at the plane with missiles and cannon fire. A missile tore into the left wing and fuselage, crippling the craft, and after a perilous ninety-minute search for a landing place, its pilot, Kim Chang Kyu, heroically managed to guide the airliner safely to a frozen lake near the White Sea fishing port of Kem, some 280 miles south of Murmansk on the Barents Sea. Two passengers were killed by shrapnel and thirteen were injured, some seriously.

In its later analyses of the incident, American intelligence would have a stunning array of raw data. A new generation of satellites, known as KH-11s, which used not film but electronic impulses that could be instantly relayed to ground processing centers, produced a series of photographs of the crash site. There was a newly deployed intelligence satellite, codenamed Jumpseat, that was capable of loitering eight or more hours a day over the northern reaches of the Soviet Union, intercepting all kinds of communications, including the voice messages from the Soviet ground personnel up to the pilots tracking the errant airliner. Americans stationed at an Air Force intelligence unit at Chicksands, England, north of London, were able to monitor the Soviet Air Defense Force as it carefully tracked the unidentified aircraft.

America's intelligence allies were also heavily involved, as they always are in crises. Voice communications from the pilots down to ground controllers were intercepted by Norwegian operators at an American-built intelligence station at Vadsø, in the northeast corner of Norway. A second Norwegian collection site, at Barhauge, located even closer to the Soviet border than Vadsø, monitored an advanced Soviet data-link communications system that enables ground controllers to exercise enormous control over the fighters above. The Norwegian intercepts, codenamed Dikter, were instantly funneled to the headquarters of the Norwegian Intelligence Service near Oslo, and from there were relayed directly to the headquarters of the National Security Agency (NSA) at Fort Meade, Maryland, outside Washington, the agency charged with the collection, processing, and protection of communications intelligence for the United States. Norway obviously plays a crucial, if little-known, role in American front-line intelligence collection.*

Within minutes of the airliner's penetration into Soviet air space, the nervous chatter of the Soviet pilots and ground controllers was relayed from the secret collection sites above the Arctic Circle to American intelligence facilities in England, Scotland, West Germany, and West Berlin. The Norwegian intercepts were the first to provide evidence that something was wrong; an aircraft, initially identified as not hostile while far out in the Barents Sea, was suddenly a target. American officers and enlisted technicians began congregating at hidden monitoring stations—at Chicksands, England; Edzell, Scotland; Augsburg, West Germany; and Marienfelde and Teufelsberg in West Berlin—to eavesdrop as the drama unfolded; the phe-

---

* There are at least eleven intercept facilities located in Norway and targeted on the Soviet Union, a few of which were initially constructed by American intelligence agencies in the 1950s. The sites, now operated by the Norwegian Intelligence Service, are still being subsidized by the United States, for obvious reasons. Vadsø, for example, is close enough to the Soviet Union to intercept the ultra-high-frequency (UHF) communications from Soviet aircraft to ground stations. Vadsø has four antenna fields to help monitor the Soviets, including one with Yagi antennas at the summit of a 397-foot hill that played a direct role in this first Korean airliner crisis.

nomenon is known in the communications intelligence business as a live-environment situation. One fascinated group of Air Force officers gathered at the Tactical Fusion Center of the newly constructed NATO Command Center at Boerfink, West Germany, located in the rolling hills of German wine country sixty miles north of the French border. The officers on duty at the four-story underground command center listened as a Soviet interceptor pilot excitedly identified the aircraft as a civilian, with easily recognized KAL insignia on the tailfin. Nonetheless, the pilot was ordered to force it down.

The full extent of the American collection capability over the western, or European, portions of the Soviet Union is not known to the public or to the press. The forced landing of the Korean airliner was reported on front pages throughout the world, as were the passenger deaths and injuries. It was not immediately clear whether the plane had crash-landed, thus inflicting the casualties, or had been fired upon, as Zbigniew Brzezinski, President Carter's national security adviser, suggested the day after the incident to a group of newsmen in Washington. The world did not officially learn that the Soviet Union had shot down the airliner until reporters questioned the released passengers. Even then, much would remain a mystery.

What was known was that while flying over the northwest corner of Greenland, just minutes from Canadian airspace, the Boeing 707 began to turn away from its polar route to Anchorage, Alaska, where it was to be refueled, and flew 112 degrees to the southeast—directly toward the Soviet Union. Its experienced pilot and navigator, who had flown the polar route from Europe to Asia some one hundred times without incident, did not realize that they were more than one thousand miles off course until their craft was approached near the Soviet border by interceptors. It was early evening and visibility was good. Korean Air Flight 902 had backtracked, as reconstructed later, on a direct route over the Greenland Sea, the northeast tip of Norway, and the Barents Sea, penetrating the Soviet border near Murmansk. The Soviets would later report that they had begun tracking the airliner from radar located at Franz Josef Land, a group of Soviet islands seven hundred miles to the north.

Two days after the shootdown, a chartered American airliner was permitted to pick up the ninety-five surviving passengers and eleven of the crew members and fly them to safety—and a meeting with the Western press—in Helsinki. (The Soviets continued to hold the captain and his navigator.) There were contradictory accounts of what had taken place. Some passengers aboard the Korean airliner told newsmen that they had seen at least one Soviet interceptor following their plane for fifteen minutes before firing, but that they did not see it waggle its wings or flash lights, the international warning signals. Those accounts were widely circulated. Yet the copilot of flight 902, Cha Soon Do, who was released with the passengers, was said by the New York *Times* to have told official investigators that he had "seen an unspecified signal that he took to mean that the Soviet pilot wanted to speak to him." The Washington *Post* subsequently quoted the copilot as telling Western diplomats that he did see a Soviet fighter "make a sign which he took to be threatening." Nine days after the shootdown, Captain Kim and his navigator were released and flown to Copenhagen. They had been questioned most of that time by Soviet officials. Just before their release, Moscow formally acknowledged in a statement from Tass, the official Soviet news agency, that the civilian airliner had been shot down by its Air Defense Force, which is responsible for protecting Soviet borders. The SU-15 interceptor, Tass said, had fired only after the Korean pilot refused to respond to international signals calling on the airliner to follow the Soviet aircraft to a landing field. Captain Kim and his airline have remained silent on the incident since 1978.

It was not until five years later, in the aftermath of an investigation by the International Civil Aviation Organization (ICAO) into the Soviet shootdown of a second Korean airliner, Flight 007, that the Soviet Union finally released a statement by Captain Kim, dated April 22, 1978. In it, he acknowledged seeing the Soviet interceptor and understanding that he had blundered into Soviet territory. "I also realized that the fighter was signaling that I should make a landing as an intruder," the captain was quoted as saying. He added, according to the Soviet account, "I lost my head" and, instead of attempting to land, unsuccessfully sought to raise the Soviet aircraft by radio, an apparent impossibility since the interceptors operated on a different frequency. Captain Kim's statement was included in a report submitted by the Soviet Union to the ICAO investigating body. The Soviets further claimed in the report that the captain did more than merely ignore a signal to land; he turned his aircraft toward the Soviet-Finnish border, less than one hundred miles to the southwest.

American military analysts have attributed the Soviet reluctance to aggressively defend their action in shooting down Flight 902 to embarrassment; its Air Defense Force not only failed to stop the aircraft as soon as it crossed the border near Murmansk but also managed to lose track of it briefly over the Kola Peninsula. The area, south of Murmansk, is a stronghold of the Soviet's strategic nuclear missile force, closely guarded by air defense batteries, and off-limits to foreigners. Within minutes of entering Soviet airspace, the Korean airliner was overflying the headquarters of the Northern Fleet, stationed at the naval base of Severomorsk. It also overflew the navy bomber base at Malyavr and the huge radar and strategic bomber base at Olenegorsk in the middle of the Kola Peninsula. The SU-15 interceptors that had scrambled were forced to loiter, burning precious fuel, while the Air Defense Force tried to find its prey.

There was little doubt that the Korean Air crew's negligent navigation had contributed to the incident. The crew members, experienced as they were, had somehow failed to notice they were flying over a landmass and not over water. Nor had the crew noticed that the sun was to the east, off the aircraft's right side—the wrong side, as some passengers had nervously realized.

The Boeing 707 aircraft, which had gone into service in 1967, was equipped, as are all passenger airliners, with a number of basic navigational aids, including LORAN—none of it state-of-the-art, but more than adequate, if properly monitored, to keep the plane on course over the North Pole. LORAN, the acronym for long-range air navigation, is based on a series of transmitting stations scattered around the world whose signals are constantly available in the cockpit, enabling the flight crew to fix its position at any time. Since the earth is rotating roughly 15 degrees an hour on its axis at the North Pole, navigational aids must be constantly updated and verified to ensure that a course anywhere near the North Pole is correct. By 1978, many commercial airliners had already turned to the far more reliable Inertial Navigation System (INS), a by-product of the American space effort, whose self-contained gyroscopes are capable of keeping an aircraft on course with no outside verification or checking, even at the North Pole.

After the uneventful return of the surviving passengers, the shootdown quickly disappeared from public view. It was easy to overlook the five-paragraph item published on April 26 in the New York *Times* reporting that officials in Moscow had privately sought to explain to a few foreign correspondents why they had acted to stop the Korean aircraft's flight. The Soviets were quoted as explaining that their Air Defense Force had feared that the Korean airliner was an intelligence intruder seeking military information and, upon consultations with senior commanders in Moscow, had ordered the aircraft fired upon after it did not react to visual commands to land. The *Times* story, published on page fifteen, quoted American officials as describing the Soviet account as "plausible."

Flight 902's flight path—barging into the Soviet Union from the Barents Sea—eventually was determined by the Soviet Air Defense Force to be consistent with that of a highly classified American Rivet

Joint reconnaissance mission. Since the early 1960s, the Strategic Air Command, working in coordination with the National Security Agency, has been routinely operating spy flights on the edges of the Soviet Union, both in Europe and in the Far East, collecting communications and electronic intelligence. A standing mission of Rivet Joint is to probe the air defense facilities of the Soviet Union, trying to collect data on the three basic types of radars—search, height-finder, and fire-control—that drive the Soviet's highly sophisticated surface-to-air missile (SAM) and interceptor air defense systems. Rivet Joint missions are also routinely flown in the Middle East. The gray-and-white planes, known as RC-135s, are specially configured Boeing 707s with distinctive black noses and externally mounted antennas. They are capable of staying in the air for ten-hour stretches before needing to be refueled, and they provide American intelligence analysts with an invaluable capability to loiter near forbidden borders—such as the Soviet Union's—or in crisis areas.

The aircraft are an intrinsic part of a secret intelligence world whose operations are known to few outside the Pentagon. Since its inception, Rivet Joint and similar airborne programs have provided American intelligence with great flexibility; the aircraft could be ordered on short notice to speed to an area of international tension and simply fly about, collecting invaluable information. The aircraft also have standing mission requirements, flying regular routes—or "tracks"—focused on the collection of intelligence about the Soviet Union and its allies.

Rivet Joint missions have continued to thrive in the 1980s, averaging about seventy flights a month in

Western Europe and the Far East, despite increasingly sophisticated satellite intelligence and occasional complaints about their enormous cost. In 1985, the Strategic Air Command's eighteen RC-135s completed a six-year upgrading program that significantly expanded the aircraft's collection-and-processing capability; Rivet Joint flights are now able to collect short-range tactical signals intelligence on Soviet naval and ground forces.* It was this added ability that, presumably, convinced the military to begin flying Rivet Joint missions over Central America in support of government troops in El Salvador and the CIA-supported rebel Contras waging war against the Nicaraguan government. By mid-1984, according to an NSA official, there were twelve Rivet Joint flights a month, originating from Howard Air Base in Panama.

From Britain, Rivet Joint flights routinely patrol north into the Baltic and then head farther north to Norway on preplanned missions, taking care to stay in international airspace. Many flights proceed over the northeast tip of Norway to the Barents Sea, where the RC-135s fly looping paths—often figure eights—while constantly monitoring Soviet communications and radar facilities. Pilots of the Rivet Joint flights are under standing orders not to get within forty nautical miles of the Soviet Union's shoreline and generally loiter one hundred miles or more out over the Barents

---

* RC-135 operations have their headquarters at Offutt Air Force Base near Omaha, Nebraska, with forward operating bases at Kadena Air Base in Okinawa, Eielson Air Force Base in Alaska, Hellenikon Air Base near Athens, Greece, and at the Royal Air Force Base in Mildenhall, England.

Sea until they intercept something of interest, which draws them closer to increase their capability to collect signals. The missions are constantly monitored by Soviet aircraft as well as by the Soviets' radar tracking system. The Soviets, in turn, are watched watching the United States.*

Even with the advent of the improved Inertial Navigation Systems in the 1970s, all Rivet Joint aircraft are under standing orders to fly missions with two naviga-

---

* The Air Force officers and enlisted men who serve on the Rivet Joint missions inevitably share an esprit de corps. One widely cited adventure shared by the men who flew from Mildenhall to the Barents Sea in the late 1970s involved a new Soviet pilot who was assigned, as is Soviet policy, to routinely check out an American reconnaissance flight as it overflew the Baltic states en route to international waters off the Soviet Union. The American aircraft was capable of monitoring the transmissions between the Soviet interceptor pilot and his ground controller, and the men aboard quickly understood, as they overheard the pilot and his controller speak in formal sentences and not in quick bursts, that a new pilot was on duty. As the Soviet interceptor drew near the RC-135, the pilot was asked by his controller whether he could "see the target." The pilot responded positively and then, to the amusement of the men aboard the Boeing 707, reported that he was in contact with a B-52, the eight-engine attack bomber that is the backbone of America's strategic nuclear forces. "Say again," ordered the Soviet ground controller, clearly not impressed. "It's a B-52," insisted the new Soviet pilot. The pilot was instructed to count engines, an obvious solution to the controller's dilemma, since Boeing 707s have four. The pilot then proceeded to slowly count to eight. At this point, any amusement abruptly disappeared aboard the unarmed RC-135 intelligence plane. "The guys were freaking out listening to this," recalled one intelligence officer. The suddenly nerve-wracking crisis ended when the Soviet ground controller, obviously as distressed as were the men aboard the aircraft, ordered his pilot to take a photograph of the aircraft and return to base. The pilot, apparently reassigned, was never heard again.

tors, one operating with INS and the other maintaining the aircraft's position with the aid of LORAN and other navigation systems, including celestial charting. The two navigators are assigned to separate compartments aboard the aircraft and plot the plane's course independently. The goal, simply, is to avoid the inadvertent penetration of Soviet airspace and thus avoid any possibility of being forced or shot down. The seizure of a Rivet Joint flight would be an incalculable loss for American intelligence, for the monitoring equipment aboard the aircraft is operated by an elite and little-known signals intelligence unit of the Air Force, known as the Electronic Security Command (ESC), which reports directly on many intelligence matters to the National Security Agency. As a component of the Air Force, the ESC is responsible for supplying the men to work the sensitive monitoring equipment in the back of the RC-135s, as well as for operating twenty-three ground intelligence stations for the NSA throughout the world. The NSA, as the prime recipient of ESC intelligence, is also responsible for helping to decide what intelligence is to be sought on Rivet Joint missions.*

---

* Any military field commander can request a Rivet Joint reconnaissance mission to collect intelligence on a specific target, but the request must hurdle an intense bureaucratic process. Such flights are very expensive and very tightly controlled. Rivet Joint collection assignments are relayed from the military commands to the Defense Intelligence Agency (DIA), which in turn "validates" the requirements and forwards them to the SIGINT (for signals intelligence) Requirements Validation and Evaluation Subcommittee (whose acronym is SIRVES) of the Director of Central Intelligence's SIGINT Committee.

Eavesdropping on the conversations of the Soviet military was routine, therefore, to the men and women of the Air Force's Electronic Security Command. American intelligence later determined that the airliner's flight path, as it appeared on Soviet radar, must have approximated the normal track of a Rivet Joint reconnaissance mission on its approach toward the Soviet landmass. Some American officers concluded that the Soviet interceptor aircraft were slow to scramble, obviously because they did not anticipate that the plane, believed to be an RC-135, would actually penetrate Soviet airspace. None had done so since the RC-135 reconnaissance missions began in the early 1960s.* Another factor, of course, was the delay created when Soviet radar operators simply lost the track of the airliner.

Once airborne, the Soviet interceptors were closely monitored by ground controllers, who instruct the pilots on the most minute details—telling them, for example, where to turn and when to change altitude. In the early evening of April 20, the Soviet interceptors, following headings provided by their ground controllers, raced to cut off the Korean airliner. The Soviet rules of engagement in peacetime are not fully

---

* The Soviets are known to have shot down at least eleven American Air Force and Navy aircraft since the Cold War began, including the U-2 spy plane piloted by Francis Gary Powers of the CIA. Pentagon statistics indicate that at least ninety American airmen have been killed in the attacks, which the Soviets insist all took place in USSR airspace. The last such incident occurred on July 1, 1960, when Soviet fighters shot down an Air Force RB-47 reconnaissance aircraft near the Kola Peninsula off Murmansk, killing four crewmen.

understood by the American military, but they are not believed to call for an immediate attack, without warning, on any foreign intruder. Eight years earlier, for example, a Soviet interceptor safely forced down a chartered Seaboard World Airways DC-8 that they claimed had flown eighty to a hundred miles off course along the Kurile Islands in the Soviet Far East. Passengers, all American GIs heading for combat duty in South Vietnam, reported seeing a MiG-21 pilot fire two gun bursts in front of the aircraft and then motion with a thumb downward. The pilot, under contract to the U.S. Military Airlift Command, chose to follow the MiG-21 to a landing field on a nearby Soviet island. The aircraft and its military cargo were released without incident two days later. The American pilot subsequently told newsmen that the MiG pilot "opened fire not at us but to show us that we must obey orders, which we did immediately."

In other cases involving military intruders, however, the Soviet rules seem to have been less flexible. On April 2, 1976, in an incident that was not publicly reported but was nonetheless carefully analyzed by the Defense Intelligence Agency, a Soviet Su-15 fired an air-to-air missile without warning at a fully marked Japanese P-2V/Neptune maritime patrol plane that inadvertently penetrated a few miles into Soviet airspace near the Japan-USSR border south of Sakhalin Island. According to the DIA analysis of intercepted Soviet communications, it took twenty-eight minutes for the SU-15 to report to his ground controller that he had "visually sighted the target." The Soviet pilot was immediately ordered to attack the aircraft without warning, and fired two missiles. Both missed, and the unarmed Japanese intelligence plane was not damaged.

In 1978, the Americans at their intelligence sites throughout Western Europe overheard as one of the Soviet pilots racing to intercept the aircraft initially identified the intruder as a Boeing 747, the popular wide-bodied passenger airliner with a distinctive hump. At the time the aircraft reached Soviet airspace the interceptor pilot still seemed to understand that his target was not an RC-135 reconnaissance aircraft; nor, in fact, was there any evidence that the intruder was a military plane. He and his colleagues should then have had a different goal, following Soviet procedures in previous incidents involving nonhostile foreign intruders: to signal the aircraft's crew to follow them to a nearby military airfield. Only if the intruder disobeyed or ignored the signals would it be fired on.

The situation over the Kola Peninsula somehow soured, and Flight 902 was targeted for destruction. The interceptor pilot now identified the airliner not as the humpbacked 747 but as the smaller 707 (also manufactured by Boeing), whose frame is utilized by the Air Force for the Rivet Joint reconnaissance missions. "As soon as I heard it was identified as a 707," recalled an Air Force colonel stationed at Boerfink, "I knew they would shoot it down." An attempt to warn the airliner was not considered feasible by the Americans on duty at intelligence sites in Western Europe, for such warning could have alerted the Soviets to the extensive U.S.

intelligence capability in that part of the world. The Americans had no way of knowing that the Soviets were tracking a civilian airliner; nor could they suspect that the Soviets would consider any Boeing 707 operating off the Barents Sea to be an American intelligence plane. It further was known that none of the Air Force's RC-135s were on duty anywhere near Murmansk that evening. The colonel had the unforgettable experience of hearing himself proven right after the fact. The Soviet interceptor pilot was ordered to destroy the airliner and began to argue against doing so. He could see, he explained, KAL markings on the fintail; this was no military aircraft. His protestations lasted over a few minutes—a very long time when a military interceptor is tracking a jet aircraft. American officers, in later interviews, were able to reconstruct this dialogue:

> Controller: Do you see the target?
> Pilot: Roger. It's a civilian airliner.
> Controller: Destroy the target.
> Pilot: Did you understand me?
> Controller: Destroy the target!

The pilot then swore at his controller, asking again: "Do you understand what I told you?" A Soviet general took charge, asking the pilot, "Do you know who I am?" The pilot said yes, and the officer then repeated, "Force down that plane." Another Air Force intelligence officer remembered the exchange as "one of most dramatic things I'd heard in years." Most searing, he added, was the pilot's tone of voice: "I could see the guy shaking his head and saying 'We don't shoot down civilians.'"

The interceptor pilot finally fired a heat-seeking missile at the aircraft, but apparently failed with his first attempt. Some American analysts concluded that the missile had malfunctioned and glanced harmlessly off the plane's fuselage; other officials believe that the pilot was too close when he fired the missile and it did not detonate. The second detonated against the left side of the aircraft's fuselage.

In after-action reports, American intelligence concluded that the pilot's identification simply did not matter, because the senior Soviet Air Defense Force officials on the scene had already decided—irrationally—that the aircraft was an American reconnaissance plane. "The Soviets didn't believe him," the Air Force colonel said, "because they thought the marking had been painted on—a false marking." The Soviets have been known to shield their military transports by marking them as civilian. There was probably a second, more primitive, reason for ordering the destruction of the plane, the officer added: the assumption that "it just can't possibly be a goddamned civilian airliner." His own conclusion, he said, is that the Soviet military were not convinced otherwise "until they went out on the ice and saw the airliner."

The American intelligence community knew immediately that it had performed remarkably well in its reporting of the incident. A closed-door Central Intelligence Agency briefing was scheduled later that spring for the members and staff aides of the Senate Intelligence Committee. It was a moment of triumph. "They bragged about it—how much they knew," one of those briefed recalled. The committee was told that the conversations between the interceptor pilot and his ground controllers had been recorded and transcribed on a minute-by-minute basis; it was told how the pilot resisted the order to destroy the aircraft after reporting that it was civilian. Taped excerpts from the pilot's argument were played for the committee, with simultaneous translations projected by slides on a screen. The agency's briefing left the impression, one participant recalled, that it "was Soviet policy to shoot it down—even after being advised that it was a civilian airliner."

But the briefers did not dwell on an essential fact—that the United States had been routinely flying sensitive reconnaissance missions over the Barents Sea and other areas overflown by the Korean airliner before it penetrated Soviet airspace. The committee further was not told of the intelligence community's conclusion that the Soviet Air Defense Force had considered Flight 902 to be an American spy plane.

Only a few in the American intelligence community would understand the link between the Rivet Joint operations and what seemed to be Soviet ruthlessness, at worst, or incompetence, at best, in the 1978 shootdown of the Korean airliner. Neither the United States nor the Soviet Union, each for its own reason, was eager to talk publicly about what had happened over Murmansk.* The United States was protecting its sources of intelligence and the Soviets were shielding their embarrassment at having performed so poorly in such a vital area of national defense.

Within a year, the Soviet General Staff initiated a major reorganization of its military structure; eventually three theater commands would be set up and each given more authority to take military action. The goal, obviously, of all the streamlining was to improve crisis control and shorten the time between the initial sighting of a target and an order to fire. The Air Defense Force survived as a separate command.

---

* Zbigniew Brzezinski distressed the intelligence community one day after the shootdown by telling a group of journalists during a background meeting in the White House that the United States knew of the Soviet attack on the airliner from secret intercepts of Soviet communications. White House aides quickly covered up the gaffe, publicly explaining that Brzezinski, in his mention of the Soviet attack, was referring only to a Japanese news agency report. NSA officials were outraged at the time, largely because it was felt that Brzezinski's statement had embarrassed the Norwegians and other allies and jeopardized their facilities.

2

A Fleet Exercise

In the early spring of 1983, Ronald Reagan, after many months of relative restraint, condemned the Soviets as an "evil empire" and challenged the legitimacy of the Soviet government, as he had done soon after taking office. The president's renewed attack came on March 8 at the annual convention of the National Association of Evangelicals in Orlando, Florida. He urged his deeply religious and conservative audience to "pray for the salvation of all of those who live in that totalitarian darkness," and then depicted the Soviet leadership as "the focus of evil in the modern world. . . . I believe that communism is another sad, bizarre chapter in human history whose last pages even now are being written."

Eight days later the Los Angeles *Times* reported on page one that the administration had promulgated a National Security Decision Directive declaring that a change in Soviet internal policies was now a primary goal. "By squeezing the Soviet Union with economic pressure," the article said, "the Administration wants to reduce the overall resources available to the Kremlin, forcing it to make tougher choices between military and civilian spending." The newspaper said that this was the first time since the height of the Cold War and the presidency of Harry S. Truman that an American government had adopted a policy calling for internal changes inside the USSR.

On March 23, the president continued his anti-Soviet campaign by proclaiming in a surprise announcement his commitment to what would become known as the Strategic Defense Initiative, or Star Wars. He described his program, which called for the development of an antimissile system based on land and in outer space, as holding "the promise of changing the course of human history." Over the next three years, Star Wars would be much criticized by some but adamantly supported by the president, and it would come to dominate strategic arms control negotiations between the two superpowers.

Thousands of miles away from the White House press corps and the presidential talk of "evil empire," the United States Pacific Fleet was beginning its largest maneuvers since World War II in the North Pacific. During the three-week exercise, Navy warplanes from the aircraft carriers *Midway* and *Enterprise* directly overflew Soviet military installations on the Kurile Islands, just north of Japan.

Little newspaper attention was paid that spring to America's aggressive patrolling and revitalized military presence in the Far East. The Navy's show of force was but another aspect of its "forward strategy" policy, initially enunciated in 1981 by Secretary of the Navy John Lehman, which called for aircraft carriers to move into "high-threat areas" near the Soviet Union. American warships were authorized by the president late in March to operate and exercise closer to Soviet borders than ever before. Three aircraft carrier battle groups, part of a forty-ship armada accompanied by Air Force B-52 bombers, specially equipped Advanced Warning aircraft (AWACs), and F-15 fighters, sailed defiantly in the icy waters off Alaska's Aleutian Islands, 450 miles from the Soviet Union's Kamchatka Peninsula. American attack submarines and antisubmarine aircraft began operating for the first time inside the normal patrol area of the Soviet submarine fleet. In all, 23,000 American military men took part. Twenty years before, such activities would have had a good chance of going unnoticed by Moscow for days, but the Soviet Union's intelligence system has been steadily modernized, to the point where, by 1983, as one expert later said, "They know we're there."

That, in fact, was one of the basic purposes of such exercises, so the Navy's most senior admiral subsequently explained to Congress: to show the Soviets who is boss. "We talk about defensive," Admiral James D. Watkins, chief of naval operations, acknowledged to the Senate Armed Services Committee in 1984 testimony, "but that is the national posture. Our feeling is that an aggressive defense, if you will, characterized by forward movement, early deployment of forces, aggressiveness on the part of our ships, is the greatest deterrent that we can have. And the Soviets really understand that. We can get their attention with that concept. . . . We can make a difference. Kamchatka is a difficult peninsula. They have no railroads to it. They have to resupply it by air. It is a very important spot for them, and they are as naked as a jaybird there, and they know it."

The Senate was not informed, however, about another bit of American aggressiveness during the fleet exercise. One night in early April, the *Midway*, after shutting off all electronic equipment whose emissions could be monitored by the Soviets, slipped away from the flotilla and steamed south toward the Kuriles. The Soviets did not track it. "When he [the *Midway*] popped up southeast of Kamchatka," one Navy intelligence officer recalled, "they were clearly surprised." The *Midway*'s next act surprised not only the Soviets but also the senior commanders of the U.S. Pacific Fleet. On April 4, a group of at least six Navy planes from the *Midway* and the *Enterprise* violated Soviet borders by overflying the island of Zeleny in the Kurile archipelago. It was a flagrant and yet almost inevitable error, triggered by the aggressive fleet exercise and the demand of senior officers for secret maneuvers and surprise activities. The Navy subsequently suggested to the State Department that the overflight was an accident—the result of shockingly poor navigation, which enraged, among others, Admiral S. R. Foley, Jr., commander in chief of the Pacific Fleet at Pearl Harbor. Nonetheless, the Navy never publicly acknowledged either the overflight or its error; it also chose to say nothing further inside the government.

The incident inevitably was viewed by the Kremlin

as highly provocative and an explicit challenge to Soviet sovereignty over the heavily fortified Kurile Islands. That sovereignty has been vigorously disputed by Japan since the end of World War II; Soviet sensitivity about the issue, as in all of its territorial disputes, was acute. Within twenty-four hours, Soviet aircraft responded with a direct overflight of American territory in the Aleutian Islands; there was no doubt in the U.S. government that the Soviet overflights were, as one State Department official put it, "clear retaliation." On April 6, a formal diplomatic note of protest, known as a demarche, was delivered to the American embassy in Moscow. The Soviets accused the American planes of flying twenty miles into Soviet airspace and staying in the area for "up to seven minutes each time. . . . [T]he said actions were obviously of a deliberate character."

There were American officials assigned to the Far East who also concluded that the Navy's actions over Zeleny had been intentional. They learned of the Soviet complaint through State Department channels and, with the Navy saying nothing, drew their own conclusions. One senior American diplomat, on duty in Tokyo in April 1983, remained convinced two years later that the Navy simply had been purposefully provocative. He believed that the goal of the Navy in overflying Zeleny Island was, as he put it, "to get some response": to force the Soviets to respond by launching its newly deployed Backfire bombers in an effort to drive off the American carriers.

The State Department did make what amounted to a halfhearted attempt to get to the bottom of the issue, but it was unable to compel the Navy to formally acknowledge its highly embarrassing error, and the United States chose simply to finesse the potential diplomatic imbroglio. Washington's overriding priority was not to try to explain away what the Soviets clearly viewed as a provocation, but to protect its diplomatic turf. Telling the Soviet Union that American warplanes had erred in overflying Zeleny Island was seen as explicitly recognizing the Soviet right to fly its flag there, a step that would enrage the Japanese. Because of that consideration, one involved State Department official acknowledged, "We never got an answer [from the Navy] and we didn't want to know. It could have been either one—a deliberate or accidental overflight. We wanted to stay away from the sovereignty issue."

There was no undue concern about diplomatic delicacy on the Soviet Union's part when it came to a dispute over sovereignty in the Kuriles: within hours of the overflight, the Soviet Air Defense Force in the Far East were put on alert. They would stay that way through much of the spring and summer. The stakes, already high, had become higher.

The Kuriles loom prominently in modern Soviet military planning. The islands, all controlled by the Soviet Union, stretch northeast from Hokkaido, Japan's northernmost island, to the Kamchatka Peninsula, thus providing a protective barrier for Soviet shipping and submarines. Only one of the three major Soviet naval bases in the Far East, at Petropavlovsk on Kamchatka, has direct access to open seas, and even that port's utility is limited: it is far to the north, away from any significant Soviet economic activity, and is iced-in much of the year. Without control of the Kuriles, the Soviet naval bases at Vladivostok on the Sea of Japan and at Sovetzkaya Gavan on the Tatar Strait would be left with only three routes to the sea, all of which are guarded by foreign bases: the Tsushima Strait between South Korea and Honshu, the main island of Japan; the Tsugaru Strait between Honshu and Hokkaido; and the La Pérouse Strait between Hokkaido and Soviet-held Sakhalin Island just to the north. In a crisis, Reagan administration policy calls for the U.S. Pacific Fleet to close off all three narrow channels of water, bottling up the Soviet fleet.

The Kuriles had been Japanese territory from 1875 until the end of World War II, when the Soviet Union, taking advantage of Japan's defeat, occupied the archipelago, with no objections from the United States. The southernmost islands, including Zeleny, known today in Japan as the "northern territories," have emerged as a chronic source of difficulty between Moscow and Tokyo and have prevented the signing of a postwar peace treaty between the two nations. In 1952, the Truman administration formally sided with Japan on the sovereignty issue, and the dispute between Moscow and Washington over the Kuriles has remained intense, if little publicized.

Washington's support for the renewed ties between Japan and China, which resulted in a Tokyo-Peking peace-and-friendship treaty in 1978, did little to reassure the Soviets. President Jimmy Carter's meeting in Tokyo two years later with the Chinese chairman, Hua Guofeng, was viewed by Moscow as an American attempt to unite Japan, China, and the United States in an alliance against Soviet interests in the Far East. By 1981, Moscow was responding to what it claimed was a unified Japanese-Chinese-American threat to its strategic access to the open sea by reaffirming publicly that the Kuriles would always remain Soviet territory and continuing to build up its military forces there. Late in 1981, Moscow also made a diplomatic protest to Washington about what it said was United States–inspired Japanese "militarism" and the continued U.S. support for Japan's claim to the Kurile Islands. The United States rejected the Soviet complaint as "outlandish."

The unyielding Soviet attitude toward the Kuriles has been counterproductive in Japan, where there is renewed anger over the sovereignty issue and the increased militarization of the islands. The Japanese have accused the Soviets of using the renewed diplomatic contact between Japan and China to justify their increased military activities in the Kuriles. The Soviet goal, the Japanese insist, is to strengthen the Kuriles as part of what one Foreign Ministry official called "a reevaluation of Far Eastern strategy" that hinged on maintaining direct access to the North Pacific. In Japan's view, the Soviets made their basic strategic decisions in 1976, before the Japanese-Chinese rapprochement, and began upgrading fighter squadrons and ground units on the Kurile Islands the next year. In early 1983, as the Navy began its renewed fleet exercises in the Far East, American intelligence reported significant modernization of the facilities in the southern Kuriles. Airfield runways were being lengthened and more advanced Soviet fighter-bombers deployed.*

On April 29, more than three weeks after receipt of the Soviet demarche, Oleg M. Sokolov, a ranking diplomat at the Soviet embassy in Washington, was summoned to the State Department by Thomas W. Simons, Jr., director of the Office of Soviet Union Affairs. Simons presented the Soviet diplomat with a terse two-paragraph diplomatic note that, Simons acknowledged, amounted to a nonexplanation of the Navy overflight. It declared the Soviet demarche to be "inappropriate" and added: "The Department of State notes that the United States fully respects the requirements of international law and the safety of aircraft operations, and affirms that its policy is to avoid intrusions into Soviet airspace." Sokolov was also presented with a formal American protest over the Soviet retaliatory intrusions over the Aleutian Islands. One involved American diplomat recalled that there was an attempt to soften the blow by accompanying the

---

* Congressional testimony on the Soviet buildup in the Far East leaves little doubt that despite constant Washington talk of Soviet superiority, the Soviet Union's basic posture remains defensive. In 1982, in secret testimony (later declassified) to a House committee, analysts for the Defense Intelligence Agency cited the Soviet's difficulty of resupply to the Far East as a major vulnerability. Rail transportation, for example, they said, "is limited to a single line. . . ." Soviet airlift capability from the West to the Far East, the analysts added, "remains limited." The basic mission of the Soviet Army troops in the Far East, Congress was told in another classified briefing that year, continued to be the containment of China, and not offensive planning. Other DIA briefings depicted the Soviet Navy's mission as similarly defensive in nature, aimed at protecting the Pacific flank.

American protests with a smirk and a quizzical shrug. "We were trying to say, 'It won't happen again,'" the diplomat recalled. "I'm not sure Sokolov got the message."

Sokolov immediately called the State Department's response to his country's demarche unsatisfactory and raised what was the critical concern in Moscow: Was the United States, by overflying Soviet territory in the Kuriles, raising an issue there of territorial sovereignty? Was it raising the stakes in the Far East?

By midsummer of 1983, the Far East commanders of the Soviet military felt completely justified in having no illusions about the goal of the United States, with its renewed fleet exercises in the North Pacific: continued military supremacy. There was obvious suspicion—also felt to be fully justified—that the United States, with its tepid official response to the Navy's overflight of Zeleny Island, was considering a renewed public attack on Soviet sovereignty in the Kuriles. Such suspicions, although incorrect, were consistent with the Soviets' general sense of being in an exposed military position in the Far East. That feeling, after all, was the one America's military leaders, so they testified to Congress, were striving for. The Soviets may indeed have believed themselves to be, as Admiral Watkins put it, "as naked as a jaybird" in the Far East by the late summer of 1983.

These factors and these beliefs were all present on the night of August 31–September 1, 1983, when an off-course Korean airliner blundered into Soviet airspace off the Kamchatka Peninsula.

3

"They Had a Right to Live"

The Japanese fishermen were cheating in the early-morning hours of September 1, 1983. They had sailed in three boats from Japan into the waters north of Soviet-held Moneron Island thirty-five miles off the southwest coast of Sakhalin Island. All of the waters north of the island were claimed by the Soviets, at least in terms of fishing rights, and the Japanese knew it. But those waters also were the best in Asia for catching squid and shellfish, and the risk was worth it. They had done it many times before, with no problem.

Their profitable and illicit adventure was shattered this day, however, by a few moments of terror. It was an unusually dark morning, with the moon blocked by a thick layer of clouds. The men were busy hauling in their catch, using bright lights to attract the squid, when they felt the whoosh of an aircraft sailing just hundreds of feet above. They could see nothing at first, but the plane's passage was followed almost immediately by a rain of kerosene. They could hear no engine noise, nor did they see any running-lights. The obviously damaged aircraft seemed to be arcing to its left —as if the engines or wing on the left side was damaged. Seconds later they heard what seemed to be the sound of the airliner's engines coughing to life. The pilot seemed to be struggling for control. Almost instantly they could see the aircraft, which had moved to the southwest, burst into flames. They watched as the plane hit the water and exploded.

One of the fishermen was an inveterate diarist, and his kerosene-drenched notes later persuaded American investigators that they finally had some eyewitness evidence about the final resting-place of Korean Air Lines Flight 007. Unfortunately, the fisherman and his notes were not located until months after the shooting-down of Flight 007. By that time, the official U.S. Navy search for the airplane and its voice and flight recorders—the so-called black boxes—had ended. The Japanese fisherman and his colleagues had been too frightened of retribution for fishing in waters vigorously claimed by the Soviets to come forward earlier; they told their story only after being promised anonymity by a senior American Navy officer. The officer kept his word, and his report remains highly classified.

Flight 007, en route to Seoul with a refueling stop at Anchorage, Alaska, had departed New York's John F. Kennedy International Airport a few minutes after midnight local time on August 31, 1983, with 269 people aboard. There was the usual mix of passengers, some of whom had barely caught the flight or had changed plans at the last minute. Twenty-seven-year-old John Oldham, a recent graduate of Columbia Law

School, had delayed his flight a day to help a group of visiting Chinese scholars at Columbia find housing on New York's Upper West Side. Oldham, a specialist in Chinese law who had been a Fulbright Fellow, was headed to Peking for a year of study. Mrs. Rebecca Scruton, of Meriden, Connecticut, was en route to what would have been a tearful reunion with her parents in Seoul. It was the first such visit for the twenty-eight-year-old mother of two, whose children were left behind with close friends, since her husband had died of cancer the previous December. Mrs. Scruton, a Sunday school teacher, had been scheduled to make the trip three days earlier, but she had forgotten her passport and had not been allowed to board that flight. She almost missed the departure of Flight 007 on August 31, for her ride to the airport fell through and she was forced to take a limousine at the last minute. Others were on the plane for equally arbitrary reasons. There was a prominent ophthalmologist from Columbia University, Dr. Jong Jin Lim, fifty-one years old, going home with his brother to attend their mother's funeral. Twenty-three-year-old Edith Cruz of Chattanooga, Tennessee, and her uncle, Alfred Cruz, had scheduled a visit with her ailing grandmother in the Phillipines; by the time they boarded the airliner, they knew that the grandmother had died, but they had decided to fly to the funeral. Some boarded Flight 007 with the eagerness of typical tourists. Jessie Slaton was one of six women from the Detroit area who were embarking on a two-week sightseeing trip to the Far East. The seventy-five-year-old Slaton, a former common pleas court judge in Detroit, had been the first black secretary hired at Detroit's City Hall and, after attending law school, had worked her way up in a field that black women had not entered before in Detroit.

The flight to Anchorage was uneventful, as such flights invariably were, with the standardized meals and the usual mediocre movie. Only four passengers, an airline freight handler named John Sears and his wife and two children, disembarked at Anchorage International Airport. The Searses were home; for the others, the scheduled one-hour stop at Anchorage was a welcome break in the long trek to South Korea. There was a chance to stretch one's legs and window-shop in the airport transit lounge, Anchorage's largest shopping center. There was a chance, too, to mingle with the passengers of Korean Air Lines Flight 015— also bound for Seoul—a sister flight that originated in Los Angeles and made a refueling stop, along with Flight 007, every morning at Anchorage.

The passenger lists of both aircraft were especially noteworthy this morning because a number of prominent congressmen and senators were en route to Seoul to attend a commemoration of the signing thirty years earlier of the U.S.–South Korean mutual defense treaty. South Korea had emerged as a valued ally in the fight against communism; the six-member official delegation to Seoul represented not only the U.S. Congress but also America's Far Right. The passengers aboard Flight 015 included Republican senators Jesse Helms of North Carolina and Steven D. Symms of Idaho. Representative Larry P. McDonald, a Georgia Democrat and chairman of the John Birch Society, was aboard Flight 007. Senators Symms and Helms looked for their conservative colleague in the transit lounge, but the congressman was not to be found—he had remained, undoubtedly asleep, in the first-class cabin of his aircraft. Senator Helms, affable and courtly, struck up a conversation instead with an Australian couple from Flight 007, Neil and Carol Ann Grenfell, and their two lively daughters, Noelle Ann, five, and Stacey Marie, three. Grenfell was the marketing director for the Eastman Kodak Company in South Korea and was returning after a visit with his wife's parents in Rochester, New York.

Flight 007 had been scheduled to take off at 4:20 A.M. local time, but departure was postponed for forty minutes when it was learned that the prevailing head winds to Seoul would be lighter than usual. An on-time departure would bring the airliner into Kimpo International Airport in Seoul some thirty minutes before the airport and its customs services opened at six the next morning, September 1. (The airplane would cross the international dateline over the Pacific Ocean). Korean Air, eager to save fuel, like all airlines, routinely delayed departures from Anchorage if the head winds aloft were not strong.

The delayed departure made it easier for the ground personnel to complete their servicing. As Senator Helms chatted with the Grenfell family, Flight 007 was being tidied up for the next leg. Carpets were vacuumed, ashtrays emptied, and fresh linen was placed on the headrest of each passenger seat. Nearly 38,000 gallons of high-grade kerosene jet fuel was aboard, more than enough to fly the Boeing 747 to Seoul. There would be a new flight crew, led by Captain Chun Byung-in, for the Anchorage-to-Seoul leg of the trip. Captain Chun and his crew, who had flown to Anchorage the day before on a Korean Air cargo plane, were picked up at a nearby hostel eighty minutes before the rescheduled departure and were given a preflight briefing by the airline dispatcher. That briefing covered, as it always did, such routine matters as ramp position, departure time, weather, alternative airports, and details of the computerized flight plan. Three minor cockpit problems had been reported during the New York-to-Anchorage leg of Flight 007: a defect in the copilot's compass system, a damaged map-table spring, and a noise in the copilot's VHF (very high frequency) radio. The ground crew, after checking, reported that the radio system was operating normally and, following usual procedure, deferred repair of the other defects until arrival in Seoul. All else appeared normal, including the plane's weight and balance.

The passengers were summoned back to the airplane, filling two-thirds of the 374 seats. Larry McDonald was one of twelve passengers who had paid $3,588 for a round-trip ticket in the first-class cabin; also in the first-class cabin were six Korean Air crew members, including three captains, who were being ferried—per usual practice—back to Seoul for reassignment. The passengers were a diverse group, including seventy-five South Koreans, sixty-three Americans, twenty-three Taiwanese, twenty-eight Japanese, fifteen Filipinos, twelve Chinese from Hong Kong, ten Canadians, six Thais, and the Grenfells from Australia. Twenty-three were children under twelve.

The flight plan was similar to one flown by Flight 007 every day from Anchorage to Seoul: the airplane would take off on a westerly heading for fifty minutes, about 350 nautical miles,* until it overflew the fishing village of Bethel near the western tip of Alaska. It would then jog 7 degrees to the southwest to pick up an international flight route, known as R-20, the northernmost of five agreed-upon North Pacific (NOPAC) commercial air routes from Anchorage to the Far East, and fly on a direct heading to the Far East. R-20, like all NOPAC corridors, was fifty miles wide, and came within twenty miles of Soviet airspace along the Kamchatka Peninsula and the Kurile Islands. Despite its proximity to the USSR, it is considered by commercial pilots to be the most desirable route from Anchorage to the Far East because the winds there tend to be lighter. Once south of Soviet territory, the airplane would turn farther to the west and head directly across northern Japan to Seoul.

Within ten minutes of Flight 007's departure, however, it began to drift off course. The flight was six miles north of its scheduled course and two hundred miles west of Anchorage when it left Anchorage air traffic control's radar coverage twenty-eight minutes after takeoff. An American Air Force radar station routinely recorded the track of Flight 007 as it overflew the Bethel area thirty minutes later; the airplane was then twelve miles off course—a not-alarming deviation for radar observers. Flight 007 never arrived at R-20, its authorized flight path, but instead flew in-

---

* Air distances cited herein will be given in nautical miles. The nautical mile is 796 feet longer than the statute mile and is commonly used in air and sea navigation.

creasingly to the north of R-20, toward the Soviet Union.

All must have seemed normal, nonetheless, aboard the aircraft. Ninety minutes after takeoff and about seven hundred miles from Anchorage, Korean Air routine called for the stewardesses to change into their native dress: long skirts known as *chima* and flared blouses called *chogori*. Snacks and orange juice and sandwiches were served to tourist passengers (those in first class were provided with more elegant fare, including chicken florentine and zucchini au gratin), and then it would be time once again for another in-flight movie. The off-course airliner was headed directly toward the Kamchatka Peninsula, which, like all coastal areas of Russia, is heavily defended and clearly marked as off-limits on all aviation charts.

In another ninety minutes, as the passengers watched the movie or dozed, with cabin lights turned off and window shades down, Flight 007 flew into the range of Soviet radar; thirty minutes later it penetrated Soviet airspace north of the major port at Petropavlovsk on the Kamchatka Peninsula. Four interceptors were scrambled by the Soviet Air Defense Force but somehow failed to locate the airliner before it overflew Kamchatka and entered international airspace over the Sea of Okhotsk, the large body of water separating Kamchatka from the Soviet mainland. Flight 007, now more than two hundred miles off course and constantly moving away from R-20, flew over the Sea of Okhotsk for more than an hour, and its crew members continued to make what they thought were appropriate weather and position reports at the usual time to air traffic control officials in Anchorage and Tokyo. Those officials took no notice of the inappropriate weather reports—such reports are routine at best and, with that discrepancy unremarked, there was no reason for those officials to have any concern about the flight, and none did.

Six more Soviet MiG-23 and SU-15 interceptors were ordered into the air as Flight 007 neared Sakhalin Island. This time contact was made by a supersonic Soviet SU-15 interceptor, which closely tracked the airliner for more than twenty minutes. Seven minutes before the end, the copilot of Flight 007 requested permission to climb to 35,000 feet, a normal procedure in a routine flight—aircraft burn less fuel at higher altitude. There still was no sign that the crew members realized how far off course they were; nor was there any evidence that they realized that their airliner was being tracked by Soviet military planes. Flight 007's course, which had not varied since leaving Alaskan airspace, would bring it—if not interrupted—across Sakhalin Island, briefly into international airspace over the Sea of Japan, and then directly over the extensive Soviet military complex at Vladivostok. Five hours and twenty-six minutes after takeoff from Anchorage, at 3:26 A.M. Tokyo time, with Flight 007 only a minute or two from the Sea of Japan, the pilot of the SU-15 was ordered to destroy the aircraft. He fired two missiles, each loaded with seventy pounds of high explosive, and reported to ground control, "The target is destroyed." One heat-seeking missile is believed to have struck the passenger plane's left wing, destroying engines number one and two and triggering a fire. The second missile, which may have been radar-guided, perhaps homed in on the airliner's tail, ripping apart the auxiliary power unit and causing all of the pressurized air in the passenger compartment to rush into the tail. The sudden surge of pressure could have blown apart the airliner's tail structure and ruptured hydraulic, fuel, and electrical lines. Even if the crew could somehow have kept the airliner under control, using the remaining engines on the right side, it would have been only a few moments before the hydraulic fluid would pour out and the aircraft would be impossible to control. It took twelve minutes for Flight 007 to spiral its way to the waters north of Moneron Island and crash. When hit, the airliner was 365 nautical miles off course, to the north and west of its intended location on R-20.

The attack came at a time when passengers would be asleep, or trying to sleep; the last twelve minutes of flight could only have been agonizing. The cabin, whether directly hit or penetrated by missile fragments, would immediately lose air pressure and would begin turning cold; some passengers, still strapped into their seats, may have been killed outright by shrapnel or debris as others watched terror-stricken. Those who suffered the most would be the ones who survived the first moments. The cabin would fog as the drop in air density caused the water vapor in the air to precipitate immediately. Within seconds the airliner's air-conditioning units, reacting to the sudden drop in temperature, would begin pumping heat into the cabin. Many of the passengers, protected by blankets and breathing through oxygen masks, would have survived the initial missile impact—and the descent to the sea—knowing that they were going to their death. The

crew members in the cockpit would be equally helpless
as they vainly tried to cope with cabin decompression,
power failure, and the incipient collapse of many—if
not all—of the airplane's systems. Within seconds, the
plane began whirling down to the Sea of Japan. It
would be almost impossible to think clearly. The
crew's report to Tokyo air traffic control, the last
known message from Flight 007, was received forty-
eight seconds after the missile struck. Not surprisingly, the crew's indistinct message—some experts
believe they had put on their oxygen masks before
radioing—indicated no immediate awareness that the
aircraft had been struck by a military missile, but, as
reconstructed by Japanese Ministry of Transportation
officials, reported the loss of cabin pressure.* Japanese
officials also concluded that the crew members may
have further reported that they were going to descend
to 10,000 feet—a level at which passengers could sur-
vive without oxygen masks.

The crew members' behavior seems to have been
amazingly unconcerned throughout the errant flight.
Even after their aircraft was struck by a missile, their
first thought apparently was of a mechanical malfunction. Similarly, to get as far off course as they did, the
crew members must have had to ignore or rationalize

---

* The fact that the crew's first radio report dealt with loss of cabin
pressure and not the seemingly more crucial damage to the engines on the left side suggests to some crash experts that the
airliner was struck by a Soviet radar-guided missile in the tail
only, and not in the wing, as widely reported. The fact is that
no one outside the Soviet military knows where and how the
airliner was hit.

many obvious clues that something was wrong. Within ninety minutes of takeoff, for example, Flight 007 had flown out of radio contact with Anchorage air control and was forced to rely on Flight 015, traveling minutes behind on R-20, to relay the required weather data and position reports. Flight 007 crew members would report twice more to Anchorage via Flight 015 without any apparent second thoughts about their radio difficulty and its possible link to the correctness of their course; the problem, they undoubtedly thought, was with the radio equipment. The crew members made no attempt to shield their true position by reporting winds and temperatures that would have been appropriate to R-20. Instead, they accurately forwarded the much-different weather conditions along their errant flight path (while continuing to report as if they were routinely flying along R-20). And finally, in the minutes before being shot down, the copilot filed a routine air traffic control request for clearance to climb from 33,000 to 35,000 feet—a standard fuel-conservation measure. The airliner was overflying Sakhalin Island at the time, with a Soviet interceptor a few miles behind.

Flight 007 was reported within hours by Japanese air control officials as overdue and missing. Anxious family members and friends at Kimpo International Airport in Seoul and around the world endured hours of errant reports, wild rumors, and waiting. It was not until 10:45 A.M. Washington time, more than twenty hours after the shootdown, that a visibly angered Secretary of State George P. Shultz went on national television to announce that a Soviet pilot had shot down the airliner over Sakhalin Island, with the loss of all aboard.

The world joined in the American outrage, and over the next few weeks the destruction of Flight 007 became a symbol of all that was wrong with the political and military leadership of the Soviet Union. The U.S. and Japanese navies would spend September and October in a tense search for the remains of the airliner and its all-important black boxes, whose built-in electronic beepers were designed to operate for thirty days. They were never found.

Senator Jesse Helms, for once representing the view of most in the U.S. Congress, would emotionally tell the Senate upon his return from Seoul of his brief encounter with the young Grenfell daughters in the transit lounge at Anchorage: "If I live to be one thousand, I will never forget those little girls. They played on my lap, giggling and kissing my cheeks. And when they went to get on that plane they waved bye-bye and blew kisses at me. That's why I'll never forget those two little girls. They had a right to live."

BOOK II

The Intelligence

4

Cobra Ball I

Air Force men call Shemya the Rock, and for good reason: assignment to the tiny island in the far reaches of the Aleutians, 450 miles from Kamchatka Peninsula, is equated with a tour of duty on Alcatraz. There are few rocks, in fact, on the island, which is geologically little more than a nine-square-mile sandpit halfway between Anchorage and Tokyo containing barracks, a few operations buildings, an all-weather airstrip, and a vast antenna field. Shemya is bordered on the north by the Bering Sea and on the south by the Pacific Ocean; the result is seemingly constant high winds and overcast conditions.

The island became home to American B-29 bombers in the last year of World War II, and the base there has remained in operation since. It was converted in the early days of the Cold War into a secret military intelligence base, whose main target was the Soviet Far East. Until the mid-1970s, intelligence specialists rotated through lonely and demoralizing twelve-month tours, primarily monitoring Soviet Air Defense Force stations on the Kamchatka Peninsula, as the Soviets, using radar, tracked all airplane traffic—civilian and military—between Alaska and the Far East. The sole mission of the Soviet Air Defense Force, a separate arm of the military known in Russian as the Voiska Protivovozdushnoi Oborony (VPVO), is to protect the national borders. It is a vast network of interceptor aircraft, radar stations, and antiaircraft weaponry.

The Americans stationed at Shemya were primarily concerned with the electronics signals that emanated from the many radars and guidance systems of the Soviet Air Defense Force on Kamchatka. Radars, whether aboard aircraft, linked to antiaircraft missiles, or at ground stations, produce distinctive high-frequency electronic emanations, or impulses, that bounce off the ionosphere and can be intercepted at long range—often thousands of miles—and analyzed almost instantly. The ability to intercept and reproduce an actual radar image, however, as opposed to intercepting the emanation of a radar signal, is limited by the curvature of the earth to about two hundred miles. In the intelligence business, the limitation is known as line of sight. The electronic intelligence specialists at Shemya thus were too far from Kamchatka to actually see on their own radars what the Soviets were tracking, but they soon learned to differentiate the various emanations from Soviet radar and other defensive systems as easily as they could tell a Chevrolet from a Ford. A quick glance could tell an alert operator whether the signal originated from a radar aboard a Soviet interceptor or from a surface-to-air missile battery.

Such monitoring had been the core of America's strategic intelligence throughout the 1950s and well into the 1960s, when America's nuclear deterrent was in the hands of the B-47 and B-52 bombers operated by the Strategic Air Command. If America's nuclear bomber fleet should be ordered to attack the Soviet Union, or to respond to a Soviet first strike, the United States would need to know the location and capability of every Soviet radar and antiaircraft site to ensure that enough planes could get through. The credibility of America's nuclear deterrent depended on the information produced by the American signals intelligence services. It was in these years that American aircraft were repeatedly ordered to violate Soviet air space—in some cases getting shot down—in order to provoke the Soviets to turn on their radars and thus enable the specialists at Shemya and at similar units around the world to collect more data. By the 1960s, the United States had mapped every significant Soviet radar site and was constantly on the alert for new facilities.

For all of its importance, monitoring Soviet electronic emanations quickly became routine. Even the occasional Soviet air defense exercise—in which Soviet MiG interceptors scrambled to defend the homeland from a simulated American attack—became humdrum. Few of the Americans knew Russian; their job consisted solely of monitoring and recording electronics intelligence, known to them as ELINT. Being stationed in the Aleutians didn't help. There was little to do at Shemya when not on duty: bingo every Friday night, all-night bowling, movies, correspondence courses, and the inevitable drinking. Outdoor sports were impossible because of the high winds and cold. Married men were not allowed to bring their wives and children. The Air Force eventually refused enlisted personnel home leave or R-and-R in the middle of their tours of duty because the men simply would not come back. There was a general belief, prevalent into the 1980s, that those who were assigned to Shemya had somehow done something wrong to be sent there.*

In the early 1960s, with the development of land-based intercontinental ballistic missile (ICBM) systems, Shemya took on an additional importance. RC-135 reconnaissance aircraft of the Strategic Air Command were outfitted with high-resolution cameras and radar and began operating from Shemya to monitor the Soviet missile test programs. The highly classified operation is code-named Cobra Ball. The impact area for many of the Soviet warheads was on the Kamchatka Peninsula, an hour's flying time from Shemya; warheads also landed to the east in the North Pacific or to the west in the Sea of Okhotsk, the large

---

* Elwin T. Williamson, of Natick, Massachusetts, who monitored Soviet radar tracking in the late 1960s as an enlisted man at Shemya, recalled as a high point of his year there the forced landing of a Northwest Orient airliner. Its crew, including at least one stewardess, was entertained briefly at the officer's club. She was the only woman, Williamson said, he saw that year. The chair on which the stewardess sat was later auctioned off to the highest-paying enlisted man.

body of water between Kamchatka and the Soviet mainland.

Cobra Ball became an essential element in America's strategic intelligence over the years, and the need for the expensive and manpower-intensive monitoring of Soviet radar stations lessened with the advent of satellites. In the early 1970s, there was an inevitable reassessment of how much meaningful information was being obtained from the ground-based operations at Shemya, and in 1975 it was decided to shut down the Army and Air Force signals intelligence sites on the island. Intelligence planners concluded that Shemya's minute-by-minute monitoring of the Soviet air defense operations could be replaced by ferret satellites capable of overflying the Soviet Union every ninety or so minutes. At least two such satellites, code-named at one time Raquel and Farrah, were in operation by the late 1970s. Their mission was to record Soviet radar activity in Kamchatka and anywhere else in the Far East and relay it on command—every day or so—to an Air Force processing station in Hawaii. "There are eleven thousand radars in the air defense system of the Soviet Union," explained Air Force Lieutenant General Eugene F. Tighe III, who retired in 1981 as director of the Defense Intelligence Agency, "and we just couldn't possibly continue to monitor all of them. At one time we did, but no more. If they do a scramble up in Kamchatka, we let it go. It might be recorded statistically as an exercise, so we can report to Congress how many are going on. A big problem," General Tighe added, "is really that the United States is made to take on responsibility for monitoring the whole world. The Soviets are convinced we know everything."

By 1983, Shemya had not been an active ground-based intelligence collection station for eight years,* but Cobra Ball was continuing to fly—more than ever. At least ten missions a month were flown from Shemya that year, with the workload shared by the two RC-135 aircraft permanently on alert there. Each aircraft carries two sophisticated camera systems: a ballistic-framing camera that can photograph the reentry of a Soviet nuclear warhead on five-inch film, and a medium-resolution system that records the wake of the reentry vehicle, an essential factor in calibrating its size. Cobra Ball also carries computerized receivers for automatically intercepting, recording, and displaying the intelligence—dealing with such matters as speed, trajectory, and rate of fuel consumption—relayed by the ICBM and its reentry vehicle to Soviet ground stations. Such signals are known as telemetry intelligence, or TELINT, and provide further data about the warhead weight, guidance systems, and accuracy of Soviet missiles. Cobra Ball is capable, for

---

* The mistaken impression that the intelligence station was still operational at Shemya would lead to confusion in the days and weeks after the shootdown of Flight 007. Former Air Force and Army intelligence operatives, including Edwin Williamson, publicly recalled their year of monitoring Soviet radar as it tracked commercial and military air traffic across the North Pacific. Flight 007, newsmen were told, must have come to the attention of the American intelligence units there as soon as the Soviets began their monitoring, two and one-half hours before the plane was shot down.

instance, of photographing the number of warheads flung from each Soviet reentry vehicle and helping to determine whether the warheads could be directed to separate targets. The information is a critical factor in monitoring Soviet compliance with the SALT I and II agreements. The SALT II agreement sets limits on the size of missiles and launchers and the number of missiles equipped with multiple warheads each side can develop and deploy.

The two Cobra Ball aircraft are flown by pilots of the Strategic Air Command, and their electronic and optical gear is manned by an elite crew of at least eight highly trained specialists from the Electronic Security Command (ESC), the NSA's Air Force component.* And, like Rivet Joint, all Cobra Ball flights must include two navigators, only one of whom relies on the Inertial Navigation System, to avoid any possibility of misprogramming or malfunction that would lead the aircraft over Soviet territory.

The similarities end there. Rivet Joint operates as an airborne sensor system, sweeping up any available radar and communications intelligence in its patrols

---

* The NSA depends on all three branches of the Armed Forces to maintain and operate the scores of NSA-controlled intelligence collection sites around the world and at sea. The Navy's component service is known as the Naval Security Group (NSG), and its primary mission, obviously, is to monitor Soviet naval activity. The Army's Intelligence and Security Command (INSCOM) is responsible, among other tasks, for collecting tactical communications intelligence on the Soviet and Warsaw Pact ground forces. An estimated twenty thousand men and women—one-third of them in the military—work at NSA headquarters at Fort Meade.

around the world. Cobra Ball's electronic equipment is specifically designed for monitoring Soviet missile reentry vehicles, and it takes up enormous space, leaving only a limited capability for tracking other aircraft or monitoring communications. In essence, Cobra Ball flies blind. Even an aircraft the size of a 747 cannot be accurately tracked by the radar aboard Cobra Ball until it gets within ten miles.*

If Cobra Ball is a highly specialized hunter, it depends on others to flush its quarry. To make the system work, the intelligence community must know when the Soviet Union is preparing to launch a missile test, and it must know far enough in advance to alert the Cobra Ball crews. Such alerts, known as tip-offs, are the responsibility of the highly secret Defense Special Missile and Astronautics Center (DEFSMAC), operated at Fort Meade, Maryland, jointly by the National Security Agency and the Defense Intelligence Agency. The elaborate—and expensive—intelligence procedures are needed because the Soviet Union, with its huge landmass, is able to fire from Tyuratam and impact in Kamchatka more than seven thousand miles away without operating outside its borders. Under the provisions of the U.S.-USSR strategic arms agreements, tests of a single ICBM do not have to be reported in advance to the other side unless the missile

---

* A secondary function of the sensory equipment aboard Cobra Ball is protection: monitoring the airwaves for approaching Soviet interceptors or other signs of trouble. Interceptors have not been a significant threat to the intelligence plane, which generally operates much farther away from the coastline than Rivet Joint does.

will impact beyond national borders. The SALT agreements thus left the United States in a position of relying on special intelligence in an effort to learn when the Soviets were planning a test. The American goal was to have enough warning to be in position to monitor the Soviet missile from the first seconds of liftoff—known in the intelligence community as first burn—until its reentry, or final burn, whose monitoring was the mission of Cobra Ball.

American ICBM testing, on the other hand, involved the recovery of warheads in international waters of the Pacific Ocean, and therefore all U.S. tests must be made known to the Soviet Union in advance. American negotiators have not challenged that aspect of the SALT agreements.

Until the late 1970s, the negotiated imbalance in SALT was not considered to be a serious disadvantage, in part because the Soviet Union decided, "as a courtesy," one former Carter administration recalled, to tell the United States in advance of its single-missile tests. By the end of the Carter years, Cobra Ball flights were succeeding more than 80 percent of the time in tracking and photographing Soviet missiles. However, a number of factors have played havoc since then with the U.S. ability to follow the burn of Soviet missile tests, military intelligence officers report, while reaffirming the importance of the Cobra Ball missions. The most serious loss was in Iran, where the new revolutionary government that seized power in 1979 from the shah demanded that the United States abandon two covert communications intelligence outposts near the Soviet border. One of the CIA-run stations in the mountains of northeast Iran, known as Tacksman I directly overlooked the Soviet space center and ICBM launch facilities at Tyuratam, 650 miles to the north. Tacksman I gave American intelligence direct line of sight to Tyuratam, where the Soviets test their more advanced liquid-fueled missiles, and thus provided first-burn data on Soviet tests. CIA analysts at the site could also monitor otherwise inaccessible short-range communications, such as the countdowns prior to Soviet missile tests, and alert the already launched Cobra Ball flight that an ICBM was under way.

The NSA responded to the loss of Tacksman I by monitoring even more intently the signals emanating from Tyuratam; there was an obvious correlation between the flow of communications and the preparation for a test. The Soviets were asked for special help to enable the United States to get the much-desired early-burn data, but relations had soured by the end of the Carter years and the Soviets refused. In the early 1980s, moreover, the Soviets further began to encode the messages from the launch range to the missile recovery area in Kamchatka and also changed their method of operation; an increase in signals traffic between the test site and the Far East command no longer automatically ensured that a missile-firing was imminent. "Now," one intelligence official lamented in a 1985 interview, "we see a communications pattern that looks good and we go—and then they don't launch [a missile]. It's expensive to launch these birds [Cobra Ball flights], and our hit rate is not that great." Some estimates put the Cobra Ball success rate at less than 50 percent by the mid-1980s.

American intelligence was forced to buttress its satellite coverage of the Soviet test ranges and the areas, many in the Far East, where warheads and missiles impact. Beginning in the early 1980s, the American intelligence community noted that Soviet missile tests—from Tyuratam as well as from the solid-fuel test center at Plesetsk, five hundred miles southeast of Murmansk—were taking place on Wednesdays, or sometimes on Tuesdays, in specific weekly patterns. The timetable held from April through November. Its effect, whether intended or not, was to ensure that the United States had sufficient notice to coordinate its collection efforts at Plesetsk and thus realize that the Soviet rocket forces were doing no more than conducting a routine test.

Cobra Ball's mission on the night of August 31 seemed no different from the hundreds before; the alert process began—as it did on many previous flights—at a secret intercept site at Vardø, a few miles from the Soviet border in the far north of Norway. There, technicians from the Norwegian Intelligence Service picked up evidence of increased activity at Plesetsk, where the Soviets had been testing a new solid-fueled missile, the PL-5 (later designated the SS-25). The Norwegian report was quickly relayed to the DEFSMAC at Fort Meade, and officials there maneuvered a KH-11 photo-reconnaissance satellite to overfly the area. The satellite's photographs, which were relayed instantly to Washington, confirmed the evidence of PL-5 activity, and the standby crew of Cobra Ball at Shemya was alerted—by the dramatic blaring of a klaxon—to take to the air.

Its mission would be to fly northwest from Shemya

about three hundred miles toward Karaginskiy Island halfway up the Kamchatka Peninsula. The aircraft would station itself off the coast and begin loitering in a familiar pattern, slowly flying figure eights at an altitude of 29,000 feet or less, taking care to ensure that the loops closest to the Soviet Union were flown with the plane turning away from land. Prudent navigation is a necessity, because the Soviets, like all coastal nations, have established an arbitrary zone off their coasts, known as the Air Defense Identification Zone, or ADIZ, that cannot be entered without prior notification. Aircraft crossing the arbitrary boundary line without clearance trigger scrambling of interceptor planes for quick identification. The depth of the Soviet ADIZ off Kamchatka varies, but it is generally believed to extend at least sixty to one hundred miles from shore, and Cobra Ball's mission plan called for it to fly parallel to the coastline, taking care always to stay outside the Soviet defense zone. The Soviets have also established an Asian Coastal Buffer Zone that extends at least twenty-five miles from the coastline in the Far East; any aircraft without clearance inside that zone is under what is known as positive control—if it flies in there, it will be fired upon.

Since the Soviets carefully track Cobra Ball, the ground rules for the flights call for extraordinary caution. If in-flight refueling is needed, the tanker aircraft is to fly outside Soviet radar range. American intelligence officials have no desire to provoke the Soviets by having a Cobra Ball and its refueler operate in the same area inside radar range. The fact that both sides watch each other and know it inevitably leads to a war of nerves. American intelligence officials have told of being forced to pull Rivet Joint missions away from the Soviet coastline in the Far East as well as along the Baltic coast when it was discovered that Soviet radar operators were purposely mistracking the aircraft— reporting the RC-135s, for example, as being twenty-five miles from the Soviet coastline when in fact the planes were thirty-five miles away, well outside the Coastal Buffer Zone. The Soviets did so knowing that American intelligence was monitoring their tracking. In such cases, American officials are under standing rules to order to pull back an additional ten miles.

There is an advantage in such predictability, for the Soviet radars, known to NATO as Tall King, are not considered especially reliable in terms of differentiation—that is, the radar cannot provide accurate information as to the height and size of a distant object. Often, while waiting for a Soviet test to take place, a Cobra Ball mission will find itself circling in and out of the Soviet radar zone in its figure eights. Because of the U.S. planes' need to refuel and the occasionally erratic loops of Cobra Ball, Soviet radar operators have become accustomed to watching the American aircraft fly in and out of radar coverage.

The Soviet Union, for reasons not known, did not fire a missile on the night of August 31. Cobra Ball was told to come home early and did so. Men who have served aboard Cobra Ball missions recall that the usual procedure after being ordered to abort a mission is to turn for home, and do one final check of the various radio frequencies for signs of Soviet activity. If that's negative, it's "Miller Time"—the crew slips off the headsets and relaxes. The pilot and crew of the Cobra

Ball told Air Force intelligence officers in Washington twelve hours later that they heard and saw nothing as they flew out of the range of Soviet radar, heading back to Shemya, where they landed less than ten hours after takeoff, shortly after 2:00 A.M. Tokyo time, September 1.

There would have been much to monitor if Cobra Ball had been equipped with different electronics gear.

5

First Signals

The intelligence started to flow in bits and pieces three hours after Flight 007 left Alaska, as the off-course aircraft drifted into the range of Soviet radar on Kamchatka Peninsula. And for the next two and one-half hours, the men and women assigned to an Air Force communications intelligence unit in Alaska and a small, secret unit in northern Japan picked up fragments as the Soviet Air Defense system tracked and scrambled first over the Kamchatka Peninsula, then over the Sea of Okhotsk, and, finally, over Sakhalin Island. Those on duty in Japan listened, too, as a Soviet interceptor suddenly fired two missiles at the aircraft and announced at 3:26 A.M. Tokyo time, "The target is destroyed." The shoot-down was overheard as it happened—in real time. But it was not understood for what it was until hours after it was over, when it was too late to do anything.

The first Soviet signals were monitored, as soon as broadcast, by the long-range antenna of the 6981st

Electronic Security Group (ESG) assigned to Elmendorf Air Force Base near Anchorage, one of the Air Force's twenty-three NSA reporting units, or "floor stations," scattered around the world. The Air Force technicians assigned to monitor Soviet Air Defense systems eavesdropped as the Soviets declared an alert and began charting the progress of an unidentified airplane through the outer edges of Kamchatka's Air Defense Identification Zone, which, for radar tracking purposes, is laid out in a series of grids. The Soviet radar technicians reported the airplane's progress both in Morse code and by voice transmissions. Since no American intelligence flights were known to be there—Cobra Ball was flying its loops well to the southeast—Elmendorf's first guess was that the Soviets were taking advantage of the quiet of the overnight shift to break in a new radar operator or to work on tracking technique by simulating an American intrusion into their airspace. It was just another exercise.

The Soviets suddenly scrambled four aircraft. Although the interceptors were far out of U.S. radar range, the electronics intelligence operators at Elmendorf could "see" the aircraft without seeing them: they were skilled at picking up the distinctive electronic emanations of the interceptors' on-board radar systems. Suddenly, as one NSA official later noted, "There was a lot of action." The intercepted data could mean that the Soviet radar operators had tracked an unidentified aircraft until it entered the Air Defense Identification Zone, triggering a scramble. What were the Soviets doing in the middle of the night over Kamchatka? Moreover, they usually scrambled only two aircraft during an Air Defense exercise, and this time there were four.

Yet, as far as the Americans could tell, there was no contact between the Soviet interceptors and any other airplane in the area. There wasn't even any evidence available in Alaska that the Soviet aircraft actually had been chasing an intruder: the incident still had the markings of a routine exercise—in which the supposed intruder does not exist, although his simulated flight path is still carefully plotted.

According to the NSA's own after-action report on the shootdown, Elmendorf took no special action on the Soviet activity during the next seventy minutes, as Flight 007 escaped into international waters over the Sea of Okhotsk and flew again into the range of radar near Sakhalin Island. The watch officer in charge filed no reports—not even the lowest NSA alert message, known as a Klieg Light—either to NSA headquarters at Fort Meade or to the 6920th Electronic Security Group stationed at Misawa Air Base in Japan, the NSA's control station in the Pacific. (NSA would cite Elmendorf's failure to properly alert higher authorities as a factor—not the only one—in what was viewed as seriously flawed intelligence reporting on the shootdown.)

Elmendorf was not alone in intercepting, in real time, the signs of Soviet defense activity. A Russian linguist at work at the 6920th at Misawa itself, which is 360 miles north of Tokyo, also picked up Soviet chatter. The operator, an Air Force enlisted man, had been scanning the various voice frequencies known to be used for low-level internal communications by the

Soviet Air Defense Force and ran across the unusual early-morning activity more than a thousand miles away. Nothing much was made of his initial finding, either, although the key role in the next twelve hours would be played at Misawa.

Not all NSA floor stations operate with the same efficiency. The 6920th at Misawa, for example, is known inside the Air Force for its ability to aggressively look for and analyze signals intelligence. The 6981st at Elmendorf, which intercepted the first Soviet tracking of Flight 007, has a much different reputation. In the fall of 1983, the 6981st was considered by its sister ESC units in the Pacific to be a marginal operation whose raw intelligence reports had to be closely evaluated. Its ability to analyze and interpret high-quality signals was not considered good enough; too often the 6981st had confounded other floor stations by filing reports based on spurious or distorted signals. By the fall of 1983, many cost-conscious senior military intelligence men were looking at the 6981st as a site to close down. The number of officers and men assigned there had dwindled over the years, along with its status: assignment to Alaska was not a boost to one's career in Air Force intelligence.

Like other American military bases in Japan, Misawa is closed to the public; those who pass its gates must have military identification cards or be formally escorted. Even this level of protection is not enough for the men and women of the Air Force, Navy, and Army who, seemingly glued to their headphones, work around-the-clock shifts intently listening to Soviet signals intelligence, or SIGINT. The intelligence specialists operate in isolation at Misawa, four miles northwest of the main base in the small 6920th operations area nicknamed, as are similar NSA facilities in other bases, the Hill. Admission to the 6920th's operational world is tightly controlled. A top-secret clearance is only an entrée: those who contribute inside the community must be cleared for, among other things, Top Secret Umbra (TSU), a high level of communications intelligence, and perhaps have Special Activities Office (SAO) clearance, enabling them to have advance information on the specific orbits and trajectories of Soviet reconnaissance satellites. The 6920th is the dominant intelligence base in the Pacific and serves as the focal point for smaller collection sites and antenna fields in Japan and elsewhere. It receives and processes information relayed from the many U.S. satellites constantly passing overhead, from Navy vessels, including submarines, and from the various intelligence aircraft, such as the Rivet Joint missions, that constantly patrol the area.

There is no real attempt to hide the kind of work that goes on at the 6920th: the Hill's trademark is a huge antenna formally known as an AN/FLR 9 Circular Disposed Antenna Array (CDAA), and commonly called a flare 9 or the elephant cage—the latter after its ungainly physical appearance. The antenna, constructed in the mid-1960s, is circular, with a diameter of about 875 feet, delineated by four rings of reflector screens and awkward receiving arrays extending as high as 100 feet. The outside ring consists of 120 equally spaced antenna elements, one for each 3 degrees of azimuth. The flare 9 played a major role in collecting intelligence on the destruction of Flight 007, largely because of its ability to intercept signals from as far as thousands of miles away in any direction; under some atmospheric conditions, especially at night, flare 9 sites in the Pacific have been known to pick up signals from Western Europe.*

There were 930 Air Force enlisted personnel and officers assigned to the 6920th ESG as of July 1983, according to the unit's declassified history for that period, making it the largest Air Force collection site—or floor station—in the world. The Air Force is not alone on the Hill. More than 700 Navy men and women are assigned to Naval Security Group Activity (NSGA) to monitor Soviet shipping and the Soviet Navy. There is also a 200-man Army Intelligence and Security Command (INSCOM) field station on the Hill, targeted at Soviet Army and General Staff activity, as well as at Afghanistan. The Navy and Army share quarters with the 6920th but operate independently. The Navy, for example, did separate reporting to NSA's headquarters on the Soviet Navy's search-and-rescue efforts off Sakhalin Island after the shootdown of Korean Air Lines Flight 007. The three intelligence services at Misawa focus their primary attention on the

---

* There are only five flare 9 sites scattered among the Air Force Electronic Security Command intelligence collection sites. Three are in the Pacific—at Misawa, Elmendorf Air Force Base in Alaska, whose flare 9 picked up the first signs of the Soviet activity, and at Clark Air Base in the Philippines; and two in Europe, at San Vito dei Normanni Air Station, Italy, and at the Royal Air Force Base at Chicksands, England.

Soviet Union but are also responsible for monitoring North Korea and China, across the Sea of Japan.*

Men and women who have worked at Misawa and elsewhere are forbidden to write about or discuss what they do. Virtually nothing is known about the operating procedures of the Electronic Security Command or its sister units in the Navy and Army. There are, for example, no novels whose protagonists spend their duty hours at work inside an NSA field station. It is difficult for an outsider to comprehend the kind of work that is carried out at such facilities: technicians and linguists spending hour after tedious hour trying to isolate valid signals intelligence from the seemingly endless barrage of chatter in the airwaves; others are constantly hunched over oscilloscopes, looking for the distinctive electrical emanations of radar activity.

---

* Misawa is more than a focal point of American SIGINT collection in the Pacific; it has international responsibility. Under a series of highly secret agreements dating back to World War II and formally ratified in 1947 as the UK-USA Security Agreement, the United States is first party to a partnership for the collection and analysis of communications and electronic intelligence, with four second parties—Australia, Britain, Canada, and New Zealand. Information is to be pooled among the five nations, with shared responsibilities for collection under a protocol known as the SIGINT Combined Operating List (SCOL). The list calls on Canadian signals intelligence to be responsible for collection in the polar regions, with British signals intelligence to handle European sections of the USSR. Britain, which has a large monitoring station in Hong Kong, and Australia, which operates out of Singapore, are to share reporting on China, and the NSA—and through it, Misawa—is responsible for reporting on Soviet Asia and the rest of the Far East. Over the years, with the advent of advanced satellite intelligence, the SCOL has become less significant, but the UK-USA Security Agreement remains a staple of the allied SIGINT world.

Those who have worked at such facilities describe their jobs as nerve-wracking and crisis-oriented: as one former Air Force man put it, "days of boredom and seconds of terror." Hundreds of men and women, perhaps as many as three hundred, are on duty at Misawa in three shifts—day, swing and mid (overnight)—monitoring raw traffic primarily from the Soviet Union and China. They are the best the Air Force has to offer. More than 90 percent of the enlisted Air Force men and women with college degrees work for the Electronic Security Command; their IQs average in the top 10 percent of all Air Force personnel. To get to Misawa, or any of the other ESC floor stations, the men and women—there is a higher percentage of women in communications intelligence than in any other Air Force field—endure a minimum of eighteen months of intensive training in languages (including Russian and Chinese) and electronics, at a cost, so the Electronic Security Command has told its recruits, of more than $250,000 per person. Merely getting the high-level security clearances needed for the handling of NSA materials takes six to eight months and costs upward of $75,000 per investigation. Many ESC recruits commit themselves to six-year enlistments.

For all of its travails, the work is uniformly described as fascinating. Those in the ESC and similar units in the Navy and Army become the ultimate insiders. There are special units at Misawa capable of monitoring and decoding the diplomatic traffic of several nations in the Far East. The 6920th can also monitor the encoded and electronically encrypted messages from a Soviet satellite in outer space to a ground station, or the telephone conversation of a Soviet GI talking smut to his girlfriend. "That's how some of the ops [operators] used to get their kicks," one former NSA analyst said with a laugh, "listening to the sex lives of the Russians."* The Soviets, of course, do all they can to shield their significant messages and signals, by encoding them and then encrypting them electronically during transmission—that is, altering the pattern of the already encoded letters or rearranging their electronic sequence. There is much value, however, merely in recording the flow of encoded and encrypted traffic between two command centers; first-rate deductions can be made by NSA traffic analysts based on significant increases or decreases in the volume of signals.

Since an enormous amount can be learned even without knowing what is said, NSA analysts are trained to determine the means of transmission, who is talking to whom, what is going on in that part of the world at that time, and, most important, what has happened in the past when those two parties have talked to each other. Inevitably, the major emphasis at floor stations is not on cryptanalysis—the breaking of codes—but on isolating and locating signals intelligence for subsequent traffic analysis at the floor station.

Finding a signal is a complicated procedure. Mes-

---

* At one point in the 1950s, apparently before women were widely assigned to the military floor stations, the NSA published a working study guide to Russian swear words. The phrases had to be censored from the classified reports going to higher authorities because, it was explained then, there were women on duty at NSA headquarters at Fort Meade and in the English cryptological service, known as the Government Communications Headquarters (GCHQ).

sages can be sent by nonverbal means such as Morse code and teletype. The NSA operator—and his Soviet counterpart, of course—must not only locate the type of signal being used but also find its channel, or frequency, of communication. Before transmission, these signals can either be compressed into a "burst" message, electronically rearranged, or simply shrouded with extraneous noise. Voice communication also can be altered before transmission in such a manner that only a prearranged receiver can unravel—or unscramble—them, as in a secure telephone system. The message itself can be encrypted to make it difficult, if not impossible, to understand even if intercepted.

The sheer volume of messages that must be exchanged in large countries such as the Soviet Union and the United States means that most communications are machine-generated, and that machines, therefore, must be invented to intercept the other side's SIGINT. One Soviet system, in use more than twenty years ago, provides an insight into the complexities that are routine in a field station. The Soviet sending machine included one television channel, one channel of manual Morse, and five channels of teletypes, all relaying communications at the same time. The actual messages to be relayed were both scrambled and nonscrambled, and usually were not inserted into the system until the communication, replete with bogus messages, was nearly completed. Sometimes the actual message, when finally separated from nonessential signals, was converted to code before being relayed; on other occasions it was converted into code and then scrambled into unintelligible pieces—to be put together by the receiving unit. Such procedures provided a double means of protecting the integrity of the message.

NSA officials, in attempting to explain the setup of a floor station such as Misawa, invariably compare it to the workings of a newspaper. Analysts, usually enlisted men, who sit at computer-driven receivers and consoles monitoring communications and electronic impulses, are said to be equivalent to beat reporters. Their job is to find a signals intelligence event as it happens and, if they deem it important or interesting, tape-record it. When they do so, it is relayed to senior analysts, or section leaders, whose function is to sort out the routine information from that which is exceptional or potentially valuable for more detailed analysis and exploitation. The senior analysts serve as editors, constantly making judgments about what is news and what is not. Communication intercepts which seem to be especially interesting or significant are forwarded to the surveillance-and-warning (S&W) supervisor, the most senior analyst on duty, who usually is an experienced enlisted man, most likely a master sergeant. He is the man on the spot who must decide whether the reports collected thus far are important enough to be rushed to NSA headquarters, and whether the event itself has been established as fact—no watch supervisor wants to report an event that later turns out not to have taken place. The men who serve as surveillance-and-watch supervisors could be considered managing editors, whose job it is to shape the final news product and make the decisions. Final analysis of the information is left to the field station's Exploitation Management operation, directed by a daytime crew of more-senior and—presumably, but not always—

more-sophisticated analysts, who further refine the raw data. They are responsible for filing the station's long-range analyses and in-depth reports to NSA. Exploitation Management is also responsible for suggesting where the station's floor operators should concentrate their future signals intelligence collection efforts.

There is a carefully maintained pecking order in the system. The operators with the lowest status are assigned to less-important units or to monitor such day-to-day activities as weather and the comings and goings of Soviet tactical units such as infantry troops and tank battalions. Other operators, because of their language skills or instinctive analytic ability to root out intelligence, are given more important assignments, or beats, as on a newspaper. The cream of the crop are those linguists (known as 208s in the Electronic Security Command) who have mastered an essential language—Chinese or Russian—and have been assigned to a major station such as Misawa. The operators at Misawa who monitor diplomatic traffic and signals intelligence from Soviet or Chinese strategic nuclear forces are among the elite. They share that status with what are known as special cells, small groups of hand-picked men and women at NSA field stations who monitor—amid secrecy stringent even by NSA standards—such activities as Soviet commando forces and the communications to and from Soviet manned-space flights. These specially trained groups also have access to America's most advanced electronic gear, capable of intercepting satellite burst transmissions and microwave signals at long distance, vastly expanding the range of American coverage of the Soviet Union.

There is nothing glamorous, however, about monitoring the constant surveillance by and exercises of the Soviet Air Defense Force. The Air Defense's field operators still rely heavily on Morse code to report unidentified aircraft entering radar coverage, as in the case of Flight 007, and the low-status task of monitoring the long and short signals can bedevil the most stoic of Morse operators, known as Dittie-bops to their field station colleagues. "Morse intercept operators are the crazies," one Air Force analyst recalled. "I've seen guys absolutely go crazy if there was interference—just pick up equipment and throw it; or start attacking people if the other guy [the Soviet operator] was going too fast." The field station's Russian linguists, invariably characterized as squirrels by their peers, were also highly volatile, the analyst added, largely because of the enormous strain of trying to comprehend spoken Russian over earphones amid static and extraneous noise. "They'd crack up all the time."

One method of dealing with the pressure of the job and the intense security measures in field stations such as Misawa was to bend the rules in little ways. There was constant personal chatter, for example, on the worldwide internal communication link—informally known as the opscom—between the operators at Misawa and their counterparts at NSA facilities thousands of miles away. Christmas became the occasion for elaborately designed teleprinter messages and greetings from one secure base to another, relayed via the encrypted opscom.

The tensions of such work have been complicated by the advent of advanced computer communications, which has led to more centralized control and has reduced the ability of a floor station to operate independently. In the late 1970s, NSA headquarters at Fort Meade set up the National SIGINT Operations Center (NSOC, pronounced "En-soc"), directed by C. Richard Lord, then deputy director for operations,* whose function is to oversee—and direct—the electronic coverage of every crisis event. NSOC has emerged as the most influential (albeit unknown by the public) intelligence command center in the United States. It is in operation around the clock and in instantaneous touch, through the opscom, with every major NSA facility in the world.

Basic decisions as to what to report, however, are still left to floor stations, although the second-guessing from NSOC, such as during the Korean Air shootdown, for example, can be enormous. The floor stations are responsible for filing the most urgent kind of intelligence report in the entire system—a CRITIC. A CRITIC is a report of such national security importance that theoretically it is to be directed to the immediate attention of the director of the National Security Agency (DIRNSA) and to the office of the president's national security adviser within ten minutes. The actual filing of a CRITIC in peacetime is a rare event; most former analysts and operators can recall every CRITIC in which they or their information played a role.

Most significant NSA information is forwarded to Washington and other intelligence facilities as an E-gram, a priority message that in theory is to be made

---

* Lord was named deputy director of NSA in mid-1986.

known to its addressees at various military and civilian commands within twenty minutes. An event that is considered important enough to be made known to its addressees within thirty minutes is usually sent as a Spot Report. The lowest-status field report, a Klieg Light, apparently is used by field stations to alert NSA to such routine events as Soviet exercises—and this the 6981st ESC at Elmendorf failed to do late on August 31.

One unresolved question that has divided the SIGINT community revolves around the proper role of a field operator. Is he merely a rote collector of intelligence for others at Fort Meade and elsewhere to appraise, or is he to make decisions about what or what not to collect? Should NSA field stations analyze or in any way politically judge or assess the validity of the information they are collecting? Senior intelligence officials acknowledge that the NSA has drawn what amounts to a hard line between the collection and the subsequent analysis of intelligence. "We do not educate SIGINT operators in anything other than in acquiring what NSA calls 'a SIGINT fact,'" one former Fort Meade official said. "And we discourage them [the operators] from knowing anything else. The basic rule is that you don't interpret SIGINT. The SIGINT guys are technicians—they run machines and can make judgments only within a very narrow background."

Such comments accurately reflect what seems to be a headquarters attitude of "us" versus "them" that would play a role in the early NSA reporting on the shootdown of Flight 007. One sophisticated military man, who worked in the mid-1980s at an Electronic Security Command station in Western Europe, recalled a visit to the field from a group of NSA civilian officials. "They had this dislike of collectors," the military man said. "They thought we make this hoopla over nothing. You got this feeling of superiority."

6

Project CLEF

The midwatch shift is usually quiet, even at a key intelligence station such as Misawa; it is an early-morning time for the training of new operators, for catching up on paperwork, and for routine maintenance. The most highly skilled linguists and operators are rarely assigned to overnight duty but work during the day, when there are more Soviet exercises and training activities to follow and more communications to analyze.

As Flight 007 neared Sakhalin, there was no immediate reason for the midwatch at Misawa to suspect that anything was amiss; the much earlier intercept of a bit of seemingly aimless early-morning Soviet radar tracking off the Kamchatka Peninsula was not followed by any additional evidence of unusual activity there. Nothing more had been reported by any other communications intelligence unit, including the one closest to the scene, the 6981st Electronic Security Group in Alaska, which had monitored the scrambling of four Soviet interceptors over Kamchatka. Furthermore, there was no evidence of a sudden surge of high-level encoded communications from Kamchatka to higher authorities. As the Americans knew, the regional officials at Kamchatka were obligated to report all significant radar trackings in a priority message to the military district headquarters at Khabarovsk, more than 750 miles away on the Soviet mainland. Such messages, known as snap-ons in the NSA—for the sudden snapping-on of a secure communications link—are invariably the most important clues that something is up.

The first snap-on was intercepted by Misawa at 2:43 A.M. Tokyo time as Flight 007, now more than halfway across the Sea of Okhotsk, again flew into the range of Soviet radar. A major Soviet radar site at Burevestnik on Iturup Island in the Kuriles filed an urgent message to Khabarovsk reporting that an unidentified aircraft was heading toward Sakhalin. At least two other Soviet radar systems in Sakhalin, at interceptor bases at Kotikovo and Dolinsk-Sokol, were on alert and constantly sweeping the area that morning; within moments there were more snap-ons and a scramble of six Soviet interceptors from two airfields on Sakhalin, Kotikovo, on the east coast, and Dolinsk-Sokol, in the south. Soviet aircraft had been alerted in anticipation of a routine Rivet Joint reconnaissance mission, code-named Burning Wind, whose early-morning flight from the American air base at Kadena, Okinawa, passed just east of Sakhalin en route to its normal patrol in the Sea of Okhotsk.

The expected Rivet Joint mission, which had been

scheduled to take off just before dawn, didn't take place, but Misawa was nonetheless awash with enciphered messages and other evidence of unusual early-morning Soviet activity. No immediate alerts were filed, perhaps because the watch officer knew of no American military aircraft in the Sakhalin area that could be in jeopardy. The Air Defense Force throughout the Kuriles was going on alert—but targeted against what? The watch officer turned to Fort Meade for advice, querying the National SIGINT Operations Center on the opscom, the secure but informal NSA communications link. The senior officials on duty at NSOC at Fort Meade had access to the NSA's powerful CRAY-1 computer, capable of transferring 320 million words per second. With a flick of a few fingers at a keyboard, they could initiate an all-points search of Soviet Air Defense Force activity, drawing on the most sensitive intelligence-collection operations in the American government. They would know or could find out within minutes whether America's satellites and listening posts had uncovered any evidence indicating that the Soviet Air Defense Force was planning a special exercise for the middle of the morning in the Far East—or elsewhere in the Soviet Union. But NSOC knew of nothing, and asked Misawa to file status reports on the scope of activity. An unusually large-scale local Soviet exercise seemed to be under way, and a mythical intruder was being tracked. NSOC's reaction was essentially the same as that at the 6981st ESC at Elmendorf.

There was disarray at Misawa—senior analysts there "didn't know what was going on," one NSA official said later. None of the conversations in Russian between the Soviet interceptors and their ground controllers, which were conducted on a shortwave ultra-high-frequency band, could be intercepted because they were outside the line of sight; Misawa was simply too far away from Sakhalin. The Japanese intelligence services were not of much immediate help, despite the fact that they maintained an intercept facility at Wakkanai on the northern tip of Japan, just twenty-seven miles across the La Pérouse Strait from Sakhalin. Wakkanai, which most certainly would have intercepted the Soviet communications, was what American intelligence officers despairingly called a nine-to-five operation, an essentially daytime operation whose recording systems were voice-activated at all other times. Furthermore, unlike the situation in Western Europe, where there is around-the-clock satellite coverage of all significant Soviet military bases, there was no American reconnaissance satellite orbiting within range of Sakhalin at the time. The 6920th thus had no real-time intelligence when it was most desperately needed.

The Soviet interceptor activity broke off at about 3:47 A.M. Tokyo time and the exercise seemed to come to an abrupt halt. And yet the message traffic between Sakhalin and Khabarovsk continued to be intense. What was going on?

The answer was provided by what was undoubtedly the most politically sensitive American military operation in Japan—a communications intelligence unit stationed side by side with the Japanese at Wakkanai, but operating entirely on its own. The unit was close enough to intercept and translate the pilots' chatter in real time. And it did. But it had no way of immediately relaying its intercepted communications, which would have made it possible to begin to put all the pieces together, to the 6920th at Misawa.

The unit, code-named Project CLEF, began operations on an experimental basis in 1982, after having been sought for years by the commanders of the three military intelligence services—the Electronic Security Command, Naval Security Group, and Army Intelligence and Security Command—stationed on the Hill in Misawa. The thirty-man Project CLEF unit had a highly specialized mission: to quietly monitor Soviet General Staff and Air Defense Force frequencies to determine whether additional collection sites were needed. Such operations are known in the NSA as readability or hearability studies and are the usual precursor of the establishment of a new collection site or remote antenna system. There was a special tension about the project, however: post–World War II Japan has considered intelligence, with its inevitable byproduct—spying—to be an illicit activity. Electronic intelligence is considered especially pernicious in a nation that remains divided about renewed militarization and the increased American pressure for more Japanese military spending. That sensitivity, NSA officials explained, made any American presence in Wakkanai politically explosive. There was fear of damaging protest.

Initially it had been hoped, in obvious deference to Japanese concerns, that enough intelligence could be collected merely by installing special gear at Wakkanai and automatically relaying what was picked up to Misawa. There would be no need for any American personnel up north. But it was finally decided, in deliberations with senior Japanese signals intelligence officers, to set up a special American unit—Project CLEF—that would operate under cover. The men involved, most of them technical sergeants, were drawn from NSA units throughout the Pacific. Each was handpicked for his language and technical expertise and each was given orders to pose as a civilian. There was to be no sign of an American military presence at Wakkanai. Knowledge of the base's existence was limited to a few Japanese signals intelligence officers who had close working ties with their American counterparts; it was agreed that the top political and military officials of the Japanese government in Tokyo had no "need to know." Even then, it took military intelligence officers months of haggling with budget-conscious bureaucrats in the NSA—and an elaborately argued White Paper—before authority was granted to move the special team into the Japanese radar facilities at Wakkanai, in the far north of Hokkaido. Americans had been there before, running a major signals-intelligence operation at the site before turning it over to Japan in 1975.* Now they would be back as ten-

---

* Wakkanai had been the first NSA station to begin to learn the scope of damage created by the January 1968 seizure by the North Koreans of the USS *Pueblo*, a spy ship on patrol for the Naval Security Group. The *Pueblo*, for reasons that are not clear, without the knowledge of senior NSA officials, had been carrying hundreds, and perhaps thousands, of highly classified documents, including detailed technical manuals for the maintenance and repair of NSA encoding and decoding machines. A week

ants, behind a cipher-lock door. Given the secrecy of the unit, it seemed logical that there would be no direct communications link between Project CLEF and Misawa.

The American intelligence leaders at Misawa were convinced that putting enlisted men under cover into northern Japan—and doing so without informing the top officials of the Japanese government—was a risk worth taking. The unit, after all, was only a research facility; it would not be permanent and, given the ambitious—and very expensive—demands for increased intelligence facilities in the Far East, its mission was consistent with the protection of both America's and Japan's national security interests. What America had now in the Far East wasn't good enough; Soviet maneuvers inevitably seemed to shut down whenever an RC-135 or a U-2 intelligence plane flew overhead. There was talk of persuading Washington to finance a new satellite that would provide the same kind of intensive real-time coverage of the Far East as was available for Western Europe. There was also talk of supplementing the proposed new satellite coverage with a series of U-2 flights; the goal would be to utilize the spy plane, traditionally considered a strategic intelligence asset, as a collector of immediate, or

---

after the seizure, Americans on duty at Wakkanai were astonished to intercept fascimile re-creations of the top-secret NSA documents. The station had been routinely monitoring the facsimile link between Pyongyang, the capital of North Korea, and Moscow. "All of a sudden there was this special transmission, and all of these secret code-word documents were coming across," one participant recalled. "All the *Pueblo* stuff was coming across. Everything was captured."

tactical, intelligence. Newer versions of the high-flying aircraft, code-named TR-1, would be in constant communication with ground stations and provide instantaneous intelligence. The concept had been tested, apparently with good results, under the code name Senior Gaze, on the Korean peninsula. The intelligence experts in the Pacific explained that the desire for increased satellite coverage, the proposed U-2 flights, and a possible new collection site at Wakkanai was linked to what they called the difficult "signals geometry" of the Far East, which made it impossible to rely on any one system for full coverage.

A cultural conflict is at the core of any account of what happened at Wakkanai in the early morning of September 1. The American signals intelligence community, in Japan and throughout the world, operates around the clock, with speed and accuracy constantly stressed. The goal is to be the first to get information on the president's desk. Japanese standards, to most Americans, seem lax. Japan's signals intelligence is not a twenty-four-hour operation, and consensus is stressed far more than speed: anxious to avoid disputes among various commands, the Japanese coordinate even their most urgent intelligence before distributing it. The shootdown of the Flight 007 focused attention not on the ways in which the Americans and Japanese worked together but on how differently they operated.

The Japanese operation at Wakkanai works smoothly, by American standards, in day-to-day operations; as it is collected, all essential intelligence in theory can be automatically relayed from Wakkanai to the 6920th at Misawa via a high-speed secure communications link. In crises, however, the Japanese become extremely sensitive to the notion that they are merely serving as collectors for American intelligence, and they invariably move significant intelligence through their own chain of command before forwarding it to Misawa. That roadblock becomes more acute during the evening and overnight shifts, when the facility is manned by a skeleton crew. If alerted in advance or during a crisis, the Japanese officer on duty can monitor the automatically recorded material, evaluate its significance, and report on it to his superiors before moving it along to Misawa. Without advance word on the shootdown, the system worked as well as it could on the morning of September 1; the destruction of Flight 007 was monitored and recorded by the Japanese at Wakkanai, but no one there listened to it—or relayed it—for hours.

It was a different story behind the locked doors of Project CLEF. Only five operators were assigned to monitor the equipment during the midwatch shift, and one of them heard it all. One official said that the operator "happened to be working on the right frequency at the right time." What he heard was the chatter of the Soviet pilots as they tracked Flight 007 over Sakhalin. The operator was listening and recording the material, the official said, "but not paying that much attention to it." It seemed to be just another Soviet exercise. Suddenly the American heard a SU-15 pilot shout the word *"Zapustkal"*—a Russian expression in the past tense for the firing of a missile. He was stunned and was said to have "bolted from his chair." As soon as the Soviet operation was over, the technician gathered his colleagues, stopped the tape record-ing, played it over and over for confirmation, and finally began to hand-copy the pilots' comments. It was then, presumably, that the phrase "The target is destroyed" also was heard. The first goal was to get what the NSA calls a gist—a preliminary transcript of the event. None of the military men at Project CLEF had any idea what the SU-15 had shot at. Furthermore, there was no secure way to communicate what they had overheard to Misawa. The solution, according to the NSA after-action report, was to make a long-distance telephone call over an open and unsecured line to Misawa.

The watch officer at the 6920th had already been thinking about the intelligence assets in northern Japan—but not about Project CLEF. He had been telephoned sometime that morning by a colleague at the Pacific Command's Intelligence Center in Hawaii and urged, as one officer recalled, to "get the Japanese triggered" at Wakkanai. The thought was that the Japanese facility there undoubtedly had monitored the all-important pilot-to-ground-controller communica-tions. Those tapes perhaps would solve the riddle of what was going on over Sakhalin, but the Air Force and NSA couldn't wait for the morning shift of Japa-nese analysts to show up for work. Project CLEF's report was timely—and electrifying. It was agreed that an airplane would be dispatched to Wakkanai to pick up the tape recordings and CLEF's preliminary tran-script for further analysis by the language experts at Misawa.

Still, it would be hours before the raw materials from Project CLEF reached the watch officer at

Misawa. One instinctive fear was that the Cobra Ball flight had somehow strayed off course and been shot down by the Soviets. But it was quickly confirmed that the flight had returned safely to Shemya by 2:00 A.M. Tokyo time, and had heard or seen nothing unusual. There seemed to be no way that Cobra Ball could have had anything to do with the events over Sakhalin. The watch officer's immediate problem was what to report to NSOC. He had learned by telephone from project CLEF of the firing of a Soviet missile, but that report would have to be held until the transcript could be analyzed. If not at Cobra Ball, what were the Soviets firing at? Could the missile firing also have been simulated as part of an exercise?

7

Two CRITICs

Flight 007's final communication to the Tokyo Air Traffic Control Center was unreadable, and Japanese Transport Ministry officials on duty there spent the next few minutes trying without success to raise the aircraft. Tokyo subsequently tried to establish contact with Flight 007 through Flight 015, which was continuing to fly blithely along R-20 a few minutes behind, or so its crew members thought. The initial concern was not over the broken-off communication—that happens all the time—but over the failure of Flight 007 to file a previously scheduled position report to Tokyo. In an earlier message to Tokyo, filed from over the Sea of Okhotsk, Flight 007's copilot had estimated that he would reach his next reporting point at 3:26 A.M. Tokyo time. Korean Air Lines Flight 015, flying along R-20, made repeated and futile attempts in the next few minutes to raise its sister ship. At 3:56 A.M., the Tokyo air traffic control center directed regional airport control towers throughout Japan and the Japanese Defense Agency to try to establish radio contact with the missing airliner. Flight 007 had not filed the position report due thirty minutes earlier; there was little doubt now that something was wrong. At 4:22 A.M., Tokyo declared an alert. With Korean Air 015 no longer in the immediate area, the control center turned to two Japan Air Lines aircraft then in flight along R-20 and requested that they try to make radio contact. That also was unsuccessful.

There was poor coordination between Japanese intelligence and the Transport Ministry. It was not until nearly 5:00 A.M. that the Tokyo air traffic control center formally notified Japanese Defense Agency officials that "something unusual" had happened and requested that a search-and-rescue (SAR) operation be mounted. The first planes and ships were not dispatched for more than four hours, and then were sent to the point along R-20 where, as far as civilian aviation authorities could surmise, the flight had disappeared.

The Japanese Air Force intelligence operation at Wakkanai was equally inefficient. Its overnight crew did not make any special effort to immediately transfer the material that had been intercepted and recorded—including the Soviet pilots' chatter—to Misawa. If that material had been handled more quickly at Wakkanai, the Japanese would perhaps have realized the significance of what initially seemed to be another Soviet exercise.

Nothing, of course, was said publicly about the snafu. In a statement to the Japanese Diet three weeks after the shootdown, Japanese Defense Agency officials acknowledged that its Air Force unit at Wakkanai had recorded radar tracks showing the sudden disap-

pearance at about 3:29 A.M. of the flight path of an
unidentified aircraft over the Soviet island of Sakhalin—a path that later proved to be that of Flight 007.
The Diet was told that it took Wakkanai "several
hours" after being informed of the missing airliner to
survey its recorded intelligence and learn what the
men at Project CLEF—just a few feet away—had listened to in real time: that the Soviets had scrambled
interceptors to chase an intruder near Sakhalin. The
Japanese lawmakers were not told that only a skeleton
crew had been on duty at the time at Wakkanai.

A major factor in the Japanese delay was the distance—365 miles—between Sakhalin, where Flight
007 was shot down, and the point on R-20 where all
involved thought the airliner had been at the time of
its last position report. It was difficult to conceive that
a commercial airliner could be so far off course. It
would be more than nine hours after the destruction
of Flight 007 before civilian aviation authorities were
told the actual area of the crash by Defense officials; the
delay meant that rescue aircraft did not begin search-
ing for survivors at the actual crash site for an even
longer period. Japanese rescue efforts along R-20,
where there was no possibility of finding anything,
somehow continued into the next day, September 2.
American intelligence officers had their own explanation for the poor performance of Japanese intelligence
in the early hours of the shootdown: the low priority
and lower budgets given to signals intelligence in the
Japanese military. The result, one Air Force general
lamented, is that at a critical moment "you find your-
self with what you've got—limited resources." The

Japanese intelligence system, this officer said, "just fell apart" over the shootdown of Flight 007.

Some information from the Japanese about a missing airliner did reach Misawa early that morning, but it was obscure and easily overlooked. Misawa's main air base, four miles down the road, also served as the headquarters for the Japanese Northern Air Defense Command. Well before the first official report of a missing airliner was made by Japanese aviation officials, one member of the 6920th recalled, a Japanese duty officer at the Northern Air Defense Command telephoned and casually asked, "Do you guys have anything?" No one linked that report to what still seemed to be a Soviet exercise over Sakhalin, more than three hundred miles away. It is not known when—or whether—an official request to Misawa for help in tracking the overdue airliner was made by the Japanese Transport Ministry; that request, obviously, would have alerted the 6920th to the possibility that the airliner was the target of the Soviet missile firing.

Sometime around 5:30 A.M. Tokyo time, after having had no contact with Flight 007 for two hours, the Japanese Transport Ministry finally announced that the Korean airliner was missing en route from Anchorage to Seoul. It was about 4:30 P.M. in New York, and such announcements always make a good news story; the missing Flight 007 was briefly mentioned on the NBC and CBS evening television news broadcasts. CBS subsequently reported on its West Coast edition of *The CBS Evening News with Dan Rather* that Flight 007's last radioed position had been off the northwest coast of Japan in the North Pacific.

By 7:00 A.M. Tokyo time, at the very latest, the watch officer at Misawa knew that a combination of things had occurred: what he initially thought was an unusual air defense exercise involving the scrambling of at least six Soviet interceptors; heavy Soviet radar activity; and an enormous number of snap-ons involving major commands. He also knew that communications intelligence was en route by plane from Project CLEF that—so the men up there had assured him—would show that the Soviets had fired a missile. And, finally, he knew that a civilian airliner was missing. All of this should have been discussed on the opscom—but apparently was not—with the National SIGINT Operations Center at Fort Meade as it was learned; now it was time to let the rest of the government know. The watch officer decided to file the 6920th's first Critical Intelligence (CRITIC) report of the year a few minutes after 8:00 A.M. Tokyo time.

CRITIC 1-83 was logged into Fort Meade at 7:10 P.M. Washington time. At the same time its urgent message came across teleprinters at the White House, the State Department, and the many intelligence agencies of the American government. The message was that an unknown aircraft, possibly civilian, had disappeared over Sakhalin and that there was preliminary evidence that Soviet aircraft had engaged in unusual activity. The CRITIC further reported that the information about the overdue airliner was based on "collateral data"—a reference to broadcast reports, Japanese government communications, and any other non-signals-intelligence information. NSOC already was aware, from the previous reports, of Misawa's monitoring of the snap-ons, interceptor scrambles, and heightened-alert status of the Soviet Air Defense Force. Misawa was identified in the CRITIC, following NSA practice, not by name but as USA-38, a special designator assigned to the 6920th (every NSA field unit is given a separate designator that is to be used in all reports).

The second-guessing began almost immediately. Within five minutes, the duty officer at NSOC convened perhaps the most highly secured communications network in the United States government—the National Operational Intelligence Watch Officers' Network, known by its acronym, the NOIWON. The network is a secure telephone line limited to the immediate Washington area that links the watch officers on duty at the U.S. government's national intelligence centers. There are terminals in the West Wing of the White House and in the secretariat of the State Department as well as at the operations centers of the CIA, DIA, and the State Department's Bureau of Intelligence and Research (INR).* The NOIWON can be activated or "convened"—as the process is called in the government—by any agency, but in practice the watch officers' network is usually summoned by NSOC, as it was in the minutes following CRITIC 1-83. The watch officers were informed that the CRITIC had been rescinded because, in the view of

---

* Other NOIWON terminals are located at the National Military Intelligence Center (NMIC) in the Pentagon, the CIA's National Photographic Interpretation Center (NPIC), Air Force Intelligence (AFIN), the Naval Intelligence Command (NAVINCOM), the Army's Intelligence and Security Command (INSCOM), and the Department of Energy (DOE).

NSOC, word of a missing civilian airliner—filed thirty minutes after it was reported on network television—was not of CRITIC threshold. Misawa was told to confine its future messages on the airliner to Spot Reports, of much lower status. The men on duty at the National SIGINT Operations Center also had initially feared for the Cobra Ball and then, upon learning it was safe, eliminated it from any scenario. "We knew that there was no reconnaissance plane there"—over Sakhalin—one NSA official recalled. "He was parked at Shemya."

By this time, five hours after the shootdown, a crowd of about seventy friends and relatives were at Seoul's Kimpo International Airport waiting for the scheduled 6:00 A.M. arrival of the delayed Flight 007. Senior Korean Air officials were saying nothing in public, but they had been in almost constant touch for hours with Japanese civil aviation authorities. They had been told that something was wrong, but no one in the Japanese Transport Ministry knew why the 747 airliner had simply disappeared. The Transport Ministry, fearing the worst, had asked their Soviet counterparts at the Civilian Dispatch Center at Khabarovsk, nearly fifteen hundred miles to the northwest, whether they knew anything, and had been informed that no information was available. The civilian officials at Khabarovsk were undoubtedly telling the truth; there was no reason for the Soviet Air Defense Force to spread the word about what they had done.

Enough was known in Japan to force the headquarters of the U.S. Fifth Air Force near Tokyo to prudently cancel most of that day's scheduled aerial reconnaissance operations. Those operations, part of what is known in the military as PARPRO, for the Peacetime Aerial Reconnaissance Program, blanket the waters of the Far East with American intelligence aircraft. The first operation to be canceled was the scheduled Rivet Joint flight out of Okinawa, whose mission was to fly past Sakhalin, collecting communications intelligence, into the northern reaches of the Sea of Okhotsk, where the Soviets maintain a submarine base at Magadan. Also curtailed were a series of naval reconnaissance flights, generically code-named Beggar, whose assignment includes the tracking of Soviet submarines and the gathering of signals intelligence in the Sea of Okhotsk. It was agreed that such flights would be exposed to enormous risk in view of the heightened tensions.

Halfway across the world, the watch office of the State Department's Bureau of Intelligence and Research, an around-the-clock operation, decided at 7:34 P.M. to issue an alert. The officers on duty did not dispute NSOC's action in rescinding the CRITIC but thought it prudent to alert some key officials of a possible airline crash. There would be American passengers on board, and a myriad of consular and diplomatic problems. The most senior official to be notified was Lawrence S. Eagleburger, the undersecretary of state for political affairs, traditionally the most senior position in the career foreign service.

By 7:00 A.M. in Misawa information had begun to pour in from all sources. The men and women now frantically at work monitored the Soviets as they began what seemed to be a search-and-rescue operation in the waters off Sakhalin, activity that was duly confirmed and reported to NSOC at 8:15 A.M. Tokyo time, as a follow-up to CRITIC 1-83. The Japanese SIGINT detachment at Wakkanai finally was becoming active, as the morning shift arrived there for duty, and Misawa was informed, apparently by a liaison officer at Fifth Air Force, that the Japanese voice-activated system had picked up evidence of some kind of Soviet military activity over Sakhalin. All of this was welcome news, for NSOC's action in rescinding Misawa's first CRITIC of the year rankled. The military aircraft from Project CLEF finally arrived at Misawa, and with it came the tape recording that provided the first hard evidence.

It took the language experts at Misawa a good hour to play the tapes and reconfirm that the Soviets had indeed fired a missile. The watch officer, although still not clear about what the pilot was firing at, decided that he had no other recourse but to file a second CRITIC. CRITIC 2-83 arrived at NSOC a few moments after 9:00 P.M. Washington time (it was now after 10:00 A.M. in Japan). The new CRITIC corroborated the initial CRITIC and added that the 6920th now had substantiation that Soviet aircraft were scrambled over Sakhalin and fired a live missile. It further said that intelligence had been obtained (also from Project CLEF) showing that a Soviet pilot had reported the target being "destroyed." Project CLEF was not cited by name in the CRITIC; it had been agreed at the outset that because of its special sensitivity, CLEF would be assigned a designator, like any other NSA reporting site, in an effort to mask its location and function.

Incredibly, the National SIGINT Operations Center, in what one official later characterized as a "fiasco," rescinded CRITIC 2-83 at 9:10 P.M., only minutes after it was logged in. It was cryptically explained in the NSA's after-action report that the duty officer at NSOC considered CRITIC 2-83 too closely related to the initial CRITIC. The watch officers at Fort Meade had argued that the second CRITIC still did not include any evidence as to what, if anything, the Soviet interceptor had fired a missile at. The initial notification of the NSOC decision apparently was made via the NOIWON, which was convened as the First Follow-up to CRITIC 2-83 within minutes. NSOC's message, as summarized in the log of one NOIWON recipient, was that "NSA determines that no alerts are necessary." Misawa, obviously distressed at Washington's vote of no confidence, filed no immediate further reports. The attitude of the NSOC duty officers abruptly changed in the next half hour. The duty officers there seemed to realize suddenly that they indeed had an international crisis on their hands. Perhaps they were responding to advice from NSA experts who had been summoned—as many were—to the Operations Center, but the fact is that at 9:40 P.M. NSA once again convened the National Operational Intelligence Watch Officers' Network. That NOIWON, officially logged as the Second Follow-up to CRITIC 2-83, explicitly made a link between the Soviet missile-firing and the missing airliner. The watch officers' talk led to this preliminary conclusion, as recorded by one intelligence agency: "It is uncertain but this missile-firing exercise may be related to the downing of the civilian airliner." Washington was finally beginning to get the picture.

By 11:00 A.M. Tokyo time Misawa was in a full-scale crunch. Men who have served at NSA floor stations during crises describe the atmosphere as chaotic and raucous. The first casualty usually is the overburdened intercom system, and operators and analysts end up standing on chairs, yelling and waving to get each other's attention. The shootdown of Flight 007 was by far the biggest event of the year, and all of the men and women assigned to the 6920th wanted in on it. Senior officers eventually had to ask those not assigned to the shift to leave the floor. There were exceptions. The unit's best linguists were immediately provided with copies of the Project CLEF tapes and feverishly began to put together a more detailed transcript. The Japanese tapes from Wakkanai also arrived sometime later that morning, translated from Russian into Japanese. A Japanese Air Force intelligence unit assigned to Misawa was asked to translate them once again—into English.

There were great difficulties at this point because of the lack of intercepted communications from the Soviet ground controllers to the SU-15 and MiG pilots. The pilots were closely directed from the ground and were overheard responding to orders—which were not on the tape recording. The American and Japanese linguists were being asked—in a hurry—to make sense out of one side of a two-way conversation. That task was further complicated by the fact that the Soviet interceptor pilots, finally on a combat mission after years of routine practice, were excited—perhaps even terrified—and were speaking less distinctly and more cryptically than usual. Breathing in such cases usually is rapid, shallow, and very noisy.

Misawa was not able to focus its energies on trying to unravel what had happened over Sakhalin hours before; there was too much going on at the moment. The Soviets began to increase their search-and-rescue operations in the Sea of Japan, and the major communication networks to and from the Far East suddenly surged with traffic, as Sakhalin, Khabarovsk, and Moscow tried to grapple with what had taken place. One Soviet General Staff message, immediately intercepted by one of the special units at Misawa, discussed the possibility of a violation of the Soviet rules of engagement. Operators at Misawa also picked up idle chatter from two apparently drunk Soviet enlisted men assigned to an air defense unit on southern Sakhalin; amid the vulgarities one asked the other whether he had heard that a Soviet interceptor had shot down a civilian passenger plane in the belief that it was an American RC-135 reconnaissance plane. Their conversation was intercepted at about 7:30 A.M. Tokyo time, four hours after the shootdown and was later seen by many in Washington as clear evidence that the Soviet military system had quickly learned the truth. (Other analysts found the conversation far less convincing, simply because Japanese and Western news agencies had broadcast reports of the missing airliner by the time of the intercept, and it was possible that the two Soviets were merely parroting what they had heard on the radio.)

By 9:30 A.M. Tokyo time, six hours after the shootdown, the crowd at Kimpo Airport awaiting Flight 007 was growing rapidly, as nervous relatives converged on the airport rather than waiting at home or at work. Amid the inevitable rumors of hijacking and a midair collision, Japanese and American news agencies suddenly announced a new development: the aircraft had been forced down on Sakhalin, with its fate unknown. The report circulated in time for CBS-TV to insert it, attributed to United Press International, in its delayed West Coast edition of the evening news. Family and airline officials were eager to believe it, as they would welcome any rumor suggesting that the airliner and its passengers were safe. The next few hours would be difficult for the anxious relatives and friends at the airport. An official of Korean Air somehow managed to confirm publicly that yes, Flight 007 was now known to have been forced to land on Sakhalin. And, a few hours later, a vice president of Korean Air announced that he would fly to Tokyo to join negotiations there for the return of the passengers. The vigil at Kimpo Airport seemed to have no more point, and the airline provided buses for those relatives who wished to go home. It would be nearly ten more hours before there would be official confirmation of the fate of the airliner. South Korean officials tried to cover their embarrassment by insisting later to newsmen that they had learned of Flight 007's landing at Sakhalin not from wire-service or television-network accounts but from the American Central

Intelligence Agency. It was a misrepresentation, as we shall see, that would linger for months.

It was well after dinner in Washington, but NSOC's Second Follow-up to CRITIC 2-83 eliminated any hesitancy: senior officials scattered around town were alerted and summoned to situation rooms and crisis centers. A C-141 aircraft was ordered to pick up the Project CLEF and Japanese tapes at Misawa and bring them to Fort Meade for further analysis. Lieutenant General Lincoln D. Faurer of the Air Force, director of NSA, was brought in, along with a key aide, Richard Lord, the operations director. At the State Department, Thomas Simons, director of the Office of Soviet Union Affairs, was summoned to his office by telephone. Simons had played a major role in the inconclusive negotiations with the Soviet Union in April after Navy aircraft had overflown Zeleny Island in the Kuriles. Simons's superior, Richard R. Burt, the assistant secretary of state for European affairs, was called to the telephone four times within ninety minutes while at dinner with his fiancée at the Four Seasons, a Washington restaurant, before heading for the office.

By 10:10 P.M., there was a separate Naval Security Group E-gram from Misawa, The Navy had its own mission at Misawa and its own intelligence requirements, geared to Soviet naval and aircraft activity. It reported a Soviet vessel and at least three Soviet aircraft conducting a search-and-rescue mission off Sakhalin. At this point, one State Department official recalled, "people in the Ops Center were saying, 'Shit. They must have shot it down.' "

Misawa, now under tremendous pressure from Washington for more facts and more details of Soviet pursuit prior to the shootdown, found that the original Japanese tape recordings were of higher quality and much clearer than those from Project CLEF, simply because the Japanese recording equipment was far superior. CLEF had been set up on the cheap, under heavy budget pressure from the NSA, and its recording and duplicating equipment was put together in hodgepodge fashion from existing stocks. It was a budgetary decision that would be much regretted in the aftermath of the shootdown. The Project CLEF tape recordings were voice-activated, as were those turned over by the Japanese, but were far more difficult to transcribe and translate, especially in a hurry and in a crisis. In those first moments, CLEF's tape was replayed again and again as the preliminary transcript, with its lapses and inaccuracies, emerged. What is known is that over the next hours, with Washington hanging on every dispatch, Misawa based much of its follow-up reporting on the Japanese intercepts. NSA operating procedures call for such third-party intercepts to be coded with the word "Druid," and it was the Druid material that ended any residual doubt in Washington as to what had happened.

Misawa filed at least three more CRITIC Follow-ups during the day (it was the night of August 31 and early morning of September 1 in Washington) providing details of the early Soviet tracking and pursuit as the SU-15 stalked its prey. At 1:53 A.M. in Washington, shortly before 3:00 P.M. in Japan, the CIA convened a watch officers' telephone conference—the first NOIWON it had summoned during the crisis—and reported, in essence, that its Soviet analysts had concluded that the Soviets had shot down Flight 007. NSA also reported during the NOIWON that it was "95 percent sure" the Korean airliner had been shot down by the Soviets. By 5:00 A.M. Washington time, there was general agreement in the intelligence community that the Soviet Union was directly responsible for the shootdown. It was a significant finding, one that would have great political and emotional ramifications for senior policymakers in Washington and Moscow. The conclusion was prudently reached, and only on what seemed—to the men in Washington, anyway—to be the most substantial evidence. The communication intercepts were seen as providing the smoking gun—indisputable evidence that the Soviet SU-15 pilot had shot first and asked questions later.

There was intense anger in Washington as word of the transcripts began to seep from the intelligence community throughout the government. The intercepts, as relayed by Misawa to Washington, quoted the Soviet SU-15 pilot as saying three times that he could see the lights of the airliner; the pilot further was quoted as saying, moments before firing his missiles, that he was "abeam," that is, parallel (so Washington would become convinced) with the intruder. America's senior officials reacted with revulsion to an event which seemed to prove, once again, that the Soviets were different from Americans. It was another reminder that the USSR was the enemy. That finding was a major watershed, and Washington, over the next few days, seemed not to want to understand anything else about the events over Sakhalin.

With only one exception—at the headquarters of

Air Force Intelligence in the Pentagon—it seemed obvious to the men on duty at the various watch offices and operations centers that the Soviets could not have mistaken a huge Boeing 747 for the smaller American RC-135 reconnaissance plane. There was anger in the field, too. Some senior Air Force and Navy officers in the Pacific, who were provided with summaries of the NSA cable traffic, "got emotional," as one officer recalled, and began formulating actions for retaliation against the Soviet Union, actions "that could have started World War III." The officer, who was stationed in the Pacific, told of being approached by an Air Force general and asked to forward an essentially fraudulent intelligence report to the Pentagon that was designed to justify acts of provocation against the Soviet Union. The general "wanted me to corrupt intelligence," the officer recalled. "I told him to go to hell."

At least one reckless decision was made in the first twenty-four hours. Six F-15 interceptors and an AWACs electronics surveillance aircraft were temporarily assigned to Misawa Air Base and ordered to orbit adjacent to Soviet territory near Sakhalin. The unstated goal was to provoke an incident: the F-15 pilots were instructed "to take advantage of the situation," one officer recalled, in the event they were challenged by Soviet SU-15 or MiG-23 interceptors. No one in Washington had cleared such instructions in advance, or knew of them. Senior authorities at Fifth Air Force headquarters in Japan quickly intervened to prevent any serious confrontation. There were many other dangerous moments in the first hours. The Soviets, instinctively angered after the shootdown by what they viewed as a deliberate American violation of their borders, immediately increased their air and sea activity around Sakhalin.

Few of the Americans on duty at intelligence posts in Washington seemed to pay much attention to the careful hedging that was coming from Misawa. Portions of the transcripts were underlined by the linguists of the 6920th in their dispatches to Washington, in an attempt to say, as one Electronic Security Command officer recalled, "We can't confirm" the accuracy of this translation. There was enormous pressure on Misawa and other NSA facilities in the Pacific. Washington wanted a constant flow of updated wrap-up reports. Some analysts working through the first hours of the crisis in the Pacific recalled their anxiety about the widespread anger toward the Soviets and what seemed to be the rush to judgment: "Those of us in the SIGINT business know how fragile SIGINT is," one officer explained. "You've got to listen to it carefully and go over translations."

One example of misunderstanding, cited later by a number of intelligence officers, revolved around the phrase, "The target is destroyed." The SU-15 interceptor pilot was overheard making that statement—widely depicted as a cry of triumph—at the moment his missile impacted. The phrase became a centerpiece in the initial press and television reporting on the shootdown of Flight 007. Signals intelligence experts read much less into that phrase, however. They had overheard it for more than thirty years while monitoring Soviet training exercises. To a communications expert, "The target is destroyed" means that an enemy interception—whether real or simulated—has been brought to a successful end. "We hear it twenty times a day in training," one Electronic Security Command officer explained. "In this case, the pilot saw something—an explosion, but it was not a confirmed kill." In the view of many American intelligence experts, the SU-15 pilot may indeed have been exultant when his missile struck the aircraft, but concluding as much because he said "The target is destroyed" is based on faulty and incomplete knowledge—and simply may not be correct.

In fact the American and Japanese transcripts showed that the Soviet interceptor pilot and two of his colleagues remained in the area for twenty minutes, apparently trying to confirm that the plane had indeed been destroyed. During that period, they repeatedly asked one another about the location of "the target." At 3:32 A.M., for example, one of the MiG pilots accompanying the SU-15 asked, "What is the distance to the target?" Six minutes later, the same pilot told his ground controller, "I don't see anything in this area. I just looked."

8

First Analysis

By the late summer of 1983, Air Force Intelligence (AFIN) had become an unhappy place to work, although the scope of its reporting was broader than ever. Its problems, and its strengths, were directly attributable to Major General James C. Pfautz, the new commander. Pfautz's overriding ambition wasn't the problem; every military man understands that all officers, even two-star generals, want nothing more than to do their job well and be promoted. But Jim Pfautz, then fifty-two years old, was seen by some of his subordinates as an insecure martinet, a general officer who always insisted that only he knew the answers, and that only his way was the right way. Such attitudes are common among senior flying officers operating combat commands, but intelligence is another matter; it is a field where, theoretically, dissent and independent analysis are essential. For those men and women, ironically, the fact that Pfautz was as bright and good at his job as he was

107

ambitious and overbearing made his personality faults even harder to accept.

Pfautz's brilliance and drive had been recognized early in his career. He had been selected as the senior military fellow to the Council on Foreign Relations in New York and later served in a key staff position during the Ford and Carter administrations in the Office of International Security Affairs, then one of the most powerful offices in the Defense Department. His first intelligence assignment did not come until 1978, when the former combat pilot—Pfautz had flown 188 missions in Vietnam—was named defense attaché to Egypt and promoted to general. His new career field was a mixed blessing for, as Pfautz understood, many of the combat pilots who run the Air Force consider intelligence to be populated by eggheads—"intel weenies"—whose only function is to tell them what they need to hear when they want to hear it.

Pfautz's rise in intelligence was meteoric nonetheless, and after a successful tour as chief intelligence officer in the Pacific Command, he was appointed assistant chief of staff for intelligence in May 1983. Pfautz's success did not sit well with his fellow Air Force generals responsible for intelligence at the Strategic Air Command and the Electronic Security Command, for his was the top intelligence job in the Air Force. Inevitably there was jealousy and much second-guessing as Pfautz began changing the way things were done—all of which would play a role in the aftermath of Flight 007.

Pfautz had direct access to men at the top as well as to much of the government's most sensitive information. It was a world in which the distribution of satellite reconnaissance photographs within an hour of a major event—such as Israel's bombing attack on Iraq's nuclear reactor in 1981—was taken for granted. Those on the inside had a special view of day-to-day world events. Pfautz had some degree of control over 33,000 men and women assigned to Air Force intelligence duties around the world. His office was responsible for coordinating and maintaining many strategic reconnaissance activities, including the Cobra Ball and Rivet Joint flights; it also worked closely with the NSA on matters dealing with the Electronics Security Command, and with the National Reconnaissance Office (NRO), the agency in charge of procuring and targeting satellites. There was a traditional internal role for Air Force intelligence, too: to help the Air Force justify its demands for new bombers and other weaponry to Congress and inside the Pentagon. The commander of Air Force intelligence was primarily seen as the loyal Air Force man whose mission was to help his service in any way he could.

Pfautz didn't see it that way. In his view, he hadn't come to Washington solely to justify new airplanes. He was there to provide intelligence on the important political, military, and social questions of the day to the men at the top of the Air Force, and especially to General Charles A. Gabriel, the chief of staff and member of the Joint Chiefs of Staff. His goal was to do an outstanding job and persuade all in the Pentagon that Jim Pfautz was the only man who could be picked for the most important military intelligence job—director of the Defense Intelligence Agency. The man who held the job in mid-1983, Lieutenant General James B. Williams of the Army, was considered inside the Pentagon to be an amiable lightweight, a former captain of the basketball team at West Point who simply did not live up to the intellectual requirements of the job. Not that Williams's acumen, or lack of it, mattered that much anyway: being director of the DIA has been considered since its inception as an all-but-impossible job.

Initially set up in 1964, during the tenure of Defense Secretary Robert S. McNamara, the DIA was designed to be a central repository and coordinator for all military intelligence, an agency that would end the eternal bickering among the Army, Navy, and Air Force. Its assessments and other reports were to serve as a counterweight to the civilian intelligence provided by the CIA and State Department. It also was designated as the primary intelligence adviser to the Joint Chiefs of Staff. But the DIA never performed as expected, basically because the three services—and their intelligence arms—could not put aside their interservice rivalries to work together.* Even an iconoclast like Jim Pfautz, who prided himself on doing things his way, developed a fierce loyalty to the primacy of Air Force Intelligence. One obvious reason for doing so was careerism: promotions continued to be the prerogative of each service. Inevitably, profound interservice disputes marred discussion of the most important issues of national security, such as the DIA's annual

---

* McNamara initially ordered a drastic reduction in the number of men assigned to the service intelligence organizations and transferred many of their responsibilities to the DIA. By 1968, however, each service had restored the manpower cuts and was able to recruit people more capable than those at the DIA.

estimates of the Soviet threat. The Air Force has argued, for example, that advanced synthetic-aperture-array radar techniques, known to be intensely researched by the Soviets, could, if perfected, enable the USSR to more accurately track and target American submarines. To meet that potential threat, the United States needed more missiles to knock out the Soviet ICBM fields. This, of course, would mean larger appropriations for Air Force bombers and missiles. Less money should be spent on nuclear missile submarines, in the Air Force view, because they were increasingly vulnerable. This has been, and continues to be, a never-ending dispute.

Other disputes often were much more petty. Jim Pfautz was enraged, a few weeks after moving to Washington as chief of Air Force Intelligence, when the DIA gave a private briefing to the top men in the Air Force on a subject so sensitive, Pfautz was told, that he was not himself cleared to attend the meeting. Pfautz was convinced that he had been, as he later put it, "blindsided" by Jim Williams, the Army officer, and made to lose face with his superiors. Williams was expected to retire in 1984, and Pfautz made it known that if and when he got the job—and the third star that went along with it—he would treat military intelligence chiefs with the respect he felt he had deserved. Few on his staff believed it.

Pfautz was in full control of Air Force Intelligence by the end of August 1983. He had completely revamped the intelligence procedures inside the Air Staff and broadened the scope of his office's daily 8:30 A.M. briefing to General Gabriel and the vice chief of staff, General Jerome F. O'Malley. Those briefings no longer focused solely on Air Force problems and systems but dealt instead with what had happened in the past twenty-four hours around the world. Pfautz expanded the use of color slides; two projectors and as many as thirty slides now dramatized the morning report to the chief of staff. If a Soviet aircraft or a foreign resort town was mentioned in the morning report, they had to be depicted in a slide. Such detail became an enormous burden for the staff. Analysts and graphics experts had to be recruited and added to the overnight intelligence team to prepare for a preliminary morning briefing of Pfautz's senior deputies, as well as to produce another Pfautz innovation—a daily two-page summary of world events known as the "Air Force Intelligence Digest." It was to be ready by six-thirty every weekday morning.

Pfautz's technique and demands may have inspired fear, anger, and hostility among his immediate staff—but they also produced results. His ritual of early-morning staff meetings, intelligence digests, and preliminary briefings was designed to get the product right for his daily 8:30 A.M. report to the men at the top. Pfautz knew he was an outsider who was called the West Pointist and Steve Canyon behind his back. He was also convinced that the Air Force intelligence staff had not been good enough prior to his arrival. Until then, it had been pro forma for a regional intelligence specialist, if unable to answer a detailed question, to respond, in effect: "Sir, I don't know the answer, but I'll find out."

Such answers, widely accepted throughout the military, infuriated Pfautz. "I gave them three days," he later recalled, "and then said: 'If I have to become the expert, I'll get rid of you.' " His constant battle, he added, was over imprecision. His intelligence officers would report an Israeli air raid over Lebanon but would not immediately know how many planes took part. Or if there was a terrorist explosion, none of his officers could—or would—venture an opinion as to who was involved. "After a while, they got the drift," Pfautz said. "And by the time I left, they were used to me and understood me. After all, I'd have to answer those same questions from the chief of staff. I was training my men to be ready twenty-four hours a day."

Many of the younger officers were convinced that the new two-page "Intelligence Digest," which duplicated the widely distributed early-morning CIA and State Department overnight summaries, was designed to curry favor with the senior Air Force staff—which it did. There was a more substantive complaint, too: the young officers, many of them graduates of the Air Force Academy, believed that Pfautz, by emphasizing current events in his daily briefings, was neglecting the basics—technical reporting on Soviet aircraft and missile systems. The officers further were dismayed by what they perceived as Pfautz's need to compete constantly with the Defense Intelligence Agency. For example, shortly after the DIA issued an elaborate study on the future politics of Ferdinand Marcos, Pfautz insisted that his staff prepare its own Philippine estimate. "He always worried about the DIA," one young officer recalled. "If DIA had something, Air Force had to include it—whether relevant or not—in its briefing."

The staff's hostility to Pfautz's ambition and drive was not helped by the general's rigid demeanor and his adherence to stiff codes of military dress and behavior. One incident became a classic: Shortly after being reassigned to the Pentagon, Pfautz was passed in a corridor by an Air Force lieutenant colonel eating an ice-cream cone. The major general marched the colonel back to his office, where, as the officer stood at attention, with ice cream dripping along the sides of his uniform, he "read him the riot act"—as one witness recalled—for conduct unbecoming an officer. The staff was agog over the incident, for the colonel was the executive assistant to one of the senior operational generals in the Air Force, and a public dressing-down of an aide to a senior general was far from politic. Pfautz, asked about it later, was unapologetic: "If it's lunch time or you're on a break, take your ice cream and lick it in a corner. But don't parade around in the Pentagon with it."

Pfautz compounded the office tensions by moving two protégés into key positions and, through them, running the organization. Both men, although full colonels, inevitably were seen by the staff as little more than spear-carriers, officers who would carry out Pfautz's orders even when they should have known better. Junior officers were reassigned jobs and work shifts at will and soon came to feel, as one put it, that "we belonged to the Air Force and it could do anything it wanted with us." Serious mistakes of judgment were inevitable; one foolish Pfautz request, if publicly known, could have triggered a political problem for the Reagan administration. At the height of the 1984 Democratic presidential primary campaign, a lieutenant colonel on Pfautz's staff spent days under cover in Chicago and elsewhere investigating whether the Reverend Jesse Jackson had, in fact, been ordained as a minister. Pfautz had raised the pedantic question during an otherwise routine briefing on the successful negotiation by Jackson, the first black presidential candidate, of the release from Damascus of Navy lieutenant Robert O. Goodman, Jr., a black navigator who had been shot down over Syria in 1984. The incident distressed many of the junior officers assigned to the office, who found it appalling that their superiors were so frightened of Pfautz and the impact he could have on their careers that they chose to look the other way. "If I had been a deputy," one junior officer said of the Pfautz protégé, "I'd have gone to see Pfautz and worked it out. Instead, he's [the deputy's] calling every half hour to find out whether we got the information or not."

Even his harshest critics inside Air Force Intelligence would agree, however, that Jim Pfautz, for all of his personal and bureaucratic defects, improved the ability of his staff to respond to a crisis. His daily intelligence reports were better than those of his predecessor, and General Gabriel and his deputies relayed word that the quality of Pfautz's reporting was appreciated. The good—and some of the bad—came together on September 1.

Only a small staff of six to eight officers and enlisted men are on duty at the headquarters of Air Force Intelligence during the evening. Their basic mission is to prepare the daily "Intelligence Digest" and to lay the groundwork for the 6:30 A.M. briefing, as the more senior officers prepare for their encounter an hour later with Jim Pfautz. The crisis in Lebanon was the dominant issue as the staff reported for duty on the evening of August 31; two U.S. marines, members of the occupying force whose mission had become less clear with each week, had been killed two days before in Beirut. One of the Air Force duty officers noted an item about an overdue airliner near Japan on *The CBS Evening News* and casually asked some of his colleagues to "keep an eye on it." Things got hectic fast. By 10:00 P.M., after the first two CRITICs from Misawa, the Pentagon was "in a tumult," the duty officer recalled. "Everyone was trying to figure out what was going on."

There was enormous pressure into the night from the senior policymakers in the government on the Central Intelligence Agency, the Defense Intelligence Agency, and the National Security Agency to analyze what had happened. The role of the National SIGINT Operations Center at such moments is that of a funnel, through which the raw material from its field stations and satellites pours forth—for others to analyze. The NSA is under a formal restriction not to interpret its data but to forward as much as possible though the NSOC without compromising the source of the information. Informally, however, there is much byplay and low-level coordination in a crisis, and analysts from all the intelligence agencies and the collection sites in Alaska, Hawaii, and Japan chatted through the night and morning on the opscom and on secure telephone systems about what had happened to Flight 007. Similarly, junior officers and enlisted men in Air Force Intelligence talked in Washington to their peers in the DIA, CIA, and NSA. But sharing at the top was a far different matter.

General Pfautz was not contacted until sometime

after 11:00 P.M. By then, Misawa had reported, in a CRITIC Follow-up, the comment of the Soviet pilot upon firing his missiles: "The target is destroyed." Pfautz recalled his reaction: "I thought to myself: 'This is going to be a big one. Get your troops out. If what I'm hearing is true, we've got a potential of war.' I told my people not to worry about the CIA or the DIA—just get on it and do the best we could. This is an air incident and I cannot wait for anybody else to get into this." Pfautz's attitude would have been understood and shared by any senior Air Force officer. He had risked his life in the air for his country—and his service. An air incident was his. "If it's in the air, it's Jesus," a military intelligence specialist subsequently explained. "If it's on the ground or in the water, it's a hippie with long hair."

As it turned out, General Williams wasn't even around. He had gone on vacation in mid-August, as he did every summer, and would not return to work until September 6. Pfautz wasn't surprised. "Jim Williams is a sweet guy," Pfautz said later, "but he doesn't demand anything. His people should have been called that night and told 'Hey, man. This thing is ominous.' " Pfautz was going to show the Pentagon what good intelligence was. He ordered his duty officers to "pull out all the stops" and start calling in staff experts on Soviet policy and the Air Defense Force.

Pfautz's team all understood without being explicitly told that the mission was to get the best story as fast as possible. Some of the men had served as electronic operators aboard RC-135 Rivet Joint and Cobra Ball missions and were experts on the radar and tracking techniques of the Soviet Air Defense Force. There

were two immediate questions: Did the Soviets know
what they were shooting at? And from which echelon
did the order to shoot originate? It would be hours, the
men in Air Force Intelligence knew, before the NSA's
field stations and satellite relay facilities could process
enough material to enable any conclusions to be drawn
about who ordered what. But there was no reason to
wait for special intelligence before attempting to analyze the shootdown itself. Jim Pfautz, they could be
sure, would demand no less.

Among those summoned to work was Major Daniel
E. Miller, a Soviet Air Defense Force analyst. Miller
would be credited by his colleagues with playing the
key role during the night and early morning. He, like
many assigned to Air Force Intelligence, immediately
recalled the 1978 incident over the Kola Peninsula, in
which the Soviets concluded that the Korean airliner
was an RC-135 Rivet Joint reconnaissance plane. The
fact that Cobra Ball had returned to Shemya more than
an hour before the shootdown over Sakhalin was not
in itself significant, in his view. The right question,
Miller thought, was where had it been in relation to the
civilian airliner. Working with colleagues on duty at
intelligence posts in Alaska and Hawaii, the major was
able to re-create the approximate flight path of both the
Cobra Ball and Flight 007. His instinctive guess was
that the Soviet radar operators had confused the two
aircraft and concluded that the plane that flew into
their airspace was an American intelligence craft.

There was little specific intelligence to back up his
theory in the first hours. While Miller and his Air
Force colleagues plotted the flight paths of Flight 007
and the Cobra Ball, senior analysts and linguists at the

CIA, DIA, and NSA were focusing most of their attention on the raw intercepts that had been obtained by the 6920th at Misawa. By early morning, the CIA and DIA concluded from those intelligence reports that the Soviet interceptor pilot had pulled abeam of his target and identified it as a civilian airliner before shooting it down. But the raw intercepts were far less persuasive, in Miller's view, if one assumed that the Soviets had initially erred in identifying the airliner as an American reconnaissance plane. Miller spent hours on the telephone that morning with his colleagues on duty at Misawa and at Pacific Air Forces headquarters in Hawaii and learned from them that the initial translation of the Soviet pilots' intercepted chatter were stopgap at best. Those officers told him that there had been a separate intercept from Project CLEF and that it would take days, if not longer, before a complete and reliable transcript—enchanced by the Japanese tape recordings—would be ready. Miller and his colleagues were convinced that even without the transcript there was more than enough available information to put together a working scenario of the shootdown.

One crucial fact stood out as the early-morning briefings were being prepared: the American intelligence system had not developed any specific evidence showing that the Soviets had knowingly shot down an airliner. Such information might turn up in the next twenty-four hours, as the NSA relentlessly searched through its satellite and field-station intercepts, but Miller didn't think it would. Meanwhile, his basic assumption was being borne out. One of his colleagues on duty at the Pentagon that morning had shrewdly telephoned several Air Force tanker pilots who had done refueling at night of Cobra Ball and Rivet Joint missions in the North Pacific. He was told that identification at night was, as he recounted, a "really goosey" procedure. The tanker pilots recalled having enormous difficulty differentiating the night running-lights of an RC-135—a modified Boeing 707—from those displayed by the widely used Boeing 747; the silhouettes of both planes appear similar when viewed from below. One tanker pilot told of approaching within five hundred yards of a Japan Air Line 747 before realizing that the aircraft was not the RC-135 that he was scheduled to refuel. The finding was important to Major Miller and his colleagues, because they suspected, from their knowledge of Soviet interception procedures and from the early bits of intercept material, that the SU-15 had always flown beneath the airliner. If he was abeam at one point, as the intercepts seemed to suggest, he was abeam—and below.

By 7:00 A.M., when Jim Pfautz was ready for the morning briefing, his staff had prepared a detailed briefing book, complete with more than thirty color slides showing, among other things, the probable flight path of the Korean airliner marked in blue and that of the Cobra Ball in red. Some slides also juxtaposed the various messages that were sent by the crew of Flight 007 as well as by the Soviet radar technicians with the progress of the aircraft along their flight paths. Other slides included the time of such messages in the context of the flight paths. There were slides depicting, in detail, Kamchatka Peninsula and Sakhalin Island, as well as an overall view of the geography of the Far East. The goal was to coordinate the slides, presented on two projectors, with the text of the briefing, as read by a junior officer. When the narrative shifted to the shootdown over Sakhalin, for example, one projector would depict a detailed map of the area while the other showed a Soviet SU-15 interceptor and discussed the capability of its weapons systems. "Pfautz liked to razzle-dazzle," one of his aides recalled. The briefing, all agreed, served its purpose well: the possibility that the Soviet radar plotters were confused was obvious.

There was some nervousness among junior staff members. They suspected that what they believed took place was not going to be what many senior officers in the Pentagon wanted to hear. Air Force intelligence was describing a tragic mistake over Sakhalin—not wanton murder. "To Pfautz's credit," one officer recalled, "he accepted it when we told him how screwed up the Soviets were. He had no problem with us going after it. When we made the call, and once he understood it, it was 'Katy, bar the door'—no matter what the president or anyone in the White House thought."

Pfautz had defied convention before. As a student at the National War College in the early 1970s, he had earned a reputation as someone who was "that way"— soft on communism—because he had refused to solve all problems in war games by calling for a nuclear strike. "Everyone's solution to a problem was 'Nuke 'em,'" Pfautz said, "and I'd object and say 'Let's try to work it out diplomatically and politically.'

"The point is that the National Command Authorities of the United States—before they take any action against the Soviets—have got to look at their forces. What is the likelihood that the Soviets would deliberately shoot down a civilian plane without any forces on alert, any forces keyed? When you look at the forces, it tells you they screwed up—they panicked. The Soviets are just like we are, with junior officers on duty in places like Kamchatka and Sakhalin, working on edge, scared to death."

Pfautz was understandably proud of the work his staff had done. The Air Force briefing book and its slide show not only explained the shootdown of Flight 007 with a sophistication that no other intelligence agency would match for days but it had been put together so quickly that Pfautz knew that he had, as he put it, "a best-seller"—the best story in town, although one not all would want to hear. A fact was a fact. "I told my people—'Look, we're not apologizing for the Soviets.' "

He said as much at the eight-thirty meeting with Generals Gabriel and O'Malley, explaining that there had been no realignment of Soviet forces in the Far East—strong evidence that "they probably screwed up." His staff had concluded, Pfautz said, that the destruction of Flight 007 was a function both of poor command-and-control and a "spastic response" by Soviet Air Defense officials fearful for their careers. One senior Air Force general later described Pfautz's initial assessment as an "extraordinarily detailed, beautifully presented briefing." The color slides, with their depiction of the Cobra Ball and Flight 007 flight paths, had been particularly effective.

The Air Force intelligence briefing ended, as it usually did, about nine-thirty in the morning. It was agreed that General O'Malley would take the AFIN briefing book, with color reproductions of the slides, and outline the Jim Pfautz analysis at a special meeting of the Joint Chiefs of Staff that was to take place later in the morning. Pfautz and the senior Air Force generals knew that the DIA would present its analysis of the Soviet shootdown at the meeting; it would be an opportunity for the Air Force staff to show their stuff to the men who ran the Pentagon.

Pfautz spoke to no one other than his own staff about the briefing, and none of the men in charge of intelligence in the Reagan administration—William J. Casey at CIA, General Lincoln Faurer at NSA, Hugh Montgomery, director of State Department intelligence, and the officer sitting in for Jim Williams at DIA—felt any need to call the Air Force. There was nothing to be learned, these men apparently believed, from a parochial group of military officers in the Pentagon. Each agency had come to its own conclusion about the shootdown of Flight 007 and made no attempt at the top to reach out.

By mid-morning of September 1, the world had no official word about what had happened over Sakhalin. Then, at 10:45 A.M., Washington time, the American secretary of state described the tragedy on national television in terms that would dismay senior government officials in Japan and many Air Force intelligence analysts in Washington and the Far East.

BOOK III

The
Politics

9

The Announcement

August 1983 was a rough
month for Secretary of State George P. Shultz. He had
been engaged in a losing bureaucratic war with William P. Clark, a long-time crony of President Ronald
Reagan, and national security adviser since January
1982; the State Department was being shoved out of
top-level policy-making in Central America and the
Middle East. Then, suddenly, early in August, Shultz's
loss of influence emerged as a front-page story. Bill
Clark's ascendancy was trumpeted within a week on
the covers of *Time* magazine and the New York *Times*
Magazine. The magazines were publishing only what
had been widely known inside the government, but it
had to be painful to Shultz nonetheless. The *Times*
story told of yet another loss for Shultz: in July the
president had agreed to place Clark firmly in control
of a newly created Senior Arms Control Policy
Group, thus bringing the U.S.-Soviet strategic arms
negotiations inside the White House. There were reports in the major newspapers and newsmagazines that

Shultz had been pressured by his senior aides to fight back and had done so, telling the president early in August that he could not be effective if major policy decisions were made without his knowledge. "I feel like going back to California," he was quoted as saying to Reagan. Shultz, former secretary of labor and the treasury in the Nixon administration, had been summoned in mid-1982 from San Francisco, where he was president of the Bechtel Group, Inc., to replace Alexander M. Haig, Jr., at the State Department. Haig had waged the same bureaucratic battle with the White House—and lost.

The president's foreign policy team was in turmoil. Clark, the man who had been unable to define détente or to name the leaders of Zimbabwe and South Africa during his confirmation hearings as deputy secretary of state in 1981, was widely seen in the State Department as a know-nothing who viewed the Soviet Union as an immoral and implacable enemy. In turn, the top echelon of the State Department was seen by Clark and some of his close aides as "professional swishes" —a phrase used by one former Clark associate in a 1985 interview—who were afraid to confront the Soviets. There were serious divisions inside the White House, too, between the hard-liners close to Clark and their enemies on the president's personal staff—"pragmatists" such as Chief of Staff James A. Baker III and senior adviser Michael K. Deaver. By the early summer of 1983, Clark seemed clearly in ascendancy; he was the man who reportedly had the president's ear, and his confidence.

The State Department's loss of influence was most evident in Central America. In July, official Washington, including George Shultz, had been stunned to learn from the morning newspapers that the president had authorized a six-month joint American military exercise in Central America, including mock bombing runs and naval quarantine maneuvers. As many as four thousand American servicemen and nineteen U.S. warships were scheduled to take part in the war games off the Atlantic and Pacific coasts of Nicaragua. With Clark leading the way, the Reagan administration seemed to be on the verge of escalation in Nicaragua. The White House was requesting an increase in covert aid for the contras, the CIA-supported opposition force, and there was an increase in the White House rhetoric against the Marxist government in Nicaragua. George Shultz was not a major player in all of this, and had even been forced in late May to go along with Clark's insistence that he fire Thomas O. Enders, the State Department's assistant secretary for inter-American affairs. Enders had angered the White House with his independence and his public talk of a possible negotiated settlement between the Left and the Right in El Salvador.

Shultz's loss of status had been hastened by the collapse of American policy in the Middle East. The secretary had staked a great deal of prestige on his ability to rescue something from the morass in Lebanon in the aftermath of Israel's 1982 invasion, which took place before he came to Washington. The basic State Department approach was to build up the Lebanese government and army of President Amin Gemayel, a Christian, and encourage Gemayel to work out a sharing of power with the many Shiite and Sunni Moslem factions in Lebanon. The policy never had a chance, as many outside experts emphatically told the State Department, simply because Moslems would never leave the future of Lebanon in the hands of Gemayel and the Lebanese Christians. Twelve hundred American marines initially sent to Lebanon as peacekeepers stayed there in an ambiguous role through the summer of 1983 as the Reagan administration sought to maintain some control over events. What had simply been bad U.S. policy became deadly policy by the end of summer, with the death of the first marines in Lebanon amid heavy shelling and fighting between Christians and Shiite Moslems.

The Lebanese crisis broke upon a vacationing Washington. It was the week before Labor Day and the president was, as usual, at his ranch near Santa Barbara, California, accompanied by William Clark and one of his hard-line NSC advisers, Vice Admiral John M. Poindexter. Policy guidance at this moment was coming not from the State Department, although George Shultz was in Washington that week, but from a quickly assembled Special Crisis Group in the White House led by Vice President George Bush. Shultz was but one of the members of the group, along with Secretary of Defense Caspar W. Weinberger and CIA director William Casey. Reporters were told by the California White House that the only solution seemed to be more of the same: to continue and perhaps increase American support for Gemayel and his Christian government.

Throughout his travails, Shultz had managed to cling to one major policy initiative—trying to expand diplomatic and economic contacts with the Soviet Union. With presidential approval, he began a series of meetings early in 1983, in secret and with limited agenda, with Soviet ambassador Anatoly F. Dobrynin. The meetings had continued, although relations between the two superpowers reached another low point in early spring, when Ronald Reagan renewed his rhetoric against the "evil empire" of the Soviet Union. Premier Yuri A. Andropov, responding a week later, accused the president in turn of telling "a deliberate lie." The name-calling came amid growing fear among America's allies in Western Europe that the Reagan administration was not capable of handling the U.S.-Soviet relationship.

On August 20, at the height of newspaper speculation about Shultz's future in the Reagan Cabinet—and perhaps because of such speculation—the president agreed to permit a previously embargoed sale of American equipment to the Soviets for the laying of oil and gas pipelines. The decision, over heated objections from Defense Secretary Weinberger, was seen as a sign of presidential support for the publicly battered Shultz. Six days later, the Agriculture Department signed a new five-year grain purchase agreement in Moscow that included an American commitment not to interrupt such sales—as had happened in 1979 after the Soviet invasion of Afghanistan—for the life of the contract. On the next day, August 27, the White House approved the reopening of negotiations between Washington and Moscow on a new cultural exchange agreement and the establishment of consulates in New York and Kiev. No one on the Soviet desk in the State Department permitted himself to think that any breakthrough was imminent, but it was progress in an area that had been stalemated. There was another positive sign: Soviet foreign minister Andrei A. Gromyko had agreed to a meeting in Madrid with Shultz on September 8 at the concluding sessions of the Conference on Security and Cooperation in Europe, with a follow-up session scheduled in New York at the opening of the United Nations Assembly in October. These were meetings badly wanted by the beleaguered secretary of state and his advisers, anxious to assure their European allies—and themselves—that they could handle the Soviets.

George Shultz was not consulted as his senior aides worked all night trying to cope with the often contradictory flow of information about Flight 007. The key players were Richard Burt, the assistant secretary for European and Soviet affairs, and his superior, Lawrence S. Eagleburger, the undersecretary of state for political affairs. Both were bright, good at their jobs, and with strong enough anti-Soviet feelings to pass White House muster. Burt had been a national security correspondent for the New York *Times* before joining the State Department in 1981. He was obsessed that summer by what had become an American public relations battle in Europe over the initial deployment of the Pershing II intermediate-range ballistic missiles in England, West Germany, and Italy. The American insistence on deploying the Pershings, as well as cruise missiles, and the Soviet campaign against those deployments—scheduled to begin in December—had turned the continent into an East-West battleground. Burt and Eagleburger saw the issue as a basic test of will between the two superpowers, a political war between communism and democracy. There was enormous pressure from the European allies, facing widespread protests over the nuclear missiles, to delay or modify the deployment. Another pressure was the fear that the Soviets would make good on their threat to walk out of the Intermediate-range Nuclear Force (INF) talks in Geneva. Europe was increasingly worried about leaving its nuclear fate to Ronald Reagan, with his tough talk and his reputation for being trigger-happy. The Soviet government, under the new leadership of General Secretary Andropov, had been doing what it could all year to make Europeans even more nervous about American control over their nuclear fate. That summer Soviet diplomats took another step and began suggesting that Moscow was willing to make concessions in the INF talks to forestall deployment of the Pershing IIs. Burt and Eagleburger were adamantly against any delays and were more than willing to call Moscow's bluff. Even reports that the Pershings had mechanical problems did not matter. "We don't care if the goddamn things work or not," Burt was quoted as saying in a staff meeting in late summer. "After all, that doesn't matter unless there's a war. What we care about is getting them in." The message was clear: deployment of the Pershings had become as much a political issue as one of national security.

Eagleburger, a career Foreign Service officer and former ambassador to Yugoslavia, shared Burt's views and worked closely with him. An expert on Europe and NATO, he had preceded Burt as head of European affairs and was intensely involved in the disarmament talks. Eagleburger had been a key aide to Henry A. Kissinger in the Nixon and Ford years and was, if anything, wise in the ways of bureaucracy and the media. Shultz trusted his judgment and relied heavily on his advice.

Burt had fought off the initial calls about the airliner he had received while at dinner; the report of a missing airliner didn't seem to be urgent, particularly since there were indications that the plane had landed safely at a Soviet airport on Sakhalin Island. At 10:45 P.M., with communications intercepts beginning to flow from Misawa, Burt was told by a senior intelligence officer at the State Department operations center that the situation was serious. He arrived within minutes, received a quick briefing, and, following his instincts, took charge of the crisis. "I wasn't the duty officer," he subsequently explained to an associate. "I just took command." There was strong reason to suspect that the Soviets had shot down Flight 007, but the intelligence had yet to be fully processed.

At 11:35 a request from the South Korean government was relayed: Would Washington ask the Soviets to help locate the airliner? There are no diplomatic relations between Seoul and Moscow. Burt telephoned the duty officer at the Soviet embassy and had him awaken Oleg Sokolov, the acting chargé d'affaires. Sokolov returned the call within minutes and was informed of the Korean request. Burt emphasized that the United States considered this to be an urgent issue; an American congressman was aboard the airliner. A similar message was forwarded to the American embassy in Moscow, with instructions that the Soviet Foreign Ministry be contacted. At this point, however, although Burt and his colleagues could not have imagined it, American intelligence knew more about what had happened over Sakhalin than the Foreign Ministry did. (It took the Kremlin four hours before it replied to the South Korean request, through the embassy in Moscow: "The plane has not been located on Soviet territory." Sokolov eventually would be summoned to a late-morning meeting with Eagleburger at the State Department but would be unable to provide any more information.)

The rest of the night and early morning became a waiting game as the Central Intelligence Agency and Defense Intelligence Agency put together their updates and situation reports. Burt telephoned Eagleburger on a secure State Department line a few moments before midnight and brought him up to date. The two men must have discussed whether to wake up the secretary of state. It was Eagleburger's call to make and he chose to wait; it was too early in the crisis for high-level decision-making.

Burt, continuing to move quickly, mobilized his staff and set up an informal working group; a first assignment was to produce a comprehensive situation report for Shultz. Burt and Eagleburger came to the realization that this was one crisis that they had a chance to control. The State Department's top intelligence expert on the Soviets, Robert H. Baraz, was a bright but cautious bureaucrat with a reputation for avoiding controversy. He agreed readily with the CIA's and DIA's view that there was ample evidence in the intercepts to conclude that the Soviet pilot had identified the aircraft before destroying it. His was an important confirmation for the senior State Department officials, because Baraz was known to be far less ideological than his counterparts in the Pentagon or at the CIA. It was becoming obvious that Shultz—if he chose to do so—would be justified in giving the Soviets a black eye in public, which could, if handled adroitly, accomplish two goals at once: improve his standing with the president and the White House hard-liners and strengthen his hand at the Madrid meeting with Gromyko. He would publicly signal that the meeting still was on. The Soviets would be eager to keep the date in the face of a worldwide outcry and a wave of anti-Soviet feeling over the shootdown. As an added bonus, European opposition to the Pershing II and cruise missile deployments would be weakened.

In those early hours, with the Soviets unable to supply any information, the only sure thing seemed to be the communications intelligence. Surely no one could question the meaning of a taped intercept in which a Soviet pilot was overheard exulting that his target was destroyed.

Like many senior government officials, Eagleburger was prepared to be skeptical about most CIA analyses and much of the diplomatic intelligence: men and women assigned to overseas posts, he understood, too often become clients of the country in which they serve. But intercepted communications are another matter: there was a special reverence for the products of the NSA. As one former associate recalled, "Larry, for all of his cynicism about intelligence, is one of those people who regard the NSA as the gospel truth." Getting access to the intercepts was an early priority. Burt was anxious about the intelligence streaming into the State Department operations center: When could the secretary of state have a complete transcript? He was told that it would take two days to fly the tapes from Japan to NSA headquarters at Fort Meade and assemble a working transcript. The initial translation, as usual, was "rough" and needed more work. The assistant secretary, caught up in the anger and moral outrage that was flooding through the State Department, insisted that the department be provided with as much of the transcript—no matter how raw—as possible, as soon as possible. Time was essential if Shultz was to take advantage of what seemed to be a brilliant opportunity. For once, the secretary of state was in the right spot at the right time. There was no ranking White House official in town; none of the president's three closest advisers was on the East Coast. Mike Deaver was on vacation in Lake Tahoe, California; Jim Baker was believed to be off hunting somewhere in Texas, and Edwin Meese III, the last member of the White House triumvirate, was in Santa Barbara, running the California White House.

By 2:00 A.M., the CIA was reporting that it was 95 percent sure that the Soviets had identified the airliner and then shot it down. The men in the State Department still hesitated. It would be another three hours before it was agreed that the evidence was strong—more than enough to make public. The next step would be up to the policymakers. The Soviets had been caught by the American intelligence network in the act of shooting down a passenger airliner. The question was no longer what had happened, nor was it—as some analysts at Air Force Intelligence and at NSA field stations thought it should be—why the shootdown had taken place. Instead, Burt and Eagleburger, convinced that they had all the information they needed, were preoccupied with the issue of how tough to make it for the Soviets without jeopardizing the enormous political and propaganda gains that were sure to come as the world responded to the shootdown. There were other voices in the State Department that morning, but they weren't being listened to. One State Department Soviet specialist, who was aware of the immense Soviet anger in April after the Navy had overflown Soviet territory in the Kurile Islands, suggested to colleagues that the destruction of Flight 007 might be linked in some way to the ealier incident. No one paid much attention.

Hugh Montgomery, director of the State Department's intelligence operation, wasn't much help. He was a longtime CIA operative who had been Alexander Haig's backup choice for the intelligence post; stronger candidates had failed the political litmus test of the Reagan administration. Montgomery was close to Bill Casey, the CIA director; many in the State Department believed that their man in charge of intelligence was simply parroting the views of the CIA. There was plenty of reason, as his personal staff understood, to suspect the independence of his judgments. Montgomery was known to make a daily stream of calls, using a secure telephone in his desk, to Casey and to Lieutenant General Lincoln Faurer, the NSA director.

George Shultz did not learn of the shootdown until he climbed into the backseat of his limousine sometime around 6:30 A.M., his normal pickup time, and began to leaf through the morning State Department intelligence reports. The initial situation report on the shootdown, as compiled by Burt's task force, had been placed in Shultz's briefing folder by nervous aides.

The secretary was an angry man by the time he arrived at his office; why hadn't he been awakened earlier? His initial pique was soon replaced by a far more profound anger as the enormity of what the Soviet Union had done began to sink in. Burt and Eagleburger had prepared their reports well. The preliminary transcript, as analyzed by the CIA and State Department intelligence, was devastating, and officials recalled Shultz's sense of outrage over what seemed to be the deliberate destruction of a civilian airliner by the Soviet interceptor. The mistreatment of innocents was one of the few issues that seemed to break through the secretary's reserve. Shultz could never understand why the Soviet chose to mistreat its Jews or refuse to let them emigrate. One of his rare displays of emotion came after learning that the authorities in Poland had somehow managed to make the children of labor leader Lech Walesa burst into tears after a visit to their jailed father. "How can they treat people like that?" Shultz asked. Similarly, Shultz's occasional anger at his own staff was triggered upon seeing his security agents push people around on official trips.

One State Department aide walked into Shultz's seventh-floor offices a few moments after 7:00 A.M. and found Eagleburger and Montgomery, among others, huddling over the secretary's desk with maps of the Soviet Union. "The implication was clear," he recalled. "The Soviets had shot down a plane and 'We've got them cold.' Right then the debate began—'We know they've done it and how do we handle it?' " The talk was of how best to make the shootdown public to ensure that the world shared the outrage of the men on the seventh floor. Should the story be put out at the noon briefing, given every day by John Hughes, the Cape Cod newspaper publisher who had been brought into the government by Shultz as his assistant secretary for public affairs? Why wait? Perhaps Hughes should do a briefing right away. Hughes was summoned, and he urged that the shootdown story be made public immediately. The story was so good that little more than a factual recitation was needed. Hughes, like Shultz's other senior aides, knew that the secretary had been suffering through a bleak period; dominating this issue could go a long way toward reviving his influence and keeping the Soviet initiatives alive. Nothing like that was said, of course; his staff knew better.

George Shultz wanted last-minute reassurance that there would be no surprises. Was the intelligence community convinced that the Soviet interceptor had shot down the aircraft, and that the downed plane was not on an American reconnaissance mission? There was at least one last-minute conversation between Shultz and Casey that morning, perhaps more. Casey was relying heavily on Fritz Ermath, the CIA's national intelligence officer (NIO) for the Soviet Union and Eastern Europe, who was known throughout the bureaucracy for his rigid anti-Soviet ideology and for his propensity during crises to consistently attribute the worst motives to the Soviets. Ermath found more than enough evidence to conclude that the Soviet interceptor pilot had identified the aircraft as civilian before shooting it down. His biases melded perfectly with those of William Casey, and it was Casey's assessment that emerged as the most important that morning, since he served not only as CIA director but also as director of Central Intelligence (DCI), bureaucratically the top official in the government in charge of the budgets and policies of *all* the intelligence agencies, military and civilian. Casey's influence, of course, extended directly into the upper reaches of the National Security Agency. (Some State Department intelligence aides were told later that Shultz took the time to consult directly that morning with the NSA, speaking either with General Faurer or with Robert E. Rich, a key deputy.) Nothing was heard from Moscow.

One essential decision was made almost casually. To erase any doubts as to the categorical nature of the American information, Shultz would make clear to the world that the communications intelligence community had the goods on the Soviets; that America and its allies had the capability to intercept and translate Soviet military communications in the Far East. Such activities are simply not talked about in public. Shultz would not specifically cite the role of the Japanese in all this, but it was not hard to foresee that the Japanese role would quickly become known. Once the subject of how America learned about the Soviet shootdown was opened, it would be impossible to prevent further revelations. (Within a few hours, in fact, White House spokesman Larry Speakes casually revealed the Japanese connection, explaining to newsmen during a press briefing in California that the administration's delay in confirming the shootdown had been caused in part by the need to translate the intercepts from Russian to Japanese to English.) All NSA Druid communication intercepts originating from allies, such as the

Japanese, are normally considered among the most sensitive national security information and designated as Top Secret Umbra (TSU), with Umbra denoting special communications intelligence. No one on the seventh floor of the State Department was troubled by the use of TSU material that morning because the Soviet wrongdoing seemed to override any diplomatic or intelligence considerations. "I don't really remember that being much of a problem," one State Department participant later said of the decision to make public the intelligence. "It went through my mind that this was a little curious." One secret was not mentioned: that an American Cobra Ball reconnaissance plane had been on assignment off the coast of Kamchatka at the time Flight 007 was first picked up by the Soviets.

Richard Burt's staff was assigned to draft the Shultz statement. It was agreed that the secretary would digest the facts and then, after clearing the statement with the California White House, go on national television to announce the tragedy. A message was also prepared for relay to the American embassy in Tokyo, assigning officials there the painful task of informing the Japanese government that the American secretary of state would be talking in public about the intelligence collected at its outpost at Wakkanai. Prime Minister Yasuhiro Nakasone's government would get less than one hour's notice. And, at 9:42 A.M., Washington time, according to State Department logs, Hugh Montgomery was instructed to telephone General Lincoln Faurer, the NSA director, to tell him that his secrets, too, would be on national television within an hour.

Getting the tough-talking statement cleared at the White House turned out to be no problem; the Soviets, after all, had done no more than prove the correctness of Ronald Reagan's view of them. The other aspect of Shultz's mission was more complicated. His goal was to save his Soviet policy and his Madrid meeting with Gromyko, and thus ward off any complaints from the Europeans—while also demonstrating that he could be as tough in public on the Soviets as any of the hardliners on the National Security Council staff.

Shultz's television appearance at 10:45 A.M. was riveting. Visibly angry and motioning with a sheet of paper in his hand, the secretary gave what amounted to a Top Secret Umbra review of the shootdown. He reported that the Soviets had picked up Flight 007 on radar off the Kamchatka Peninsula at 1:00 A.M. Tokyo time. The first visual sighting, he said, took place at 3:12 A.M. off Sakhalin. Fourteen minutes later, "the Soviet pilot reported that he fired a missile, and the target was destroyed. . . . We know that at least eight Soviet fighters reacted at one time or another to the airliner." A Soviet search-and-rescue aircraft subsequently reported spotting a kerosene slick on the surface of the Sea of Japan, Shultz said. The statement concluded with strong words: "The United States reacts with revulsion to this attack. Loss of life appears to be heavy. We can see no excuse whatsoever for this appalling act."

Under questioning, Shultz went further and—relying on the intelligence assessments of William Casey and Lincoln Faurer—purposely revealed that the United States had intelligence showing that the Soviet pilot had deliberately shot down what he must have known was a civilian airliner. The Soviet interceptor, he said, "moved itself into position where it had visual contact with the aircraft, so that with the eye you could see what it was you were looking at . . . the aircraft that shot the plane down was close enough for visual inspection of the aircraft." Asked whether he could offer any explanation for the Soviet action, Shultz responded: "We have no explanation whatever for shooting down an unarmed commercial airliner, no matter whether it's in your airspace or not." As planned, Shultz buffered the tough words by explicitly stating in response to a question about the future of U.S.-Soviet relations that he intended to keep his appointment in Madrid with Gromyko to "hear what he has to say about this."

George Shultz was not a headline-seeker and the Washington press corps knew it. His rage and his willingness to go public with the most sensitive intelligence information in the government, as symbolized by the piece of paper he waved (really a prop), was completely convincing. The networks had interrupted their morning broadcasting for the Shultz television appearance and the emotion of his statement carried the television reporters beyond the facts. Bill McLaughlin, CBS's State Department correspondent, stayed on the air after the news conference to describe Shultz as being in a "moral rage" over the shootdown. McLaughlin then said: "The Secretary emphasized that the . . . fighter that shot down the airliner had visual contact. He could see the airliner, perhaps could even see the other pilot. He could identify it. He could see that it was a 747, clearly marked KAL, Korean Air

Lines. This is not a bomber. They were up there for a long time. For about two and a half hours, the Soviet ground people were able to track it. They were talking back and forth. The conclusions that the Secretary seems to have made, I may be reading between the lines, is that this was a premeditated act."

On NBC, Roger Mudd, a seasoned and skilled journalist, had his own embellishments. In an exchange with a colleague after Shultz's appearance, Mudd asked: "Was I wrong to conclude that the Secretary was claiming Soviet enticement? . . . If visual contact was made, it appears from the Secretary's rendering of events that they really sort of enticed that plane and shot it down within its own space."

Secretary Shultz also was watched that morning halfway across the world by analysts of the Air Force's Electronics Security Command, on duty in Hawaii and Japan, men who knew what intelligence had been forwarded to Washington and what it showed. Many had been on duty for twenty-four hours or longer, filing reports and assessments to the National SIGINT Operations Center. They were appalled by Shultz's insistence that the Soviet pilot had knowingly fired at a civilian airliner.

"We were all saying," one intelligence officer recalled, " 'How can the son-of-a-bitch do this? He's disgracing us all. He's making political and corrupt use of intelligence—waving that paper around as if the hard intel[ligence] backs him up.' People will never appreciate the blow that we—who consider ourselves to be technical intelligence officers—suffered when Shultz stood up and made his statement."

Another Air Force intelligence officer, also on duty in the Pacific, recalled thinking as Shultz spoke that "the guys advising him have got to be as smart as I am and have got to know it was totally wrong. How can he, as secretary of state, say what he did?" His thought was that Shultz's hard line was linked to developments elsewhere; perhaps a serious violation of SALT I or some other international understanding.

There was far better intelligence available, in the Air Force office of Jim Pfautz, but it wouldn't be presented to the top echelon of the government for another two hours.

10

"We Ate Their Sandwich"

Air Force Intelligence stole the show at the Joint Chiefs of Staff's meeting late Thursday morning.

Jim Pfautz's briefing book had been taken into the "tank"—the secure Pentagon room used for JCS meetings—by Jerry O'Malley, the Air Force vice chief of staff. O'Malley knew that the first order of business would be an assessment of the shootdown of Flight 007 by representatives of the Defense Intelligence Agency, officially designated as the senior intelligence advisers to the Joint Chiefs. O'Malley had not even considered the possibility of bringing Pfautz and his briefers to the tank; under military protocol, Pfautz could not give a briefing to the JCS unless officially invited. But O'Malley also knew that John W. Vessey, Jr., the Army general who was chairman of the Joint Chiefs, eventually would ask, as he always did, what information the Air Force had to contribute. After all, it was an air incident.

The Air Force general said nothing as the DIA

representative briefed the Chiefs. The DIA had received the same raw intelligence from the NSA's National SIGINT Operations Center as had the other intelligence agencies and concluded that the intercepts proved that the Soviet pilot had at one point pulled abeam of the airliner and must have identified the intruder as a Boeing 747 passenger plane. Its report closely mirrored the version made public two hours earlier by George Shultz. When he finally got his chance, O'Malley's analysis not only disagreed about the ease with which a 707 and a 747 could be differentiated at night but also went far beyond communications intelligence and dealt with what Pfautz and his aides were convinced was the crucial issue—the link between Cobra Ball and Flight 007. There were no slides to project, but O'Malley did have a sequence of color charts showing the flight paths of both aircraft, as well as all significant communications and the time of those messages. The Air Force version had momentum and plausibility: it seemed clear that the Soviets had made a terrible error. O'Malley's obvious confidence in the analysis also may have played a role. O'Malley, as most in the room knew, was no innocent to intelligence; he had flown U-2 and SR-71 missions while serving in the Strategic Air Command and was considered one of the most forceful advocates of improved intelligence in the Pentagon.*

There were many in the intelligence community

---

* O'Malley, his wife, and two aides were killed in the crash of his Air Force T-39 passenger plane on April 20, 1985, near Scranton, Pennsylvania.

that day who concluded that Pfautz had contrived—
perhaps with O'Malley—to make the DIA look bad.
One Air Force colonel described O'Malley, who was
Pfautz's classmate at West Point, as a strong supporter
of Pfautz's ambition to succeed Jim Williams as DIA
director. Such maneuvering (if that's what it was) is an
intrinsic part of Pentagon politics, with the services
anxious to get their man in the top echelon of intelligence. The DIA job was all the more important to the
Air Force because Lincoln Faurer at NSA, an Air
Force lieutenant general, was scheduled to be reassigned or to retire in a year or so, and his replacement
would undoubtedly come from the Army or Navy.
O'Malley was doing his part for the Air Force, the
colonel explained, by taking Jim Pfautz's briefing book
into the JCS meeting, where he "sprang a trap" and
"overwhelmed" the poorly prepared DIA representative.

   Pfautz and his senior aides were given a blow-
by-blow afterward from O'Malley's office and were
told that Vessey had asked for the Air Force briefing
book. After leafing through it, he exclaimed, "Why the
hell don't I know this? Where are you getting all this
information? This is more complete than anything I
have." The JCS chairman then turned to the DIA
representative and asked why he was getting so much
more detail from the Air Force than from the Defense
Intelligence Agency, whose sole mission—under Robert McNamara's 1964 reorganization—was to provide
the Joint Chiefs with the best available intelligence.
   Vessey ended the meeting by grabbing the Air
Force papers and rushing with them over to the office

of Secretary of Defense Caspar Weinberger; the two men usually met, each accompanied by senior military aides, every working day at 11:30 A.M. Their meeting that Thursday was delayed by the JCS session and didn't take place until a few minutes after noon. It had been a hectic morning and would get worse. Vice President George Bush had called a meeting of his Special Crisis Group for 2:00 P.M. at the White House; the issue would not be Lebanon, as it had been all week, but the Korean shootdown. Vessey and Weinberger knew that the Pentagon would be expected to provide a full-scale briefing; there was an extended discussion of the intelligence for the next thirty minutes, with the critical issue being whether the Soviets had indeed identified the airliner before shooting it down, as George Shultz had said publicly, or whether the Air Force version of events was correct. "Halfway through the first day," one participant recalled, "it was clear that we had a reconnaissance plane up there and it was clear that the Soviets could have gotten the tracks mixed up"—as the Air Force had told the Joint Chiefs of Staff. Weinberger and his military aides somehow came to the conclusion, however, that the Air Force's view couldn't be correct. For one thing, the participant said, the radar tracks of the RC-135 and the airliner "were so far apart and so different in nature" that it was hard to imagine that the Soviet Air Defense Force had confused them. A second factor was the communications intercepts, which seemed to show clearly that the Soviet pilot had pulled close to the airliner for a look and had then drawn back to attack. "The guy who was up there—tracking it, getting ready to pickle it," the participant recalled, "had to know" he was targeting an airliner. "It was not believable that he could have had it so screwed up. Our own view was that they knew what they were doing. It seemed to us to be beyond reasonable doubt."

In a crisis, the men at the top of the Pentagon chose to become their own intelligence officers.

Neither Vessey nor Weinberger deigned to attend the 2:00 P.M. Special Crisis Group meeting. Vessey recalled later that he had a prior engagement that could not be canceled.* There was no such excuse for Weinberger, whose appointments calendar for the day, as supplied by his office, showed that he remained in his office all day and even hosted a late-afternoon reception for a departing aide. Weinberger chose to pass up the meeting, Vessey acknowledged, primarily because President Reagan wouldn't be in attendance. In Weinberger's view, it was a low-level meeting. There was another factor, Vessey said: "George Bush isn't going to make any decisions." It was eventually agreed, Vessey said, that his senior aide, Admiral Arthur S. Moreau, Jr., who normally accompanied the chairman to all White House meetings, would be sent alone to brief George Bush and the Crisis Group.

General Vessey was untroubled by his decision to send a junior aide to fill in for him. He had come to

---

* Vessey's official log for that day, which the general kindly agreed to review after his retirement, incorrectly showed that he had been out of Washington from early Thursday until late the next day, September 2. In fact, he was in meetings on the shootdown with the secretary of defense until after 3:00 P.M. on September 1.

the personal realization sometime that day, he recalled, that "on the face of it, [the shootdown] had all the elements of a major screwup. Whether the pilot identified the airliner or not, it had to be a screwup." Vessey also knew that the full story wouldn't be known for days. The first intelligence reports, including the Air Force's, were little more than "part of a mosaic" whose pattern was impossible to discern immediately. If the White House wanted to play hard ball with the Soviets over the shootdown, that was its business. "As far as we in the armed forces were concerned," he said later, whether the Soviets had identified the airliner or not "wasn't going to make any difference in what we did. We weren't going to go over there and bomb Moscow."

Pfautz learned later that afternoon that his briefing had gone to the White House; his informant was a senior aide, a colonel, who had been assigned responsibility for the highly classified Air Force briefing book and, as usual, had waited for Generals Gabriel and O'Malley to return with it after the JCS meeting. The colonel was told that Vessey and Weinberger had ordered the Air Force's briefing taken to the Special Crisis Group. Pfautz, who did not know that his intelligence already had been discounted by the secretary of defense and his military aides, was ecstatic. "We ate their sandwich," he said of the DIA.

The Air Force intelligence finally made it into the White House at 2:00 P.M., Washington time, twenty-three and one-half hours after the shootdown of Flight 007. The Soviet destruction of the airliner was a concrete issue for the Special Crisis Group, a problem that could be handled. George Bush may have been the nominal leader of the group, but all involved—as well as the men running the California White House—understood that the real player in the crowd was Bill Casey. The CIA director emerged in the first hours as among those advocating that the government take every step it could to tell the world what the Soviets had done. Some in the administration would later call the process Russian-bashing.

Under any circumstances, Casey's opinions would be difficult to question. Of all those at the meeting—including the vice president—he was the only one who had a close personal and working relationship with Ronald Reagan. Any challenge to his beliefs would have to be made on the basis of hard information. Even without Casey's imprimatur, it would have been difficult to challenge a CIA assessment in the Special Crisis Group, for the CIA was more than merely well represented there—it was dominant. George Bush, who ran the group, had been CIA director in the Ford administration, and his two aides at the meeting both had CIA ties. Donald Gregg, Bush's national security adviser, was a longtime field operative and former CIA station chief; and retired Admiral Daniel J. Murphy, Bush's chief of staff, had served as a deputy director of the CIA in 1976, under Bush, and in 1977. Admiral Moreau represented the Pentagon; Larry Eagleburger, sitting in for the very busy George Shultz, represented State, and the National Security Council was represented by its forth-ranking member, Robert M. Kimmitt, a former Army major. Kimmitt, who had been appointed executive secretary of the NSC in May, was running the NSC staff that week, as William Clark and

Admiral Poindexter were in California with the president and Robert McFarlane, another of Kimmitt's immediate superiors, was in the Middle East.

The meeting focused on the essential point that had been raised a few hours earlier by George Shultz: Did the Soviet interceptor pilot know he was shooting down a civilian airliner? It was generally agreed that the answer was yes. One member of the group recalled Casey speaking with certitude about what appeared to be hard technical intelligence showing that the Soviet pilot had identified Flight 007 as civilian. "Casey was strong on something like this," the group member said. Casey brought up the fact—or what was widely accepted as fact—that the intercepts showed that the Soviet pilot had pulled abreast of the Boeing 747 just moments before shooting it down. "This guy's a fighter jock," he recalled, in summarizing the consensus. "He's up there for a reason—to shoot a plane down. He's got to have seen the silhouette." The conclusion was that the pilot knew that his target was a Boeing 747 and not the much smaller Boeing 707.

At some point after Casey's presentation, the views of Air Force Intelligence were briefly outlined by Admiral Moreau. The situation could have been very awkward. Here he was, a special assistant to the chairman of the Joint Chiefs, preparing to present an intelligence scenario that—if described fully—directly conflicted with the stated views of the president's secretary of state and the known belief of his director of Central Intelligence. It wasn't every day that a vice admiral filled in at the White House for both the secretary of defense and the chairman of the Joint Chiefs of Staff. Jim Pfautz's technical analysis, with its complicated charts and minute-by-minute account of the airliner's flight path, must have seemed to be a poor match for an NSA interpretation that had the endorsement of the CIA director. The admiral's presentation was further limited by the fact that he had not witnessed Pfautz's original Air Force briefing but had relied on a summary presented by General O'Malley. In other words the Navy man—who was doing nothing more than operating as the system operates—was twice removed from the original intelligence.

Any enthusiasm the admiral might have had for the Air Force analysis had been diminished by Weinberger and Vessey before he even came to the White House; Casey's seemingly definitive review of the communications intelligence couldn't have made things easier. In any case, Moreau discredited the very intelligence he was supposed to be representing and provided only a cursory account of the Cobra Ball mission and its proximity to Flight 007. One crisis group member recalled Casey making a point of "explaining that this was kind of far out. The Soviets had lots of time and should not have been confused." In essence, the Air Force version "was pooh-poohed by the briefer on the grounds that the Soviets should have known." The Air Force information "just didn't play a significant role in the total briefing. The issue was 'How could these guys have shot down an unarmed passenger plane?' " The flight paths of the Cobra Ball and Flight 007 "may be a big thing to the Air Force," the participant thought at the time, "but why is it a big thing to me?" He left the White House meeting convinced that the Air Force intelligence had been "pretty well debunked."

A second member of Bush's Special Crisis Group similarly remembered "some discussion of plane tracks and all that," but he found it very unpersuasive: "Everybody came back to the point: 'What difference does it make? Let's worry about what they [the Soviets] did. How could a pilot fail to make an ID? Why find reasons to excuse the Soviets? Let's not worry about explicating them.' "

There was general satisfaction with the hard information from the intercepts, as well as a pro forma agreement that much more needed to be learned about the Soviet decision to destroy Flight 007. One group member recalled an insistence by Bush that the intelligence community be urged to "run to ground all the facts."

Thus, by mid-afternoon of September 1, the Air Force's intelligence had crash-landed. It had been discounted even before it had gone to the White House and been uninspiringly presented there by an aide to the JCS chairman who could not have been familiar—and had every incentive to not want to be—with all of its implications. The men who were involved in the discussions that afternoon in the White House soon moved on—as did the intelligence community—to other crises and other analyses. Unknown to Jim Pfautz, his "scoop" had been a nonstarter from the moment George Shultz went on national television to suggest that the Soviets had knowingly shot down a civilian airliner.

George Shultz's televised news conference unleashed a wave of public revulsion and anger. The Soviets had been caught out, and no one at the top of the Reagan administration was interested in any information that would make the story more complicated. Within hours, the government initiated what amounted to a public relations campaign against the Soviets, involving extensive private briefings for the press and extensive public appearances and television interviews by senior officials, who were suddenly being made available to all who asked. The Voice of America was assigned to tell the story of Flight 007 around the world and around the clock, as was the United States Information Agency.

At the early-afternoon press briefing at the State Department, Richard Burt began what would become a series of public appearances to discuss Flight 007. The issues involved in the shootdown went far beyond the knowledge of John Hughes, the official spokesman. Burt, as the senior official most deeply involved, was brought in to answer newsmen's queries. One of Burt's goals in the briefing was commendable: to reinforce the State Department's view that the shootdown should not be permitted to destroy the ongoing U.S.-Soviet arms talks. Another goal was to keep the heat on the Soviets, and Burt did so, although he didn't always know what he was talking about. Asked, for example, what he could say about the American intelligence capabilities in the Far East, the assistant secretary said he would not go into detail but added: "I can tell you that we did not have real-time information." In fact, the 6981st Electronic Security Group at Elmendorf Air Force Base in Alaska had picked up the Soviet tracking as soon as Soviet Air Defense Force began monitoring the airliner off the Kamchatka Peninsula. Asked whether the United States had monitored communications making it clear that the Soviet interceptor pilot knew he was targeting a civilian airliner, Burt answered: "I think that it was understood that it was a commercial aircraft." Burt would become even more emphatic in private briefings later in the day for newsmen, categorically telling a senior correspondent for one of the weekly newsmagazines that the American intelligence community was sure that the Soviets had identified the plane as a civilian airliner before destroying it. Other newsmen were told during background sessions that the intelligence community had concluded that it was "almost inconceivable" that the order to shoot was issued without the knowledge or approval in advance of the senior Air Defense Command in Moscow.

All of this played the major role in the unrestrained and inflammatory television news coverage that marked the first day of the crisis. By mid-afternoon, for example, the networks had gone on the air with what they told the American public was the final radio transmissions between the Soviet SU-15 interceptor pilot and his ground controller. As widely publicized, those conversations went like this:

> Ground: Take aim at the target.
> Pilot: Aim taken.
> Ground: Fire.
> Pilot: Fired.

This spurious pilot-to-ground-controller conversation had initially been published by Kyodo news service in Japan and represented nothing more than one unsubstantiated news report in a highly competitive breaking story. Nonetheless it was introduced by anchorman Dan Rather during a *CBS News Special Report* that day as having originated from "Japanese intelligence sources." The line between fact and fiction, initially broken by the secretary of state, had been erased.

Within hours of George Shultz's news conference, leading members of Congress took to the Senate and House floors to denounce the Soviet action. There were few voices of caution. "If that's not cold-blooded, outrageous murder," Senator Patrick Leahy, Democrat of Vermont and ranking member of the Senate Intelligence Committee, said of the shootdown, "I don't know what is." Senator Carl Levin, Democrat of Michigan, called it a "despicable and a barbaric act." Former vice president Walter F. Mondale, the leading candidate for the 1984 Democratic presidential nomination, similarly called the shootdown "barbarous and despicable." Senator Alfonse M. D'Amato, Republican of New York, told newsmen that the destruction of Flight 007 was nothing less than murder. Representative Thomas F. Hartnett, Republican of South Carolina, equated the shootdown to an attack on a school bus. Senator Orrin Hatch, Republican of Utah, announced, "We know what happened. We know who did it. We know how it was done, and the Russians do, too." Leahy, Levin, Hatch, and the others were behaving no better or worse than the secretary of state and his assistant secretary for European affairs—or the news media, for that matter.

In the early afternoon, Tass, the official Soviet news agency, put out a statement acknowledging only that Soviet interceptors had tracked an unidentified aircraft over Kamchatka Peninsula and Sakhalin Island. The aircraft, flying without navigation lights, Tass said, "did not respond to queries, and did not enter into contact" with Soviet air control officials. The Soviet fighters, the statement concluded, "tried to give it assistance in directing it to the nearest airfield, but the intruder plane did not react to the signals and warnings . . . and continued its flight in the direction of the Sea of Japan." The statement, which made no mention of the shootdown, was seen as further evidence of Soviet culpability.

Newsmen were summoned to a special late-afternoon press briefing at the State Department and told by John Hughes that the U.S. government "finds this reply totally inadequate, and the United States reiterates its demands for a satisfactory statement." The United States was considering its options, Hughes said, but that was a matter for the president—still in California—to consider.

The drama in the Far East was far from over. Soviet and American military commands throughout the Far East had gone on heightened alerts as both sides struggled to cope with the shootdown. Some American commanders had done more than merely get angered by what was seen as Soviet brutality and had authorized six F-15 interceptors to fly to Misawa and participate in the early—and fruitless—search-and-rescue operations in the Sea of Japan, just off the southeast coast of Sakhalin Island. The interceptors were accompanied by an airborne E-3a AWACs aircraft, filled with radar gear that could guide the fighter planes to any target in air or at sea. The message to the Soviet General Staff was clear: "If you try anything more, we'll shoot you down." The Soviets responded in kind, by escalating their air and sea activities as well as flying two of their most advanced interceptors, known as MiG-31 Foxhounds, to Sakhalin. The interceptors, never before deployed in the Far East, had increased range and improved radar and weapons systems that gave them better capability to conduct operations over water and thus—so the U.S. Navy concluded in a series of urgent intelligence reports—escalated the threat. Moscow's decision to bring the MiG-31s to Sakhalin seemed to be far from a sign of regret over the destruction of Flight 007 and signaled, at least to some intelligence officers in the Electronics Security Command, that the Soviets were convinced that they had been provoked into shooting down the airliner. One experienced officer described the Soviet message, in essence, as this: "We know what you did to us. We know you knew what you were doing. In effect, we are treating this behavior in a way to ensure the continuance of poor relations."

Amid the posturing and escalation of forces on both sides, a jurisdictional struggle broke out between the American Navy and Air Force over operational control of the air and sea search-and-rescue forces. The dispute was not resolved until cooler heads at the top of the Fifth Air Force in Japan agreed that the Navy commander at sea would have operational control of all Air Force assets.

Jim Pfautz and his staff at Air Force Intelligence weren't worrying that afternoon about George

Shultz's botching of the intelligence. There was more work to do and eagerness to get on with it; Pfautz's fourth-floor Pentagon offices were still filled with excitement over the fact that the Air Force's briefing—and not the DIA's—had gone over to the White House. The junior officers who had spent much of the previous night and morning preparing the elaborate slides and charts for the 8:30 A.M. briefing to the top brass in the Air Force shared Pfautz's pleasure in a job well done. "Pfautz was happy about what we did," one officer said. "We were out in front on it. It was like press time. We scooped everybody—had the best story in town and got it out faster than anybody else." One of Pfautz's senior aides pinned a long note to the office bulletin board recounting how the Air Force intelligence had been praised by General Vessey at the JCS meeting earlier in the day.

Not everyone was persuaded, however, that the right thing had been done. At a staff meeting later that day, a lieutenant colonel working for Pfautz reported that he had telephoned one of his counterparts in the DIA and "apologized for taking the initiative" and for the embarrassment of having an Air Force Intelligence assessment brought over to the White House instead of a coordinated DIA position paper. "I told him," Pfautz said, " 'Look, don't ever apologize for that again. We put the book together for the [Air Force] chief of staff. And then we've done our job.' "

Pfautz's failure to share his information immediately with DIA or anyone outside the Air Force would become a source of controversy over the next weeks, as word of what seemed to be a Pfautz power play spread through the Pentagon. Pfautz was accused of putting career interests before the nation's security in not immediately sharing what he knew with the DIA. "What Pfautz did was not right," said one ranking Air Force intelligence officer. "You don't play with the possibility of war. He goes to the DIA and says, 'I got this and I'm going with it.' They can disagree, but his information needs to get told in order to prevent—in a crisis—serious miscalculation. You go in and talk it out. It demands coordination—that the top people know that Air Force and the DIA have differences of opinion. He's playing fuck-around when there's a possibility of the use of force in a major conflict."

There were some Air Force generals who later claimed that Pfautz's handling of the Flight 007 intelligence played a role in his failure to be named DIA director and early retirement. One difficulty in assessing the subsequent backbiting is the fact that Pfautz was no more popular with many of his fellow general officers than he was with the men who worked under him.

None of Pfautz's senior staff recalled being troubled by the failure to brief the DIA early that morning. "It was all so hectic," one aide said. "There was no time." Pfautz acknowledged later that he never considered making a call to DIA and, even if there had been time, would not have done so. In Pfautz's view, his job description did not call for any outside sharing. He believed his mission was solely to produce intelligence for the senior operational officers of the Air Force, with whom he was scheduled to meet—as he did every weekday morning—at eight-thirty. Those officers, of course, were free to relay word of the Air Force's findings to any office they chose. At no time, before or after that meeting, Pfautz said, did he consider wasting his time by volunteering a briefing for General Williams or any of his associates in Defense Intelligence. "If Jim [Williams] had come to me that morning on his way to breakfast," Pfautz insisted, "I'd have given him the book. Even if he had been an enemy, I'd have given it to him. We didn't do this to embarrass DIA; we did it to get the chief of staff the best intelligence. It's not my fault that we did better. Don't blame Jim Pfautz for this.

"Was I out for Jim Williams's job? The answer is yes. Did I torpedo anybody on 007 in order to get the job? I didn't have to—because it was coming to me."

Pfautz spoke bluntly about a process known to all senior intelligence officers in the Pentagon: the armed forces collaborate, as one officer put it, "on everything except the hot stuff. They just don't do it if it's hot." Flight 007 was hot and Jim Pfautz had the best story. The system, as it was working in mid-1983 and had worked for years—and will, no doubt, continue to do for years—was geared to such conduct in crises.

Meanwhile, the National SIGINT Operations Center was still processing raw intelligence on the shootdown of Flight 007 and would continue to do so for many days; and returns were pouring in from some of the government's most sensitive Soviet satellite-intercept programs, which had been requested to search out Soviet General Staff communications and other data relevant to the shootdown. All of the evidence supported the initial Air Force thesis. For example, one of the second-day intercepts, apparently from a U.S. satellite, showed that one of the Soviet pilots who failed to intercept Flight 007 over the Kamchatka Peninsula referred to the airliner as an RC-135. "The second day was much better than the first," one Air Force officer recalled. "We had made assumptions that were borne out by hard copy that we didn't see until twelve hours later." None of this would immediately affect the debate over the shootdown.

The truth was that by the first afternoon of the crisis Jim Pfautz's staff was at work in a vacuum—and didn't know it. They hadn't paid much attention to George Shultz's statements, in part because they were too busy, but also because Shultz had spoken out, after all, hours before their first intelligence report was forwarded to the White House. The facts eventually would emerge, so the young officers thought. The White House announced late on Thursday that Reagan had decided to return to Washington from his California ranch and would preside over a meeting Friday night of the National Security Council. In the meantime, Air Force Intelligence had dramatically improved its initial reporting. The evidence was no longer problematical; it was empirical: the Air Force now had intercepts demonstrating that the Soviets had not knowingly targeted a civilian airliner.

The new information didn't matter. The administration was committed to its anti-Soviet public relations campaign. Eagleburger, in an appearance that night on ABC-TV's *Nightline*, acknowledged that he was not an "expert" on what pilots could see at a distance of two kilometers, but added nonetheless: ". . . clearly I think they had to know it was a 747, and I myself believe that at that distance they must also have known it was a civilian airliner. I don't see any way to avoid that."

The Russian-bashing continued on other networks. For example, newsman Marvin Kalb served as moderator for a thirty-minute late-night NBC-TV special report called "Shot From the Sky." Kalb, relying—as would any good journalist—on what senior government officials were saying publicly and privately about highly classified information, declared at the opening of the show, "One of the [Soviet] jets got close enough to see unmistakably that the 747 was a passenger plane." Later in the broadcast, however, NBC Pentagon correspondent Jack Reynolds reported on the conflicting theories among Defense Department officials, noting skeptically that there were some who viewed the shootdown as a military plot to embarrass Soviet premier Andropov and try to reverse his arms control policies. Reynolds, turning to another point of view, then accurately summed up the Air Force information: "So I think that basically what they've come to over there is a theory that because of the confusion, the lack of information, the hour of night that it happened and so on, that it probably was a snafu. And that the Russians made a mistake which has caused them enormous embarrassment." At that point, Chris Wallace, NBC's White House correspondent, in California with the president, took it upon himself to interject the official Reagan administration view: "Marvin, if I could jump in here. I must say that some of my sources at the White House offer a dissenting opinion. They say that our intelligence indicates that there were communications that they intercepted between the ground in that area of the world and Moscow. They say that the command structure, the Russian command structure, was working well."

11

The President

Ronald Reagan first learned of the missing Korean airliner and the possibility of Soviet involvement by telephone from William Clark, his national security adviser, on the evening of August 31. The first CRITICs had been filed from Misawa and rescinded by the NSA; there was still doubt as to the aircraft's fate. It was 7:30 P.M. California time. A second call from Clark came three hours later as the devastating intercepts quoting the Soviet SU-15 pilot were circulating throughout official Washington. Reagan reacted with characteristic anger but authorized no immediate response. Larry Speakes, the White House spokesman, told newsmen later that the senior aides in California found the intelligence "so incredible" that they insisted it be checked and double-checked overnight. The president apparently went to bed at that point. It could wait until morning.

The intelligence community was still hours away from reaching any consensus on the incident; many Americans had gone to bed thinking that the airliner was safe somewhere on the ground in the Far East. Reagan was provided with a much more detailed briefing a few moments after seven o'clock the next morning by Edwin Meese, his counselor and the only one of the senior presidential advisers on duty in Santa Barbara. Bill Clark was spending the night 150 miles north of Santa Barbara at his 888-acre family ranch at Shandon, in San Luis Obispo County. Precisely what information the president was given at any point during the night and morning will have to await his and other's memoirs, but Clark, Meese, and CIA Director Casey had a close working relationship with the president and shared many of his conservative attitudes, especially those concerning the Soviets. Casey's belief that the Soviets had identified the airliner before shooting it down was undoubtedly relayed in some form to the president. Similar findings were being presented at about the same time to Secretary of State George Shultz. It was much too early to discuss policy options: the government was still struggling with the most crucial question of the moment—just how to tell the world that the Soviet Union had brutally shot down a planeload of civilians. The president had approved Shultz's news conference solution—the secretary's statement was read to Bill Clark in advance—but he did not speak to his secretary of state until after the successful broadcast.

By midday, official Washington was consumed with both growing anger at the Soviets and growing unease over what Ronald Reagan, the hipshooter, might do in response. Leading members of Congress, including Senator Howard H. Baker, Jr., of Tennessee, the Republican majority leader, and Representative Thomas P. O'Neill, Jr., the Democratic Speaker of the House, had already been in contact with White House aides and urged caution. One basis for caution, in the post-Watergate era, was the fear that, perhaps unknown even to the White House, some intelligence agency—American or South Korean—was responsible for Flight 007's seemingly insane deviation over the Soviet Union. Many newspapers were flooded with tips to that effect, and there were some Americans who believed—as some still believe—that the Korean airliner must have been secretly outfitted with cameras and listening devices to spy on the Soviet Union.*

Fears about the president's reaction were not valid. Indeed, Ronald Reagan had spent much of his political career trying to educate the American people about the threat he believed the Soviet Union posed. And now, in a few desperate minutes over Sakhalin Island, the Soviets had demonstrated to all—even his most severe critics—that his crusade had been justified. But unlike

---

* For example, I was telephoned on the night after the shootdown by a military employee and told that the Korean airliner involved had been parked at Andrews Air Force Base in suburban Maryland the week before. The implication was that the plane could have been outfitted with sensitive intelligence equipment. The story surfaced repeatedly in subsequent months. An editor in the Washington bureau of the New York *Times* also telephoned me to ask if I would help determine whether Flight 007 had somehow been arranged by American or South Korean intelligence. At the time it seemed to be a very logical and prudent request. No evidence emerged over the next two and one-half years to support the thesis, but it remained a favorite theory of the many journalists who continue to do research and write about the Korean airliner. It should be said that in all of my reporting inside the NSA and military intelligence I found no evidence of any advance word on the Korean flight, and advance notice to

George Shultz, who was in a struggle for his political life, Reagan felt no immediate need to denounce the Soviets or in some other way to seek vengeance. Reagan, in fact, never seriously considered any direct retaliation. How he made that decision, which was reached almost immediately, is not known; perhaps, as some close aides seriously suggested later, the president himself did not know. One aide who discussed Flight 007 with Reagan depicted the president's thought process at such moments as not reasoned but instinctive: "Reagan rises above all of his rhetoric and all of his ideology in moments of crisis and moments of decision. It's not as if he thinks it through himself—he just instinctively rises up."

In any case, his unwavering hostility to the Soviet Union and his willingness to speak out against the "evil empire" in public had given him a flexibility that would not have been available to a different president. There were no Ronald Reagans in political opposition

---

such units would be essential to monitor the flight's progress if its mission was—as some suspect—to activate Soviet radar activity. Furthermore, any plan calling for the airliner to divert inside Soviet territory would have to assume that the aircraft would be fired at and shot down in the waters east of the Kamchatka Peninsula, where Flight 007 would have been destroyed if the Soviet Air Defense Force had not stumbled so badly. The rationale for planning an intelligence mission that would end even before the spy plane got over Soviet territory is difficult to comprehend. Finally, officials of the International Civil Aviation Organization (ICAO) found no evidence that members of the cleanup or maintenance crews were denied access to any portion of the airliner while it was serviced at Anchorage prior to takeoff for the Far East. If the aircraft had been scheduled to serve as an active spy plane and not a passive provocateur, it would have required huge amounts of electronic and/or camera equipment.

to call for immediate action. As a close aide crudely but accurately put it, "Nobody's ever called Ronald Reagan a pussy." Reagan, if anything, became more serene as his government began its attack on the Soviet Union. He not only concluded that there was no need for him to make any immediate response, he also decided there was no reason to leave his beloved California and return to the White House. He could handle the crisis from the ranch. He didn't have to prove that he could stand up to the Soviets.

Reagan's instinct that no immediate retaliation was called for provided a bottom line for the inevitable bureaucratic infighting over what to do. The administrative apparatus of the presidency, with its options papers and analyses, would be limited to dealing with diplomatic or economic sanctions.

The bureaucratic turmoil below was, in essence, a traditional one in the Reagan administration: between the hard-liners on the National Security Council staff and their enemies in the State Department, the "pragmatists." Over the next thirty-six hours there was a heated argument over options.

The most restrained recommendations, originating from the working groups set up by Larry Eagleburger and Richard Burt in the State Department and supported by the moderates in the White House, urged an international anti-Soviet propaganda campaign, to begin immediately by taking the issue of Soviet culpability to the Security Council of the United Nations. That move would be followed by a United States–orchestrated drive to organize a worldwide boycott of Aeroflot, the Soviet civil airline. No serious economic or political sanctions were proposed. The just-announced consular negotiations between Washington and Moscow would be dropped, but it was essential that the Geneva talks continue, particularly since the shootdown of Flight 007 had immensely improved the administration's standing with its European allies.

Most administration hard-liners, including Defense Secretary Weinberger, insisted that the president retaliate by breaking off the disarmament talks at Geneva or, at the least, aborting the recently signed contract for the sale of pipe-laying tractors to the Soviets.

There were a few who wanted even more. The most fervent faction was headed by John Lenczowski, one of Bill Clark's Soviet experts on the NSC staff. Lenczowski, son of George Lenczowski, the Russian-born conservative scholar, was viewed with respect by his conservative colleagues throughout the Reagan administration. He insisted to all who would listen— Clark among them—that a military response should not be ruled out.* Lenczowski went so far as to assemble a small rump group of conservatives from through-

---

* William Casey's recommendations could not be learned, but he supported, according to a Washington *Post* account, a suggestion by the president—said to be made early in the crisis—that the United States respond to the shootdown by shipping U.S.-made antiaircraft missiles to the Afghan rebels fighting the Soviet Union. The thought was, so the *Post* reported on March 3, 1986, that the rebels would then be in a position to retaliate for the destruction of Flight 007 by shooting down a Soviet military aircraft. The recommendation was rejected, the *Post* said, after senior CIA officials argued that the new weapons would dangerously escalate the civil war in Afghanistan and alienate Pakistan. Two years later the Reagan administration changed its mind and approved the clandestine shipment of the antiaircraft missiles to Afghanistan.

out the government to talk about specific military steps. "We wanted action—military action," one member of the group recalled. "We discussed everything from attacking Cuba to rolling back the Soviets in Eastern Europe. For example, what's the cost of Cuba? The answer was Berlin." Lenczowski eventually prepared a formal options paper for the president that included some possible military responses as well as such harsh reprisals as a break in U.S.-Soviet diplomatic relations and the shutting of all Soviet consulates in the United States. "We were willing to trade [the American consulate in] Kiev for [the Soviet consulate in] San Francisco," the Lenczowski associate added. "John spent a lot of capital on this and he got it on the table—and it was considered." The Lenczowski proposals were appended, at Clark's direction, to the formal NSC options paper on the crisis. Lenczowski wanted much more than merely getting his views on the table, however, and later told colleagues that the president's refusal to take some drastic action in the Flight 007 crisis was America's worst foreign policy failure since 1933, when the Soviet Union was formally recognized by the administration of Franklin D. Roosevelt. For all of his tough talk, Lenczowski would stay on in the White House as one of four NSC "directors" of European and Soviet affairs.

The first-day issue for the president's senior advisers in California was far more mundane: how to persuade Ronald Reagan that the Korean airliner issue was significant enough to warrant his return to the White House and his personal attention to the debate over what to do next. It was leadership by telephone in the first hours of the crisis, as the president's aides called, one by one, with their guidance. His immediate staff understood that if anything was sacrosanct to the president, it was his time alone with his wife, Nancy, at their ranch. It's difficult to judge how much of Reagan's initially prudent response to the shootdown—his decision to wait and see—was abetted by his desire to do nothing that could interfere with his stay in California, where he was scheduled to remain through the weekend. During the week, he had handled the first deaths of marines in Beirut and the escalating civil war in Lebanon from the ranch without complaint from the press or the public.

In the midst of crisis, his staff believed, Reagan truly seemed to be guided by a high sense of patriotism, a belief—almost too corny for outsiders to accept—that the only acceptable decision was one that felt right to him and right for America. One adviser recalled a sharp conversation he had with the president after Reagan had refused all staff entreaties that he attend the funeral of Soviet Premier Andropov in 1984. The major argument was a political one: no matter what the president thought of the Soviet leader, or of that society, 1984 was an election year and it made good sense to go. "Why?" the president said, bridling. "I never knew the guy." The comment seemed more appropriate to the argument of a suburban couple over going to the funeral of a distant relative. The adviser understood, nonetheless, that the battle was over: Reagan would stay home. The president's approach was similarly personal and apolitical on all big issues: Reagan truly does not like the Soviets, the adviser added, "and never will—but he also understands that it's a big world and we have to live with them."

That view seemed to sustain Reagan early on September 1. George Shultz had done a first-rate job in making the administration's case and in depicting the Soviets for what they were. Until more was known, and the Soviets publicly explained what had happened, he and Nancy could continue their vacation. Ed Meese had been severely criticized in August 1981 for allowing Reagan to sleep through his first national security crisis, involving the destruction of two Libyan warplanes by U.S. Navy interceptors in the Gulf of Sidra. Then, as now, Reagan had been away from the White House, in California, with Meese as the senior aide in charge. If the president once again seemed to be out of the loop of decision-making and at the mercy of his staff, it could be a damaging issue in the 1984 reelection campaign. Larry Speakes was given a brief—and temperate—initial statement to read at an early-afternoon briefing of the White House press corps, which was staying at the nearby Santa Barbara Sheraton Hotel. Drafted in part by Meese, the statement seemed to anticipate a quick Soviet explanation: "The President is very concerned and deeply disturbed about the loss of life aboard the Korean Air Lines flight overnight. There are no circumstances that can justify the unprecedented attack on an unarmed civilian aircraft. The Soviet Union owes an explanation to the world about how and why this tragedy has occurred." It was the mildest language the president would use in public to describe the shootdown. Speakes, obviously anxious to avoid any notion that the president was not on top of matters, also provided reporters with a summary of the earlier presidential contacts with Clark, Meese, and Shultz on the shootdown and added that Reagan "is being kept abreast and will be kept advised throughout the day as the assessments proceed by officials in Washington."

The most effective—and ultimately successful—impetus to get the president back to the White House originated with one of Reagan's junior aides, Lee Atwater, a deputy assistant to the president for political affairs who had nothing to do with the great issues of foreign policy, such as U.S.-Soviet relations. Atwater, a native of South Carolina who had worked for Senator Strom Thurmond, got involved because of the president's sensitivity to one of his traditional constituencies, the Far Right, which had lost one of its leaders, Larry McDonald, on the Korean airliner. Atwater was the White House contact point for senior Republican officials and worked closely with Stuart K. Spencer, the president's trusted political adviser who—despite not being on the White House staff—was considered to be one of the few men capable of telling Ronald Reagan what he didn't want to hear. It was natural that McDonald's congressional staff would turn to the seemingly always available Atwater upon hearing that Flight 007 was missing. Some of McDonald's followers were convinced that the Soviets had targeted the airliner solely to get rid of McDonald, who, as chairman of the John Birch Society, was a rabid anti-Communist. There was fear that Ronald Reagan, who, in their eyes, had betrayed McDonald since becoming president by continuing to negotiate with the Soviet Union, would not take strong action to avenge his death.

By the time Atwater was contacted, McDonald's

staff was in the ironic position of having not too little but too much information. Someone in the Pentagon had decided, perhaps in deference to McDonald's renowned anti-Communism, that the government's most sensitive intelligence information could be shared. Just before midnight on August 31, Tommy Toles, McDonald's congressional press secretary, was told by a Pentagon duty officer that secret information on the flight was available, but it could be disclosed only over a secure telephone and to someone with a top-secret clearance. Toles turned to Frederic N. Smith, McDonald's administrative assistant, who had served twenty years as a Navy officer and still held a clearance. Smith made a call from his home in suburban Virginia to the Pentagon's National Military Command Center (NMCC), the clearinghouse for all military activities, and was invited to pay a visit. He was amazed. "I spent five years in the Pentagon [as a Navy officer] and had never been there," he recalled. He took along his sixteen-year-old son, Colin. Both were given a brief tour that included a look at the famed hot line between Washington and Moscow. "I'd seen a few briefing rooms in the service, but this was the fanciest one I'd ever seen." About a dozen officers were at work, surrounded by screens, displays, and telephones. He was sworn to secrecy by the NMCC duty officer, a Navy commodore, and flatly told that "the Soviets had shot down Flight 007." The officer was holding a group of what were obviously raw intelligence messages and depicted them as "pretty good information." Smith was relieved to finally get some facts. Honoring his commitment not to talk, he telephoned Toles after the meeting and said only that the outlook was poor. McDonald's aides had been given a more optimistic assessment a few moments earlier from an official at the State Department operations center, who assured them that the Korean airliner was safe on Sakhalin.

By early morning, there still was no State Department confirmation of the plane's fate, and McDonald's aides managed to convince themselves that information was deliberately being kept from the president in California as part of a State Department effort to avoid a confrontation with the Soviets. It was then that Frederic Smith telephoned Atwater at home and told him McDonald had been shot down. Atwater, initially skeptical, made a call to the White House situation room and learned the dimensions of the tragedy. A quick thinker, he immediately realized that any strong diplomatic or military response to the incident posed enormous political risks to the president. There would be plenty of hard-line advice, but only a few willing to tell the president that a strong response could hurt in 1984. "American politics are controlled by Big Events, and this was definitely a Big Event," Atwater later said. "What was important was not how it would play out in the next three or four weeks, but over the next few months. You've got a president with a reputation of having an itchy finger; a mad bomber who will react recklessly in a crisis." There would be enormous political usefulness in reacting calmly and responsibly. Atwater was well aware that his views weren't necessarily the views of some of the men around Ronald Reagan in California. He was getting in over his head; he did not have the clout to get involved.

But Stuart Spencer did. Atwater found Spencer by

telephone and expressed his fear that Reagan and his close-by aides didn't understand how important it was for him to get back to the White House and run the government during the crisis. Spencer, a California politician who had directed President Gerald R. Ford's successful primary campaign in 1976 against Reagan for the Republican presidential nomination, had become close to Nancy Reagan and had been brought into the 1980 primary campaign at a critical moment and served throughout as a key strategist and *éminence grise*. In a crisis, the president's immediate staff understood, Reagan often was reached by an outsider—such as Spencer—who could work through Nancy Reagan and deal with the most important issues in personal terms. Reagan's willingness to listen to an outsider's advice over that of his immediate staff did little to encourage presidential aides to take issue with their boss, even when dealing with the most sensitive issues of foreign intelligence.

Spencer believed that the president had marvelous political instincts, but he shared Atwater's immediate concern that Reagan, outraged over the brutality of the Soviet action, might be convinced to act in haste. He assumed that there would be plenty of tough advice available and his message in a brief telephone talk early that afternoon with Reagan was direct: "Make sure you have all the facts before you do anything. Don't overreact. Be calm, cool, and collected." He had been informed by presidential aides of the early intelligence assessments concluding that the Soviets had deliberately shot down the airliner after identifying it as civilian. Spencer knew that his advice might be gratuitous, but his basic concern was political. Having said his piece, Spencer no longer dealt with the substantive issue of what to do and how to respond. He stayed in touch with the president and his wife that day because he also shared Atwood's belief that Reagan had to return to Washington. He had learned in an earlier telephone talk with Ed Meese that the president was intent on staying at his ranch and running the crisis from there. Mike Deaver was located at a resort in Lake Tahoe and he was asked to intervene. Deaver had been at a party late the night before and hadn't even known of the Flight 007 crisis until a friend suggested that he turn on a television set. He called Santa Barbara and quickly learned that the big issue was getting the president to change his mind and return to Washington. It was hard going; Deaver later told Spencer that the president was "in concrete" on the issue. There was a second, much longer telephone call to the increasingly annoyed Reagan. "Whatever you've got to do," Spencer told Reagan, "you've got to police this thing. You've got to get back to Washington so the American public knows you're on top of it." Spencer understood that his best argument—stating the president's options in terms of the 1984 election—simply could not be used. "If you put something in a political context with Reagan," he said later, "you're dead." The goal was to work around him. There was a third call to Nancy Reagan, whose influence on such decisions, as widely reported, can be decisive. Spencer could speak more directly to the First Lady, and did. She agreed that he had to return, and the process of turning Ronald Reagan around was well on the way.

More support came from Kenneth M. Duberstein, the president's highly respected chief lobbyist. Duberstein, who had just returned to Washington after a weekend meeting with Reagan and other advisers at the ranch, informed Meese that the senior Democratic and Republican leaders of Congress wanted the president back in Washington and wanted to be consulted on his future plans. Eager to reassure the leadership, and with the president unavailable to do so, Duberstein prevailed on George Shultz to telephone Howard Baker and Tip O'Neill to brief them on the administration's initial actions. Most significant of these was a decision to urge an immediate convening of the U.N. Security Council to discuss the Soviet shootdown. Duberstein also managed to locate Jim Baker at an out-of-the-way duck blind in Texas. Baker's later call to Reagan duplicated the advice already given by Spencer and others: "Let's not overreact and let's get back to Washington." The president finally gave in. He would cut his vacation short by two days and return to Washington in time to chair a National Security Council meeting Saturday night and a bipartisan briefing of congressional leaders on Sunday.

With the president now committed, the gloves could start coming off. A new, much harsher statement was drafted and released by Larry Speakes in time to dominate the evening network news broadcasts. The tougher language was a reflection of the need, as seen by the president's men, to reestablish control, as well as a legitimate expression of deepening anger over Moscow's refusal to accept responsibility for the deaths of the passengers aboard Flight 007. The initial Soviet statement, as relayed through Tass, was seen as a blatant evasion of responsibility—and as an opportunity. The Soviets had demonstrated that Ronald Reagan had been right in his denunciations of the Soviet empire, and he would take that message to the world. It was a message that would be repeated by presidential spokesmen and briefers for the next week.

Speakes, emphasizing that his words were those of the president, stood in front of the network cameras at Santa Barbara and heightened the rhetoric: "I speak for all Americans and for the people everywhere who cherish civilized values, in protesting this Soviet attack on an unarmed civilian passenger plane. Words can scarcely express our revulsion at this horrifying act of violence. The United States joins with other members of the international community in demanding a full explanation for this appalling and wanton misdeed." The reporters further were told that the president had ordered all flags at federal installations and U.S. military bases flown at half-mast. There was an assurance from the president: "I will make every effort to get to the bottom of this tragedy."

Any reluctance the president had about his decision to return to Washington ended abruptly upon that night's broadcast of *The CBS Evening News*. With the nation, the Congress, and much of the world up in arms over the Soviet shootdown, Ronald and Nancy Reagan were shown—as photographed by cameras stationed three miles away—enjoying their usual afternoon horseback ride at their ranch. There were angry protests to CBS from the president's staff about "cheap shots" and sensationalism, but the long-range television cameras were known to be there and no one had compelled the president and his wife to go riding. The staff wanted the president off his horse and back in Washington. It was decided after the newscast that

Reagan would delay the inevitable no longer and return not on Saturday but on the next day, Friday, to the White House and a meeting of the National Security Council, which would now be moved up to Friday evening. It was also decided that before returning at midday Friday he would make his first public comments on the shootdown, and that he would be tough. William Clark arranged for John Lenczowski, still at work in Washington trying to generate support for direct retaliation, to forward some ideas. The nation would finally hear directly from its president.

Reagan's statement came shortly after noon California time from the airport tarmac at Point Mugu Naval Air Station in California, where he was scheduled to board Air Force One for the return to Washington. It was his strongest denunciation of the Soviet Union since taking office. The shootdown, Reagan said, was more reprehensible than the 1979 Soviet invasion of Afghanistan: "While events in Afghanistan and elsewhere have left few illusions about the willingness of the Soviet Union to advance its interests through violence and intimidation, all of us had hoped that certain irreducible standards of civilized behavior, nonetheless, obtained. But this event shocks the sensibilities of people everywhere.

"What can we think," the president asked rhetorically, "of a regime that so broadly trumpets its vision of peace and global disarmament and yet so callously and quickly commits a terrorist act to sacrifice the lives of innocent human beings? What could be said about Soviet credibility when they so flagrantly lie about such a heinous act? What can be the scope of legitimate and mutual disclosure with a state whose values permit such atrocities? And what are we to make of a regime which establishes one set of standards for itself and another for the rest of humankind?"

The president had dropped a gauntlet. He had escalated the crisis and turned an international tragedy into a superpower contest. Not having been informed—even at this point—of evidence to the contrary, he had labeled the Soviet attack an act of terror. He had also made public the essential outline of his policy for responding to the shootdown. The National Security Council meeting later that evening in the White House would be public relations, designed to placate those in the Congress, the press, and the public who are reassured by such events. Bolstered by Shultz's newfound determination to take the offensive, the State Department, with its pragmatic options, had won out, to the disgust of many of Ronald Reagan's more fervent supporters inside the government and elsewhere. Flight 007 would remain primarily a media issue, and the Reagan administration would kick off an international anti-Soviet propaganda campaign at, of all places, the much-reviled United Nations. The harshest goal would be to temporarily shut down Soviet civil aviation. There would be no boycott of the disarmament talks at Geneva, for Flight 007 had given the United States improved bargaining leverage there. Cancellation of the recent grain deal or the pipeline-equipment transaction would be counterproductive—the Soviets simply would buy elsewhere—and would also put the president in the position of adopting trade policies he had criticized during the Carter administration.

There were, in fact, few real retaliatory options, and

the president had chosen the most effective. Reagan truly believed that words were important and would be seriously considered by the Soviet Union. In his view, the real fear of the Soviet Union was the truth; they could not tolerate public exposure. Triggering worldwide condemnation of the Soviet Union was now within reach. He had been right all along in his public emphasis on "evil empire"—the Soviets were an immoral society, and the most dramatic response possible to Flight 007 would be to say that over and over again. Ephemeral acts such as boycotts or walkouts, or even a military attack, would pale besides the presidential rhetoric.

Ronald Reagan had instinctively avoided any direct action in the Flight 007 crisis for more than a day and had reassured many in the nation and the world who had feared a trigger-happy response. He was thus free to talk, to say anything he wished about the Soviets, without being perceived as intemperate. There is a frightening irony in all this: the president of the United States, relying on information that was wholly inaccurate and misleading, was accusing the other side of telling lies, and was perceived as being moderate in so doing.

The Soviets played right into the hands of their harshest critics in the Reagan administration by their inability to face up to their error. Moments after Reagan's speech on the airport tarmac in California, Tass distributed a statement claiming that its interceptors had done nothing more than track an intruder that had flown into Soviet airspace without clearance and without navigation lights and had ignored warning shots. The statement made no specific mention of the Soviet role in the shootdown but included an expression of regret from the "leading circles of the Soviet Union"—a euphemism for the ruling politburo—"over the loss of human life and at the same time a resolute condemnation of those who consciously or as a result of criminal disregard have allowed the death of people and are now trying to use this occurrence for unseemly political gains." Moscow was accusing the United States, in effect, of having deliberately organized Flight 007's intrusion into Soviet airspace as part of a provocation: "[T]here is reason to believe that those who organized this provocation had deliberately desired a further aggravation of the international situation [and were] striving to smear the Soviet Union, to show hostility to it and to cast aspersions on the Soviet peace-loving policy. This is illustrated also by the impudent, slanderous statement in respect of the Soviet Union that was instantly made by President Reagan. . . ." The reference was to the White House statement issued in the president's name by Larry Speakes the night before. *Pravda*, the Communist Party newspaper, eventually would elaborate on the Soviet view that all of the initial American responses, from Shultz's news conference to the presidential statements, were part of a well-orchestrated anti-Soviet plot: ". . . facts demonstrate convincingly that the crude violation of the Soviet state border by the South Korean plane and its deep penetration into the Soviet Union's airspace was a deliberate, preplanned action pursuing far-reaching political and military aims."

The rigid Soviet bureaucracy, pushed into a corner by American rhetoric, was unable to make the best and most sensible response and admit that the Soviet military, exalted for its role in World War II, had made a mistake. The Soviet leadership, in choosing to appear indifferent to human life rather than admit incompetence, was doing its part to heighten the crisis. It was much easier to insist publicly that the military had performed its mission well in destroying what could only have been a plane sent as a provocation by Ronald Reagan. There would be no apology. The Soviet leaders, including such experienced men as Marshal Nikolai V. Ogarkov, the military chief of staff, came fervently to believe that Flight 007 had been a provocation, just as Ronald Reagan fervently believed that the Soviet interceptor pilot had known that the aircraft was a civilian airliner when he shot it down.

Friday afternoon's Tass statement, by attempting to shift the blame for the shootdown to the Reagan administration, revived all the worst American fears about the Soviet Union and was widely condemned. Most American newspapers published scathing editorials on Friday about Flight 007, invariably focusing on the fact—as initially enunciated by George Shultz—that the Soviet pilot knew he was shooting at a civilian airliner. The usually cautious New York Times, for example, took Shultz's account at face value—there was no reason not to—and wrote: "After tracking the South Korean intruder for more than two hours, and then observing him at close range, Soviet air defenders had to know the identity of their target—which means someone in the Soviet chain of command is guilty of cold-blooded mass murder." Anti-Soviet demonstrations took place in front of Soviet embassies and consulates in the United States and across the world, as anger over the shootdown continued to mount. One of the largest demonstrations, involving an estimated two thousand Korean-Americans, took place in front of the United Nations building in New York, where the U.N. Security Council debated a resolution in mid-afternoon condemning the Soviet shootdown of Flight 007. Mayor Edward Koch of New York City addressed the crowd and depicted the Kremlin as "a gang of murderers" who should "get down on their knees and apologize for what they have done."

The decision to turn to the United Nations, a forum for which the president and his top aides had little respect, was the clearest sign of the administration's ultimate policy in the crisis: to flay the Soviets publicly wherever and whenever possible. Charles M. Lichenstein, the senior American delegate in the absence of the vacationing ambassador Jeane Kirkpatrick, went beyond even Ronald Reagan's rhetoric. Lichenstein, a political appointee known for his strong anti-Soviet views, as were many on Mrs. Kirkpatrick's delegation, had no way of knowing that most of the facts he relied upon were wrong. His hastily written speech began: "Let me note here that hour by hour these last two and one-half days, more and more facts have become and are becoming available to my government, and as they do, our concern deepens and our outrage grows." Borrowing from the president's airport statement, Lichenstein characterized the Soviet action as a "heinous crime" that had been compounded by the Soviets' continuing denial of responsibility. The evidence showed, Lichenstein said, that the Soviet interceptor pilot "had the Korean 747 in his sights, clearly identified as a civilian airliner . . . for more than ten minutes running, prior to launching the destructive missile. The crime committed was, indeed, calculated; and, indeed, it was deliberate. . . ." He added: "Let us call the crime for what clearly it is: wanton, calculated, deliberate murder."

Lichenstein subsequently acknowledged that the final draft of his speech had not even been completed when he began his denunciation of the Soviets; a conclusion had been left to an aide and fellow hard-liner, Carl Gershman, who took his time, forcing Lichenstein to slow down his delivery to the Security Council. When the last page arrived, the final paragraphs of a major American policy address delivered before an international forum in a moment of crisis amounted to perhaps the rudest possible cultural attack one could make against the Soviets, quoting Aleksandr Solzhenitsyn on his former country: "Anyone who has once proclaimed violence as his method must inexorably choose the lie as his principle." It was as if the Soviet ambassador to the United Nations had quoted Benedict Arnold as a moral authority and expert on the United States. Lichenstein was not trying to resolve an international dispute with his words; he was trying to whip one up.

George Shultz, his status inside the Reagan administration dramatically revived, continued to play a prominent role and joined in Friday's public criticism of the Soviets for their failure to acknowledge responsibility for the shootdown. He made a brief voluntary appearance at the State Department's press center and, with cameras rolling, directly accused the

Soviets of knowingly shooting down a civilian airliner and then lying about it: "The aircraft was a commercial airliner on a regularly scheduled flight—and the Soviet fighter came close enough to see that. . . . No cover-up, however brazen and elaborate, can change this reality—or absolve the Soviet Union of its responsibility to explain its behavior. The world is waiting for the Soviet Union to tell the truth." They were strong words for a man who had spent much of the year trying to prompt continued relations between the two superpowers. Shultz also denied Tass's statement that its interceptors had attempted to warn the airliner by firing tracer shells along its route. "There is no indication," the secretary of state declared indignantly, "that the Soviets tried to warn the plane by firing tracers."

It was impossible on that Friday to conceive of any ambiguities, or any possible explanation for the deliberate Soviet shootdown of a passenger airliner. The administration, convinced of its information, pressed the advantage all over Washington. Midday Friday, there was a hastily assembled briefing on Capitol Hill for all congressional staff members with high-level security clearances. More than fifty aides were given a hard-line briefing by a team led by Richard Burt. "It was a real militant, tough briefing—'this heinous crime,' " one aide recalled. "But then, everyone of us felt that it was. And these guys were genuinely convinced of the immorality of the shootdown." The aide did notice one bit of caution: Burt and his colleagues no longer were categorical in insisting that the Soviet interceptor pilot had identified the aircraft as an airliner before shooting it down. "They were clearly leaving the question of Soviet identification as an open question," he recalled, "with a nudge in the right direction." Burt, in fact, had learned earlier that day of the American reconnaissance craft that had flown near Flight 007. Obviously aware that the issue was much more complicated than initially thought, he began on Friday to modify his comments in public, saying only that the Soviets must have or should have identified the airliner before shooting it down. The hard-driving assistant secretary, smoking constantly and seemingly on the verge of exhaustion, did not stop with Congress. He summoned senior embassy representatives from America's NATO allies to an afternoon meeting at the State Department and urged their nations to support the administration's tough line against the Soviets. Burt seemed very confident, one diplomat recalled: "He was totally in command, as if he'd cultivated a mystique."

That night, Burt, the administration's newest media star, appeared on ABC's *Nightline* to restate the government's claim that the destruction of Flight 007 was not merely a U.S.-Soviet problem—although the United States had spent two days trying to make it just that—but a problem for all the world. "The Soviet Union in a sense has told the United States as well as every other country in the world that it doesn't care about world opinion," he told anchorman Ted Koppel. There was one nuance, however. Asked whether the Soviet pilot perhaps had not been able to identify Flight 007 as a civilian airliner, Burt—who had been so emphatic in earlier private briefings with newsmen—would say only that it was "very, very implausible, to say the least." The quibble paled when juxtaposed with a telephone call-in conducted that night by *Nightline*. The question was direct: "Should the administration take strong action against the Soviets?" More than 220,000 viewers voted yes during the next hour, and 14,700 voted no—a 15-to-1 plurality. America clearly had made up its mind on the crisis.

Richard Burt and the State Department were not alone in lobbying that day. Obviously operating at the behest of Bill Casey, CIA officials allowed Senator Patrick Leahy of Vermont, a member of the Senate Intelligence Committee, to read the intercepted communications from the Soviet pilot. Leahy had been among the severest critics of the shootdown the day before, and his comments, as a moderate Democrat with a reputation for being hardworking and thoughtful, had been widely quoted and broadcast. Leahy was impressed, and told other guests at a Canadian embassy dinner a few days later that he had seen "hard and specific evidence" convincing him that the Soviets absolutely knew what they were doing when they destroyed Flight 007.

Friday night's National Security Council meeting was pro forma. The president, still wearing his California clothes—boots, a Western-style leather jacket, and a yellow polo shirt—listened courteously for more than an hour as the various options were debated. Before the meeting Bill Clark's NSC staff had presented Reagan with an options paper that had included John Lenczowski's hard-line recommendations in an appendix. It was all wasted work. The president had already exercised his option. As expected, there were strong recommendations from Caspar Weinberger that the disarmament talks in Geneva be frozen and that George Shultz not be allowed to meet with Andrei Gromyko in Madrid. There also were calls for economic sanctions. The president made no response to the substantive issues but instead spoke movingly on the virtues of the American system. One participant recalled Reagan declaiming that the shootdown "shows that we have the better system." From the moment Reagan walked into the room, the participant added, "I could tell that he was only going to talk. It was clear that he had a pacific instinct on this." At one point, the president turned to Charles Z. Wick, his personal friend and director of the United States Information Agency (USIA) and said, "You guys get this out." Wick, always eager to please, ordered his agency's Voice of America to beam ninety additional hours of transmissions daily toward the Soviet Union, despite a warning from engineers that the VOA's transmitters could not sustain the additional effort for more than a week without breakdown.

There was one nagging problem that no one seemed willing to deal with. By late Friday word had begun seeping out, even among the junior staff members of the National Security Council, of the Cobra Ball mission that had operated off the Kamchatka Peninsula on the night of August 31. It was a matter of hours, many officials believed, before the Soviet Union—desperate to improve its credibility—would make public the existence of the intelligence plane and link it to the airliner.

W. Scott Thompson, a deputy director of USIA who accompanied Wick to the NSC meeting, recalled a discussion about the RC-135 with a group of senior NSC advisers shortly after the National Security

Council meeting. Thompson had learned about the intelligence plane from one of Bill Casey's aides a few moments before and immediately concluded that the administration had better announce it before the Soviets did. His views on such matters usually were not lightly dismissed; he was a senior member of the administration's highly touted Special Planning Group for Public Diplomacy, an NSC-directed operation aimed at combatting Communist propaganda with American propaganda. The operation, run out of the White House but with an extremely low profile, was said to be one of the president's favorites. Its action officer was Walter Raymond, Jr., a longtime CIA operative who had been assigned to the National Security Council on the strong recommendation of Casey, who played a major role in getting the propaganda operation off the ground. Thompson and Raymond worked closely and effectively together: "I remember sitting on the edge of a desk outside the sit-room kicking it around," Thompson recalled, "and I was trying to force the issue of the recce [reconnaissance] plane. I said we've got to limit the damage and make a virtue of it. Nobody listened to me."

12

A Good Ally

In Japan, as throughout the world, the destruction of Flight 007 produced a renewed wave of anti-Soviet feeling. Twenty-eight Japanese citizens were aboard the airliner, and their deaths seemed to symbolize all that was unstable in Japanese-Soviet relations. Spontaneous demonstrations took place in front of the Soviet embassy in Tokyo, and Japanese officials were forced to increase the embassy's police guard. The fact that the shootdown had also revealed Japan to be America's secret partner in the collection of communications intelligence seemed insignificant, to the immense relief of Japanese officials, when compared with the enormity of Soviet wrongdoing.

Publicly, Prime Minister Yasuhiro Nakasone's government joined the United States in strongly condemning the Soviets and, within days, it would do more than talk: it voluntarily associated itself with the Reagan administration's spectacular at the United Nations centered on the Japanese tape recording of the

Soviet pilot's radio transmissions as he tracked and destroyed Flight 007. (Using Project CLEF's tape recording at the United Nations was out of the question; it was of poorer quality and, more important, Washington could not make it public without possibly compromising the unit and without officially explaining to Tokyo that the NSA had been clandestinely collecting intelligence on the Soviet Union from Japanese territory.)

Privately, the Japanese government was appalled and disappointed by what it perceived as the arrogant American handling of the shootdown. The Nakasone government, which viewed itself as a loyal American ally, had been given no more than one hour's notice of George Shultz's initial announcement unraveling the close U.S.-Japanese intelligence ties. Furthermore, there was skepticism over what was viewed as a faulty American conclusion in terms of the critical issue— whether the Soviet interceptor pilot knew he was shooting down a civilian airliner. The Japanese intelligence community knew of no evidence to support the Reagan and Shultz contention and was convinced that the United States had no evidence either. America's insistence on making the incident public was understood, but why do it so prematurely, well before any thorough analysis could be prepared? How could the United States mishandle intelligence so blatantly, with the mere goal of embarrassing the Soviet Union?

Still, the Japanese government remained silent.

The key policymaker in Japan in the days after the shootdown of Flight 007, along with Nakasone, was Masaharu Gotoda, one of Nakasone's closest associates. Gotoda was then serving as the chief Cabinet secretary, which, under his direction, had emerged as the most powerful position in the labyrinthine bureaucracy of Japan's Cabinet government. He was both the spokesman for the prime minister and chief of domestic policy. He also had a thorough background in high-level intelligence matters that dated back to his pre–World War II service—along with Nakasone—in the powerful Ministry of the Interior, which controlled Japan's secret police.

It was to Gotoda—as the political confidant of the prime minister—that the Japanese Defense Agency (JDA) and the Foreign Ministry turned after the loss of Flight 007, when the first suggestion of Soviet interceptor activity became known. Gotoda recalled being telephoned at home by his secretary at 8:30 A.M. Tokyo time, and informed that a Korean airliner was missing. He was told that there was disagreement among military and civilian agencies about its possible location. Military radar had isolated what seemed to be a scramble of Soviet interceptors, but it was hundreds of miles from the last reported location of the airliner. Ninety minutes later, Gotoda, still not in direct contact with anyone from the military, was telephoned again by his secretary with further intelligence—obviously from the Japanese facility at Wakkanai—indicating that "it was likely" that the airliner had been shot down by a Soviet interceptor. He ordered his secretary to relay the information to Nakasone's private secretary. At this moment it was nine o'clock in Washington on the night of August 31 and the first CRITICs had been filed from Misawa to the National SIGINT Operations Center. Ronald Reagan had finished his afternoon horseback ride at the California ranch and George Shultz was less than fourteen hours away from broadcasting much of the intelligence.

Gotoda then did what no action-oriented American in his position would ever take the time to do: he spent the next hour in contemplation. If the Korean airliner had, in fact, been shot down by the Soviets, it could provoke a major superpower crisis—and one that could not be controlled by Japan. "Although Japan has a great deal of economic power and political influence," Gotoda explained later, "when it comes to questions of power politics, Japan is not a major player, and the issue had to be handled very carefully, especially since it involved intelligence." The Japanese role would be to join with the United States in trying to force the Soviets to acknowledge their responsibility, make apologies, and pay reparations. "It would be essential," Gotoda recalled concluding, for Japan "to coordinate its intelligence with the United States as much as possible."

Another factor surely was at work: There had been increasingly sharp American criticism of Japan—predating the Reagan administration—for what was perceived as its willingness to enjoy the security of America's nuclear umbrella without fully committing itself to the region's defensive needs.* The shootdown

---

* Japan's outlays for its Self-Defense Forces (SDF) have been frozen by Cabinet decision since the mid-1960s at 1 percent of the nation's gross national product. The Japanese constitution, adopted after World War II, has a "no war" clause, and the issue of limiting defense spending to 1 percent has become a measur-

of Flight 007 gave Prime Minister Nakasone an opportunity to do something in return for Washington: remain steadfast.

The first report to the American embassy in Tokyo—that an airliner was missing—came from Japanese civil aviation authorities, and was made directly to Dennis H. Wilham, the Asian representative of the Federal Aviation Administration. Wilham was an old hand who had been on the job at the American embassy in Tokyo since 1962; Japanese officials had no hesitancy about waking him up before dawn at home and alerting him to a potential problem. Any flight from New York to Seoul undoubtedly would have many Americans aboard.

Ironically, it was Wilham's experience that tripped him up that morning. He had been on duty in July 1968 when the first word came—early in the morning, as now—of a missing airliner over Soviet territory in the Far East. It was the chartered Seaboard World Airways DC-8, ferrying more than two hundred GIs from the United States to combat duty in South Vietnam, that had been forced down over the Kuriles by the Soviets. Wilham and others in the embassy had

---

ing rod of Japanese defense policy. Prompted by the Reagan administration, Japanese officials began in the early 1980s to discuss the possibility of raising the de facto ceiling, but have held back because of the political risks. More than 70 percent of the citizenry, according to a November 1983 poll, opposed any alteration of the 1 percent limit. The budget restriction means that military activities deemed to be less significant, such as communications intelligence, do not get the funds for equipment and manpower that are sought.

"panicked" and somehow persuaded themselves that the Soviets had shot down the airliner. In fact, the soldiers and crew were detained without incident for two days on Iturup Island before being flown to Tokyo; the GIs, many of them carrying souvenir packets and tins of Soviet-made cigarettes, were described by newsmen as tired but cheerful upon their arrival.

Thus, Wilham said, when Japanese air traffic control officials alerted him on Thursday to the missing Flight 007, his first thought was that the airliner had been forced down. "I remembered vividly the emotions that I had in 1968, and I said 'I'm sure there are airports along the way and you'll find them there.'" There had been no distress calls from the Korean airliner, and it was difficult to believe that the crew would not have had time to make a radio report or—even if in a total crisis—to radio "Mayday."

Wilham assumed that the airliner's final position report had been correct and reasoned that it was possible Flight 007 had simply made its scheduled turn to the west—toward South Korea—too early. Instead of overflying northern Japan, as the flight plan had called for, it could have overflown a military air base on one of the Soviet-held Kurile Islands and been forced down there. Within an hour of his arrival at his office at the embassy, his telephone started ringing. It was the press, routinely turning to the FAA's man in Tokyo for public comment and private guidance. Wilham sought to downplay the initial reports and told the reporters of the many airports in the Kuriles where Flight 007 could have landed. "I was determined to get the panic level down. We were all running around. I'm probably responsible," Wilham sadly acknowledged during an interview in Tokyo, "for the stories about the airliner being 'down on Sakhalin.' " It was not until mid-afternoon that the embassy people were told that there was intelligence showing that the Soviets were conducting active search-and-rescue activities north of Sakhalin.*

---

* Unbeknownst to Wilham, it was his early suggestion that Flight 007 could have landed safely that triggered similar published reports a few hours later in South Korea, which were said at the time to emanate from the American CIA. Those stories would later be cited by the Soviet Union and some American journalists as evidence of high-level Reagan administration involvement in the incident; the safe-landing report was alleged to have been aimed at providing the administration with enough time to perfect a cover story. What actually happened is far more mundane, and involved Jangnai Sohn, the station chief for the Korean Central Intelligence Agency in Washington. Sohn, who operated under cover with the rank of minister from the Republic of Korea's embassy in Washington, had a tragic link to the downed airliner; his sister-in-law was on the flight, and Sohn's wife had in fact gone to see her off at John F. Kennedy Airport. CIA officials were aware of his personal interest in the flight, and one of Sohn's close friends in the agency was telephoning him at home periodically during the night to keep him up-to-date. Sohn naturally considered the information, which he knew came from the CIA's Operations Center, to be reliable, and was in turn relaying what he learned by telephone to his intelligence colleagues in Seoul. His CIA ally telephoned as soon as the first press reports were filed from Japan indicating that the airliner may have landed on Sakhalin. Sohn promptly passed along the good news to the Korean CIA, apparently communicating in the process the fact that his information had come from the CIA. By the time he was told, a few hours later, that the airliner had definitely been shot down, word of the airliner's safe landing had been passed from Korean intelligence to the Foreign Ministry. It went from there to officials of Korean Air Lines, who made the information and its source public. Sohn returned to Seoul in 1985 as a high-level official of its Agency for National Security Planning.

Even as Wilham was innocently relaying his inaccurate information to newsmen, Gotoda left home for his office at the Kantei, the official quarters in Tokyo of the prime minister and his closest aides. En route, he telephoned the Foreign Ministry and ordered an immediate formal study of options, based on the possibility that the Korean airliner was indeed shot down by the Soviet Union.

Shortly after eleven in the morning, Hauro Natsume, vice minister of the Japanese Defense Agency, gave Gotoda his first detailed report on the crisis, based on the intercepts from Wakkanai. Gotoda was told, he recalled, that it was "likely" that the Soviets had shot down the aircraft, "although the reason for the Soviet act was not yet known. In other words," he added, "we did not know whether the downing was intentional or by mistake." Gotoda was present two hours later when Natsume made his first formal report to the prime minister at his office; there were still more questions than answers. Also present was Toshijiro Nakajima, a deputy foreign minister who had been placed in charge of the newly set-up task force on the shootdown. Gotoda recalled that he was easily able to dominate the briefing: not only was he a powerful political figure with enormous bureaucratic expertise but he had also taken the time to consider which questions had to be answered first. There had been no high-level contact yet with the United States, although Gotoda assumed, as did all at the briefing, that the usual coordination was taking place at lower levels between the Japanese and American intelligence agencies. Gotoda did not know of the existence of Project CLEF at Wakkanai, of course. Nor did he know that, just as the meeting began in Nakasone's office, the first intercepts from Project CLEF were beginning to circulate in Washington.

Gotoda did not trust the late-morning reports from South Korea that the airliner had safely landed at Sakhalin Island. He assumed they originated with the South Korean government and realized that such reports—reassuring at first to the family and friends of survivors—eventually would create more distress. He scheduled a news conference for 4:00 P.M. Tokyo time—it was 3:00 A.M. in Washington and George Shultz had yet to be informed of the shootdown—and informed newsmen then that Japan had radar and communications data showing that the airliner had disappeared. Gotoda deliberately avoided using the phrase "shot down" but made a point of stating that the Soviets had insisted that the airliner was not down on Sakhalin, as publicly reported.

By late evening Tokyo time, the American embassy was confronted with an embarrassing diplomatic problem. At 10:45 P.M. Tokyo time, the State Department instructed the embassy to alert Prime Minister Nakasone and Shintaro Abe, the foreign minister, not only that in about one hour Secretary of State Shultz was going to tell the world about the Soviet atrocity, but also that, in order to be persuasive, he would unilaterally release information on some of Japan's most sensitive intelligence activities—those specifically targeted at the Soviet Union. In essence, one senior American diplomat recalled, it was a mission impossible; the embassy would have to tell the Japanese government that they "were going to be burned." Even before that step, there was another concern: Had the Japanese intelligence community, with its insistence on consensus, reached the point of sharing all its information with Nakasone? It was just not clear how much the top men of the Japanese Foreign Ministry, with whom the American embassy was in constant contact, had been told. There was every reason to believe that Prime Minister Nakasone and his key aides, including Gotoda, would have been briefed in part, but the Japanese intelligence agencies were known to be very slow to fully share information with Cabinet departments. There was a great potential for confusion inside the Japanese intelligence community, with each service—Army, Navy, and Air Force, as well as the civilian police—exerting control over its own branch of communications intelligence. Given the redundant bureaucracy, did the senior executives in Japan know that the Soviet pilot had been overheard declaring that the target was destroyed? Did they know that the intercepts also showed that the Soviet pilot had not identified the aircraft as a civilian airliner before shooting it down? There were other questions. Did the Foreign Ministry, or anyone in the prime minister's office, for that matter, know that the United States had its own secret collection facility in Wakkanai? Did they know the extent to which the Japanese intelligence operations had been laggard in analyzing and evaluating the information automatically collected overnight?

The Americans believed, rightly or wrongly, that the answer to most of their questions was no, and one of their immediate concerns was how best to prevent George Shultz's news conference from inadvertently triggering embarrassment and loss of face throughout the Nakasone government. It was for that reason that the embassy chose to touch base with its loyal contact in the Japanese Defense Agency, Vice Minister Shinji Yazaki. "We had to tip him off," one American recalled, "because we knew he had not yet briefed the Foreign Ministry. He would have told only the prime minister, and he hadn't told the P.M. everything because he doesn't have enough of a feel for it. The Japanese system doesn't work the way we do. They get it and play with it. They'd say to us—and they did: 'What are you doing making this public?'" The Americans understood that Vice Minister Yazaki would, as one official put it, "want it all back in the intelligence community. Impossible," the official added, because "our system works too quickly for the Japanese." The Americans knew that Yazaki would immediately tell Nakasone, Gotoda, and Abe what specific details they needed to know before the embassy telephoned with the news that the United States was going public.

The Americans were convinced that the next few minutes were extremely difficult ones for the Japanese, with their emphasis on consensus and face-saving. Being warned by the American embassy to hurry his briefing process amounted to a loss of face for Yazaki, but, in a sense, the Americans were saving his face, too—helping him avoid an even greater embarrassment in front of his superiors. There had to have been a desperate and mortifying attempt to pass information up the chain of command. When finally contacted by the embassy, Nakasone was "disconsolate," one American recalled. "He'd like to have been asked rather than being told; after all, it's their stuff." The prime minister had asked what Shultz would say, and embassy officials could only lamely reassure him that they were certain it would be "good things."

It was an awkward moment for the American embassy. Discussing communications intelligence with senior Japanese officials posed risks, simply because the embassy was far more involved in the processing of such intelligence than the Japanese government knew—or was supposed to know. A special National Security Agency collection unit was assigned to the embassy and operated from a sealed compartment there. The special NSA unit, whose linguists were highly skilled, had been provided with copies of both the Japanese and Project CLEF tape recordings very early in the crisis and had been asked to help improve their quality as well as work on translation. The embassy was very much in the loop that day.

There was little doubt that the American intelligence system, with its emphasis on speed and getting information to the top, had outgunned the Japanese. Embassy officials in Tokyo later were told that Nakasone, displeased by the slow-moving Japanese intelligence community, had made his displeasure known, through Gotoda, to Vice Minister Yazaki. Some Americans were themselves distressed by what they saw as George Shultz's precipitous rush to judgment in the crisis, which left some of the embassy's closest allies in the Japanese military exposed. "Yazaki didn't do anything wrong," one official recalled. "He followed the rules and, most important, even modified the rules when he had to. He had every reason to be pissed."

Gotoda and Yazaki understandably disputed the American embassy's contention that Yazaki and his colleagues had been slow in relaying significant information to important offices in the Foreign Ministry and elsewhere. Citing national security, they were reluctant in later interviews to say precisely what had been learned when—but Yazaki insisted, "We provided information in an appropriate fashion."

As for the news conference itself, Gotoda refused to discuss his personal reaction to Shultz's disclosures, and Vice Minister Yazaki, choosing his words carefully, said only, "We did not know what the basis was for Shultz's statement. I think it might be true that the American side was a little bit hasty." Japanese diplomats, requesting that they not be cited by name, later quoted Gotoda and Nakasone as being distressed by what the diplomats called Shultz's "manhandling" of intelligence. The Cabinet officials, assuming that Shultz did not have a private source of intelligence not known to the Japanese government, were said to be disturbed at the thought that the United States would distort intelligence to make what amounted to an untenable situation for the Soviet Union even worse.

There was yet another complication, involving Project CLEF. One of the by-products of the NSA's collaborative and secret arrangements with the Japanese communications intelligence officers is divided loyalty: an American Air Force Electronic Security Command officer can become more closely aligned with his Japanese counterpart than with NSA officials at Fort Meade. Many officers assigned to the 6920th and other ESC units in the Far East knew that

their Japanese colleagues had from the beginning
shielded the existence of the secret American base from
what the military men viewed as the politically suspect
bureaucracy in Tokyo. The Americans had been
warned by their Japanese colleagues that even the top
Japanese defense officials could not be trusted to keep
all secrets inside the military: Project CLEF, if made
known to the political leadership in Tokyo, inevitably
would find its way into the Japanese Diet and provoke
a political donnybrook.

Thus, in the days following the public revelation of
the U.S.-Japanese intelligence link, the main concern
of the Americans in communications intelligence was
not, as widely reported at the time, the potential loss
to national security in terms of the ability to intercept
Soviet signals in the Far East. It was conceded that the
Soviets would alter the frequencies on which the pilots
communicated with their ground controllers, but the
new frequencies could be discovered in a matter of
hours. Anything more complicated would make it too
difficult even for the Soviets themselves. The immediate fear of the Americans was much more subtle:
Would the existence of Project CLEF become publicly
compromised and damage the careers of those Japanese Air Force officers who had helped shield the operation—with or without tacit assent of the Japanese
military—from the scrutiny of higher-ups? Key officials on duty at the U.S. Fifth Air Force headquarters
and at the NSA's civilian headquarters in Japan were
contacted and, as one officer put it, "reminded that we
weren't supposed to be up there"—at Wakkanai. They
were asked to intercede at the highest levels of the
Japanese military and do whatever could be done to

protect those lower-ranking officers who had—perhaps foolishly—not informed their superiors of Project CLEF. In subsequent weeks, one American Air Force general recalled, "everybody went back and diligently tried to mend fences—with some success. The Japanese seemed to understand that we didn't intend to do harm." It was later learned that none of the Japanese intelligence officers who helped shield Project CLEF from their higher-ups were punished, or in any way suffered professionally for having been extraordinary allies.*

Washington's precipitous action left a bad taste, but it was short-lived. On Friday, Ambassador Mike Mansfield visited Nakasone and relayed a warm written message of support and thanks from President Reagan. One American described the note as intended "to take the sting out" of the aggressive U.S. action the day before. The ambassador, in a subsequent interview in Tokyo, described the note as an expression of "our appreciation for the extraordinary effort they made to keep us informed." It's easy to be critical in hindsight, Mansfield said, but "This called for quick action and Shultz did the right thing in presenting the informa-

---

* Senior policymakers, both in Japan and the United States, refused to discuss Project CLEF with outsiders, and it could not be confirmed that the men at the top in Tokyo had not known of the secret base prior to the shootdown. There were some clues. Vice Minister Yazaki, asked later whether he had been told of Project CLEF before the shootdown of Flight 007, pointedly responded: "Your question is about American intelligence activities, and we're not in a position to know *all* about U.S. activities."

tion" to the American people. He added: "Sometimes you just haven't got the time to think things through before you make a case."

Two days later Mansfield, a former Montana senator, who was extremely popular in Japan, returned to Nakasone and his senior aides with an awkward request: Could the United States play the Japanese tape recording of the Soviet pilot at a session of the United Nations Security Council? Permission would undoubtedly further set back Soviet-Japanese rapprochement, already grievously damaged. The Japanese were already sensitive about not being a permanent member of the Security Council. Mansfield, aware he was on delicate ground, suggested that the United States would merely play the tape recording without identifying its origin, if the Japanese chose. "They were very tough when that was what was needed," one American diplomat said appreciatively of the senior Japanese leadership, "and said yes"—the United States could play it and should identify it. The Japanese agreed, he said, knowing that regarding the USSR, "they were shooting themselves in the foot."

Not quite. The Japanese intelligence service was being credited with providing the first evidence of the Soviet shootdown—which it did not do—and Nakasone himself agreed with many of the political and military objectives of the Reagan administration. A public display of anger or disappointment over Washington's handling of the crisis was unthinkable, both for cultural and political reasons. Any such complaint would cause a loss of face and could involve the Nakasone government in a fight with the United States on an explosive issue—electronic spying on the Soviet Union. There was nothing to gain by letting the United States or anybody else know how shabbily the Japanese government had been treated.

13

Defending the Faith

By Saturday, the third day of the crisis, the Reagan administration was operating with unanimity, pulled together by the stunning propaganda victory over the Soviet Union. There was, for once, no backbiting between the staff members of the National Security Council and the State Department; George Shultz, as if being rewarded for his newfound public toughness, was invited to lunch with the president in his private residence in the White House. Correspondents were informed later that the secretary of state would keep his date in Madrid with Soviet foreign minister Andrei Gromyko, all right, but the first topic of conversation would be the shootdown. There were bristling network television accounts that night of Shultz's determination to confront the Soviets: "Shultz will insist," said NBC, that "Gromyko come clean with the facts."

That same weekend the administration began to pressure its allies in NATO and around the world to deny landing rights to Aeroflot, the Soviet state airline, for at least sixty days. International airline trade associations and pilot groups were contacted by high-level officials, including Eagleburger, and urged to join the boycott. It was further decided to seek condemnation as well as an investigation of the shootdown at a special session of the International Civil Aviation Organization, a United Nations agency based in Montreal that is responsible for setting aviation policy for its 151 member states, which include the Soviet Union and its allies. J. Lynn Helms, the tough-talking administrator of the Federal Aviation Agency, was summoned to the White House meeting and ordered to Montreal to keep the pressure on the Soviets. There was nothing ambiguous about the instruction to Helms, recalled Scott Thompson, who helped coordinate such activity through the NSC's Special Planning Group for Public Diplomacy. "We sent Helms up there to beat the shit out of their guys," he said. "We essentially told him, 'No holds barred.' " It was a legitimate crusade, so Thompson and many of his anti-Soviet colleagues thought. Airline groups, such as the Air Transport Association, whose members include most of the world's airlines, similarly were eager to help take steps against a nation that had deliberately shot down a civilian airliner.

A new and very much unwanted element began to emerge over the weekend, however, as it became known inside the administration that the events surrounding the shootdown were far more complicated than initially believed. Word of the Air Force's RC-135 off the Kamchatka Peninsula had spread and it was only a matter of days before someone in the press—or, perhaps, in the Soviet Union—reported the fact that there may have been a basis for confusing Flight 007 with another aircraft. And for the first time there were published doubts about the administration's account of what happened above Sakhalin Island. That morning Michael Getler, the Washington *Post*'s national security correspondent, quoted government officials as speculating that the interceptor pilot "may have thought" the Boeing 747 airliner was an RC-135 military reconnaissance aircraft.

Reagan was briefed in the morning by officials of the National Security Agency. The meeting could only have been reassuring: he was told that the Cobra Ball reconnaissance flight had nothing to do with the destruction of the airliner. By that time, the headquarters analysts at NSA—ignoring, as did the rest of the government, the findings of Air Force Intelligence—had determined, according to an account provided later by General Lincoln Faurer, NSA director, that the "most profitable way of looking" at the issue was "to say that there is no reason why the Soviets couldn't have known it was a civilian airliner." There was "absolutely no way," Faurer said, that the Soviet interceptor pilot could have failed to differentiate the military reconnaissance aircraft from the airliner.*

---

* One NSA official who was directly involved in the analysis of the shootdown initially applauded Faurer's approach to the issue. "Why should we want to be fair?" he asked. "We get so few opportunities to put them in the worst light. Why should the United States try to make the Soviets look good when the Soviets

One of the goals on Saturday was to depict the president, just back from his California ranch, as the man in charge. Television crews were called in and given a rare opportunity to videotape the president's weekly Saturday-morning radio talk to the nation. In that talk, he seemed to expand his criticism to suggest that all who lived in the Soviet Union were lacking in values. The destruction of Flight 007, he declared, posed a serious issue between "the Soviet Union and civilized people everywhere who cherish individual rights and value human life."

The White House also struck hard at the Getler story in the Washington *Post*. "We find it difficult to believe," spokesman Larry Speakes told the press on Saturday afternoon," that a Soviet fighter aircraft could approach and have visual contact with a 747 civilian airliner and mistake it for another type of aircraft." The 747, he added, "is just unmistakable and clearly the Soviet pilot had visual contact with this airplane." Asked specifically whether that assessment was supported by the tapes, Speakes said yes.

He was taken, as he had to be, at face value. Later in the briefing, Speakes volunteered that he had yet to see the intercepted communications between the Soviet ground controllers and the pilots. No such intercepts existed, of course, a fact that Speakes did not fully understand for four more days. At this early point

---

do everything in their power to make us look bad?" The official, who was on assignment in the Pacific in September 1983, finally supplied his own answer: "Intelligence people have no choice but to tell it straight." Faurer's views, he added, were, "of course, a political judgment."

in the crisis, the White House press office did not have direct access to the intelligence but was being briefed by others in the White House, including two of Clark's aides on the NSC staff, Kenneth E. Degraffenreid, who handled intelligence issues, and Admiral John Poindexter, the senior military aide. Speakes himself was relying heavily on the newest employee in the press office, Leslie A. Janka, a former NSC aide to Henry A. Kissinger and, before that, a deputy assistant secretary of defense in the Ford and Carter administrations. Janka's first assignment after the president's return from California was to coordinate the intelligence on Flight 007 for Speakes's daily briefings. A sharp critic of the Soviet Union, Janka thought shooting down the airliner without identifying it made the Soviets "brutal, insensitive thugs regardless of whether they mistook it for an intelligence plane or not. That was beside the point." Janka had been around Washington long enough to recognize, however, that the initial rhetoric on the issue, particularly by George Shultz, had been too hard and had led to a growing sense of vulnerability in the White House, heightened by the disclosure in that morning's Washington *Post*. "There was fear," he recalled, "that the media was so ready to jump on the White House for blowing this up into a major crisis."*

---

* The most senior government officials seemed to be involved in zealously protecting Washington's view that there could be no possible explanation or mitigation of the Soviet shootdown. Stephen M. Meyer, a Soviet arms expert and professor at the Massachusetts Institute of Technology, was stunned to get an early-morning telephone call at home from Kenneth W. Dam,

The White House's response was not to assess the criticisms objectively but to rally ever more around the president and the secretary of state and publicly reinforce their stated belief that the Soviet pilot knew what he was doing when he destroyed Flight 007. The president would continue to believe that account. To buttress its case, the White House decided to release the NSA's tape recording of the shootdown. The administration that had emphasized the need to protect secrets and had proposed tightened national security laws was reversing itself to help the president fight his war of words with the Soviet Union. The release of the tape recordings was an attempt to abort the just-beginning public debate over the government's account of the shootdown. Prime Minister Nakasone had granted permission for the tape to be made public at the United Nations on Tuesday, but the White House couldn't wait that long; it would be aired on Sunday at a closed briefing Reagan would personally preside over for the six senior leaders of the House and Senate. What the Japanese didn't know wouldn't hurt them. It was decided during the weekend that the president would

---

the deputy secretary of state, bitterly complaining about a statement issued by Tass that weekend quoting the academic as saying that the Soviets had every right to suspect that Flight 007 was on an intelligence mission. Dam "was really angry at the thought that somebody at MIT would do this," he recalled. "He started berating me for what he'd read." Meyer, in fact, had said almost the opposite—that the Soviets were likely to make a spy charge—and the New York *Times*, which published the Tass statement without verifying it, printed a clarification two weeks later. The MIT professor was left, however, with a strong sense of the administration's sensitivity to any possible challenge to its version of what had happened.

make an address on Flight 007 to the nation on Monday, and play a portion of the NSA tape recording to demonstrate that the United States had evidence to back up its charges. The most dramatic moment would come at the United Nations on Tuesday, when Ambassador Jeane J. Kirkpatrick, who had been summoned from vacation in Morocco, would make the whole tape public at a special session of the Security Council. Such raw intelligence had always been withheld from public release, essentially because it was considered by NSA professionals to be often misleading unless it was evaluated and put into context. The intercepts sent to the White House would become a classic example of why raw intelligence should be carefully screened before going to policymakers; it simply did not prove what the president and his aides thought it did. One NSA official who was directly involved in the processing of the tape recording acknowledged that initially "we didn't do a good job of translating and ordering the chronology." The final version was "much different" from that made public by the White House—a not-unusual situation, the official said. "There's a reason you see so many versions of COMINT," he said. "It's like the problems in translating the New Testament scriptures into any language. There's more than one rendering of what Mark said."

Another former NSA official pointed out that there was a strong general rule inside the agency that analysts "do not use raw data—do not try to make too much of it. We violate our own rules by trying to draw conclusions from such data," the official analyst said. "It's important to recognize," he added, "that when left to their own devices on normal reporting, the

SIGINT community considers anything that's less than three days old to be a current event. It often takes you that long"—three days—"to get something creditable to say."

Leslie Janka knew enough about the NSA to be surprised at how easy it was to get such sensitive materials cleared for release to the media. He also understood the White House's urgency to make the tape recording public: "The big problem was that it was clear that the press didn't believe us, so therefore we had to release the stuff. There was nobody of sufficient stature to say, 'Look, we can't talk about the following things to protect intelligence.' " Janka was directed by David R. Gergen, the assistant to the president for communications, to start giving private briefings to the press and put "the proper spin" on the intelligence. Janka was bitter, in a later interview, about his assignment and Gergen's role: "Gergen, with less experience and less knowledge, was just feeding everything he could to the networks. He was going over the heads of the correspondents"—to producers and network executives—to provide "the proper interpretation" of the intelligence. "David was just putting out a constant drumbeat of anti-Soviet and pro-Reagan information," Janka recalled. "Nobody set policy as to how far we should go."

Policy guidance on that issue certainly did not come from the top of the NSA. General Faurer, asked later why he did not caution against the publication of the intercepts, explained, "It all flowed from our first agreement"—a reference to his conversation on Thursday morning with William Casey and Hugh Montgomery, which resulted in George Shultz's public release of the intercept information at his dramatic news conference. "It was not only my personal decision," Faurer added, explaining that the two senior civilian deputies of the NSA, Richard Lord and Robert Rich, also were "comfortable" with the release of the tape recording. "It was a corporate decision."

It was more than that, surely: Faurer and his deputies understood that the White House and the president—convinced of the morality and correctness of their position—were waging what amounted to a renewed Cold War against the Soviets, and the tape recording would play a major role.

At Sunday's meeting the congressional leaders* were appropriately respectful when the Japanese tape recording was played; after all, they were being provided with NSA information of the highest order of classification and had promised not to reveal the data. They were also informed that an American RC-135 intelligence plane, the Cobra Ball, had been airborne on a routine mission off Kamchatka Peninsula on the night of August 31–September 1. Flight 007 and the RC-135 had been within a few moments' flying time of each other near the Kamchatka Peninsula, which may initially have confused the Soviet Air Defense Force. But the legislators were assured by Ameri-

---

* At the meeting were Howard Baker, the Senate majority leader; Tip O'Neill, Speaker of the House; Senator Strom Thurmond of South Carolina, president pro tempore of the Senate; Senator Robert C. Byrd of West Virginia, Senate minority leader; Jim Wright of Texas, the House majority leader, and Robert H. Michel of Illinois, House minority leader.

can intelligence officials, who were not to be publicly identified, that the intelligence community had monitored the Soviet radar operators as they tracked both planes and carefully assigned separate track numbers to each. In other words, the confusion—if there was any—had disappeared by the time Flight 007 overflew Sakhalin Island, where the Soviet pilots had to have seen—visibility was said to have been good—that the aircraft they were tracking was a Boeing 747 civilian airliner and not the much-smaller military reconnaissance plane. (The administration provided similar, although far less detailed accounts, that day to correspondents for the major networks.)

One of the goals of the briefing was to build up support to counter the inevitable second-guessing that would occur when the existence of the American intelligence plane became known. The lengthy meeting with the president was a flattering sign of importance and presidential respect for the three congressmen and three senators; they, in turn, would loyally support the administration's analysis of the intelligence. The intelligence itself—the tape recording and other data—remained almost magically above the fray, as if beyond dispute.

The White House must have known that the presence of the reconnaissance aircraft would be made public by one or more of the legislators to someone in the press that day. What the White House did not anticipate was the extent to which the briefing had confused the legislators. House Majority Leader Jim Wright, Democrat of Texas, threw the president's men into a panic afterward by mistakenly telling a cluster of reporters outside the White House that the

Soviets had been recorded as twice referring to Flight 007 inside Soviet airspace as being an RC-135. His comment, as he obviously did not realize, implied that the Soviets had misidentified Flight 007. Within hours a White House statement was rushed out, defending the faith: "[W]e do not think this was a case of mistaken identity. . . . The SU-15 and MiG-23 aircraft pilots, whose voices are on the tape obtained by the United States and played for the congressional leadership, never refer to the Korean target as an RC-135, only as the 'target.' They made no serious effort to identify the aircraft or to warn it."

Wright's mistake provoked sharp questioning from the press about just what information the NSA had collected, and Larry Speakes was forced to confirm a published report that there were other intercepts—not briefed to the legislators—showing that the Soviets initially identified Flight 007 over Kamchatka Peninsula as a military plane. It was a contentious briefing, with Speakes insisting that it was "clear from the evidence, which I will not go into, that . . . the Soviets had no reason to doubt that they were tracking a civilian airliner. . . . The evidence is irrefutable and unmistakable because the SU-15 had visual sighting within three kilometers and . . . literally circled the plane, circled the Korean airliner. There is no margin for error. . . . The Soviet pilot should in any way, under any circumstances, have known that it was a civilian airliner, unmistakably a 747 and in no way could be mistaken in its shape for a U.S. reconnaissance plane." Speakes did concede, in response to a question, that the administration had no specific evidence that the pilot described the aircraft as a civilian airliner before shooting it down: "We never heard the pilot say to his ground controller—'That is a civilian airliner.'" Asked by another reporter whether the administration had "at least entertained" the theory that the Soviets may have made a mistake, Speakes responded, "Yes, but we feel that our evidence, particularly the words of the pilots, indicate that it's irrefutable."

In a later interview, Leslie Janka acknowledged that he and Speakes, relying on information supplied by others, had inadvertently misled the press corps. Janka, who resigned his White House job in October 1983 after assuring newsmen on the eve of the invasion of Grenada that the administration had no plans to invade, had served as the go-between from the NSC to the press office on Flight 007. "If Degraffenreid or Poindexter say to us [in the press office], 'Look, we've got the evidence,' we have to take their word for it," Janka explained. "Until Grenada, I believed everything they told us." Speakes's claims that there was "irrefutable" but unavailable evidence to back up the administration's allegations, Janka added, "was a rhetorical cover: to say we know a hell of a lot more, but we're not going to tell you. We weren't seeing everything." At the time, Janka said, he was convinced, after a briefing on the intelligence, that the Soviet pilot knew that he was shooting down an airliner.

It was Speakes's worst day in dealing with the shootdown and an anxious moment for the administration, but the press was still without a smoking gun— without any way to learn the truth. Major General Jim Pfautz and his aides would continue to promote their version of events, but only in highly classified briefings with members of the Air Staff and others inside the Pentagon.

On Sunday, Tass published a new account of the incident by Colonel General Semyon F. Romanov, chief of the headquarters staff of the Soviet Air Defense. Romanov depicted Flight 007 as a provocation and described the airliner as resembling an RC-135, in terms of both its flight path and its appearance at night. Moscow, after failing for days to acknowledge the shootdown, had finally found its version of the truth: Ronald Reagan and his agents in the American "special services"—the CIA and other intelligence agencies—had sent Flight 007 to its death.

Those few reporters who tried to learn whether the Soviets had in fact confused Flight 007 with the RC-135 now found themselves in the unenviable position of seeming to lend credibility to Tass in so doing. There was an ugly bottom line in all of this, too, one that was not mentioned in any of the newspaper or television accounts: what the White House now seemed to be acknowledging—that there was no specific evidence that the Soviet pilot knew that he was shooting down an airliner over Sakhalin—was inconsistent with the prior statements of the American secretary of state and the president.

The contradiction arose on a day on which Reagan was being hailed by newspapers across the nation and the world for his statesmanlike response to the shootdown. The New York *Times*, for example, editorialized Sunday: "For once, President Reagan and his advisers are showing an admirable understanding of that delicate balance. They have used their impressive powers of intelligence and publicity to pursue the truth and to stir a proper revulsion around the world. And now they are groping for a measured and constructive response."

Confusion and suspicion about what the White House or CIA may have known or planned about the destruction of Flight 007 would be implanted and reinforced over the weekend and, for a few, never disappeared. A joint CBS and New York *Times* poll in mid-September suggested that the nation was profoundly conflicted by the shootdown. Sixty-one percent of those queried said they doubted that the Reagan administration was disclosing all the information that the public should have, and yet 56 percent said that they were in overall agreement with the president's handling of the issue. In addition, 55 percent said they didn't think Reagan had been tough enough. The public seemed to be saying that it had reached a decision on what had happened without knowing—and without insisting on knowing—all the facts; if the additional information was good enough for Ronald Reagan, it was good enough for them. In an effort to quell any remaining doubts, the State Department commissioned a White Paper on the shootdown, emphasizing the Soviet guilt and the American innocence, but distribution of that document was vetoed in mid-September by William Casey and others in the intelligence community, including Lincoln Faurer, on the grounds that too much classified information already had been released.

Touting the White House press corps away from the question of what the president and the secretary of state knew and when they knew it was anything but difficult, despite the skepticism of many reporters. The congressional leadership played a major role Monday in defusing the issue, telling newsmen—who knew that the legislators had received top-secret briefings—that there was little connection between the presence of the RC-135 and the shootdown of Flight 007. "I'm sorry it was even mentioned," Senate Minority Leader Robert C. Byrd was quoted as saying. "It is not pertinent at all to this situation. It has confused the situation, and it need not. The Soviets cannot hide behind it." Representative Jim Wright, as if seeking redemption after his error of the day before, praised the administration for making public the existence of the military plane and reassured reporters that the RC-135's presence did not weaken the administration's case against the Soviet Union. "It is far more important that the truth be known than that one side make debaters' points at the expense of the other," Wright added.* The top leadership of the NSA, normally unavailable to the press, suddenly began returning telephone calls. On Monday, the New York *Times* was able to publish this assurance from a senior intelligence

---

* Wright further observed, according to the New York *Times*, "Even if it were an RC-135, I would take very unkindly to the idea of its just being summarily shot down simply because it invaded Soviet airspace." The congressman's point was unassailable and an approach that had been advocated by some well-informed members of the American intelligence community in Washington, Hawaii, and Japan. The fact remains, however, that neither Wright nor any of the Democrats challenged the administration for taking a much harder tack and claiming that the Soviet pilot had to have deliberately shot down the airliner.

official, one of Lincoln Faurer's military aides: "There's no way that the Soviets could have confused an RC-135 with a Korean 747." Similarly on Monday, John McWethy, the Pentagon correspondent for *ABC World News Tonight*, quoted other American officials as saying, "Once visual contact was made . . . it would have been nearly impossible to mistake the two types of planes." Robert Hager, Pentagon correspondent for *NBC Nightly News*, flatly told his viewers that the distinctive size and shape of a Boeing 747 "would seem to make it easy to tell from the Korean plane even in the black hours of early morning, and there was supposed to have been a moon that night."

The initial draft of the president's Monday speech was written by Bentley T. Elliott, a former CBS news producer who had joined the White House speechwriting staff early in 1981. Elliott recalled the action of the Soviet pilot in shooting down the airliner as being "so vividly imprinted on us. The tapes were so conclusive. There was no way this could be explained away." Elliott was no expert on NSA intercepts, and had satisfied himself of the unassailability of the tape recordings in discussions before writing the speech with Les Janka and others on the staff of the National Security Council—none of whom, as Elliott could not know, had any idea what the intelligence from the Far East really showed. The harshest rhetoric had been slipped into Elliott's speech by Anthony Dolan, a presidential speechwriter whose dislike for the "pragmatists" around the president had put him at odds with many in the White House. Dolan was determined to add a few phrases that were as tough as possible. "The Soviets are like the mob," Dolan said in a later interview. "They're scared; afraid somebody knows the truth." He didn't bother to seek a briefing from anyone on the NSC staff or in the intelligence community to understand what had happened; he was sure he knew.

Sometime during the day, President Reagan signed National Security Decision Directive 102 formally outlining the government's response to the destruction of Flight 007. The basic goal of American policy, a declassified version of the document shows, was to "advance understanding of the contrast between Soviet words and deeds. Soviet brutality in this incident presents an opportunity to reverse the false moral and political 'peacemaker' perception that their regime has been cultivating," the NSDD said. "This image has complicated the efforts of the Free World to illuminate the USSR's true objectives."

The president, not concerned or, more likely, unaware that the intelligence community was divided over the question of what the Soviet interceptor pilot knew, followed the script and tore into the Soviets on Monday night. It was an enormously effective speech, dramatized by the playing of four brief excerpts from the Japanese tape recording in which the SU-15 pilot reported to his ground controller, as translated by Reagan, that he was "closing in on the target," had "executed the launch," had "destroyed" the target, and was "breaking off attack." Hearing the actual words of the pilot, even if in Russian and unintelligible, seemed to provide all the proof most Americans needed to conclude that what the president depicted as the "Korean airline massacre" was a reality. Reagan conceded nothing on the issue of whether the pilot knew he was shooting at a civilian airliner: "Let me point out something here having to do with [the pilot's] close-up view of the airliner on what we know was a clear night with a half-moon. The 747 has a unique and distinctive silhouette unlike any other plane in the world. There is no way a pilot could mistake this for anything other than a civilian airliner." The president also had an answer for those who believed the Soviets had been confused by the flight path of the American RC-135: the Soviet confusion could not have taken place, he said, because the American aircraft "had been back at its base in Alaska, on the ground, for an hour when the murderous attack took place."

Having resolved that issue to his satisfaction, the president went to the heart of his speech: "Make no mistake about it, this attack was not just against ourselves or the Republic of Korea. This was the Soviet Union against the world and the moral precepts which guide human relations among people everywhere. It was an act of barbarism, born of a society which wantonly disregards individual rights and the value of human life and seeks constantly to expand and dominate other nations." Reagan then publicly linked the shootdown for the first time to more congressional support for defense spending, and especially for the controversial MX missile. He urged Congress "to ponder long and hard the Soviets' aggression as they consider the security and safety of our people, indeed all people who believe in freedom." Such linkage could only have been seen by the Soviets as further evidence that the overflight of the Korean airliner had been a deliberate provocation aimed ultimately at the Geneva strategic arms talks.

In their reports, the White House press corps

focused on the few minor specific sanctions announced by the president, none of which were unexpected. American landing rights for Aeroflot, which had been suspended in 1981 when the Soviets threatened Poland, would continue to be denied, and the United States would seek a worldwide boycott against Soviet civil aviation. The president said that he had ordered a delay in the U.S.-Soviet negotiations on the establishment of new consulates; also to be suspended were further talks on renewed cultural and scientific exchanges as well as a civilian transportation agreement. Most journalists, reflecting widespread relief that Ronald Reagan had not done something more drastic, emphasized the sanctions in their dispatches—depicting them as the sign of moderation they were. The president's rough language was mentioned almost in passing; it was seen as a rhetorical smoke screen and not the essential policy. The Washington *Post*, for example, reported on the disappointment of the New Right at the limited sanctions and described the president's speech as being "delicately balanced" in tone between harsh words and restrained action. The same point was made by most network television commentators.

The success of the speech obviously was keyed to the tape recordings, which—even as briefly played—seemed to provide damning evidence against the Soviets. White House aides were quick to press the advantage. Chris Wallace, the White House correspondent for NBC, quoted aides that night as being convinced that the president's speech would put to rest any belief that the Soviets had confused Flight 007 with the RC-135. "It took three or four days after the event for this to dribble out, and clearly it muddies the waters," Wallace said. "It allows the Soviets to claim with at least some measure of credibility that there was some legitimate confusion between an American spy plane and the Korean plane. They [White House aides] say now they've made it all clear, that there really shouldn't be any confusion, that the planes were far apart, they have completely different shapes. And they don't think that the Soviets have a legitimate opportunity here to show some confusion."

The shootdown left Moscow reeling. A state commission was assembled within twenty-four hours and took testimony directly from involved military men and officers at Sakhalin Island, Kamchatka Peninsula, and in the Kurile Islands. Marshal Nikolai V. Ogarkov, chief of staff of the Soviet armed forces, said later that he talked "with all directly involved in this incident." American intelligence officials carefully monitored the signals traffic from Moscow in the first days of the crisis as the commission and the Soviet General Staff struggled to get a straight story from the field commands in the Far East. The proceedings quickly turned into what NSA officials came to call a witch-hunt—a drive to find and remove those officers who were responsible for the worldwide embarrassment of the Soviet Union. After several weeks, Moscow began to reshuffle senior personnel in the Far East and revise its operational rules of engagement there. Many senior NSA officers quickly understood what seemed impossible for the policymakers and newsmen in Washington to grasp: that the intelligence apparatus of the Soviet Union would study the shootdown and

Washington's response to it and immediately choose to argue—and perhaps even believe—that Flight 007 had been sent over Soviet territory to make trouble. It was a short step to much harsher judgments. One American official, who spent much of his intelligence career analyzing the Soviet Union, later described three factors that probably triggered Soviet suspicion even before Washington began its propaganda campaign: "One, the Soviets routinely load up Aeroflot flights out of Berlin with all kinds of [intelligence] shit; two, they know that the United States has tried to do the same thing [in military aircraft] in the past, and three, the U.S.–South Korean relationship is very close." The question for a Soviet analyst then becomes—no matter how unrealistic, the American added—"Why not have the South Koreans carry a black box [special intelligence gear]?" on Flight 007.

The quick and harsh response from Washington, beginning within twenty hours of the shootdown, could only have heightened the initial Soviet embarrassment and helped trigger Moscow's suspicions. Washington did more than draw the world's attention to the shootdown; it indicted and sentenced the Soviet leadership for the murder of the passengers aboard Flight 007, before any significant information was known in the Kremlin. Moscow might well have chosen to proceed as it did in any case: admit nothing for six days and then blame the destruction of Flight 007 on the United States. But the instant prosecution by the United States had the effect of guaranteeing the worst from the Soviet Union, whose leaders would have found it difficult under any conditions to fault the military. Moscow could easily have concluded that whether or not it lied made little difference after the first days of blanket condemnations by the United States. The men who run the Soviet Union waited six days before publicly insisting that Flight 007 had been deliberately sent into their airspace. There undoubtedly were some senior officials in Moscow who resolutely believed that claim to be true. As described by Tass, "The plan was to carry out without a hitch the . . . intelligence operation but if it was stymied, to turn all this into a political provocation against the Soviet Union. . . . The entire responsibility for this tragedy rests wholly and fully with the leaders of the United States of America." The Soviet government expressed "regret over the death of innocent people" and said it shared "the sorrow of their bereaved relatives and friends." Moscow was finally admitting that its aircraft had shot down the Korean airliner. But the Kremlin insisted that the passengers aboard Flight 007 had been used by "American special services for their dirty aims" and had fallen "victim to a fresh crime."

The president's speech offered final proof, in Moscow's eyes, of American culpability: "This conclusion is confirmed by all subsequent actions of the U.S. administration. Its leaders, including the U.S. president in person, launched a malicious and hostile anti-Soviet campaign over a very short time, clearly using a prearranged script. Its essence has been revealed in its concentrated form in the televised speech of U.S. president R. Reagan on September 5—to try to blacken the image of the Soviet Union and discredit its social system, to provoke a feeling of hatred toward Soviet people, to present the aims of the foreign policy of the USSR in a distorted perspective, and to distract attention from its peace initiatives."

Those officials in Moscow who truly believed that Flight 007 had been a provocation could only have been reassured and strengthened by the American decision to make public the highly classified tape recording the next day at the United Nations. State Department and White House teams, prodded and encouraged by Eagleburger, had worked through the weekend to put together what amounted to a brilliantly conceived propaganda show. A video was prepared that depicted the shootdown through the words, in Russian, of the Soviet interceptor pilot. As the pilot spoke, his comments were spelled out in both English and the Cyrillic alphabet on the video, which was shown on a TV monitor. Eleven minutes of the voice-activated tape recording were played, and it made for effective theater. Mrs. Kirkpatrick did not claim that the tape recording showed that the Soviets had deliberately shot the airliner after identifying it. Her accusations instead dealt with what she said was evidence on the tape recordings of the failure of the Soviet interceptor to make any significant attempt to warn the airliner or to identify it properly. The complaints about failure to identify were valid—the same complaints, as the NSA knew, that were being made inside the Soviet chain of command. Mrs. Kirkpatrick made the point that "no nation has the sovereign right to shoot down any person or vehicle that may stray across its border in peacetime. There are internationally agreed-upon standards for intercepting unwelcome aircraft." The initial basis for the American protests against the Soviets had been altered: the issues were now being framed in terms of the Soviet failure to issue warnings and to make a careful identification. That change was lost, however, amid a very tough speech that repeatedly accused the Soviets of lying. "(I)f pilot error was responsible for this tragic mistake," Mrs. Kirkpatrick said, "why has the Soviet Government not said so? Why has it lied, and why is it complementing the murderous attack on KAL 007 with a lying attack on the United States for provocation and aggression?" She quickly answered her questions: "The fact is that violence and lies are regular instruments of Soviet policy. Soviet officials regularly behave as though truth were only a function of force and will—as if the truth were only what they said it is; as if violence were an instrument of first resort in foreign affairs. Whichever the case—whether the destruction of KAL Flight 007 and its passengers reflects only utter indifference to human life or whether it was designed to intimidate—we are dealing here not with pilot errors but with decisions and priorities characteristic of a system."

The American government had utilized an international forum to deal directly with the peoples of the world and share seemingly incontrovertible state secrets. There was no way for outsiders to know that there had been basic doubts among some who worked on the U.N. presentation over the translation and interpretation of many of the Soviet pilot's comments. It was decided to make minimal clarification in the translation, one State Department official recalled, "with all of its vagueness," out of a concern that any alteration would have to be discussed and approved by the Japanese and that, in turn, could prompt the Japanese government to usurp the American show-and-tell by deciding unilaterally to make the tape recording public prior to the Security Council meeting. The general attitude toward Tokyo, the official added, was "The less said the better." There were inevitable gaps and inconsistencies in the translation, including one absurdity that was apparently aimed at avoiding blue language. The Soviet pilot's phrase "Yolki palki," said just moments before he shot down Flight 007, which means "Holy shit!" or perhaps "Oh, my God!" was benignly translated as "Fiddlesticks."

Some of those closely involved in planning the U.N. initiative became the most skeptical. Scott Thompson of the USIA, who had grown familiar with sensitive intelligence as a special assistant to the secretary of defense in the Ford administration, recalled having few illusions about the administration's goals at the United Nations. "The tape was unclear and really didn't prove anything," he said, "but if you give out something in real time; if you present it and orchestrate it so nobody could catch his breath . . . We tried to package it and we succeeded. We made a calculated decision that we were going to pretend that this tape was going to be the be-all and end-all. We figured no one would challenge it—'the emperor has no clothes.' " The weekend was one of around-the-clock work and Thompson recalled a conversation about the tape recording's significance with Robert Kiernan, one of his very conservative aides at USIA: "I remember Bob laughing and saying, 'It's almost as if there's something there.' Bob said, 'Let's play this as if it's real.' " Kiernan subsequently confirmed that he had shared Thompson's skepticism about the tape recording: "It's not something that either of us would take as scholars or academics and hold credible, particularly if you were trying to justify a military response" to the shootdown. But, Kiernan added, he felt the "Security Council was another matter"—and the tape recording, with all of its flaws, was good enough for that equally flawed, in his view, political institution.

The president's speech and the use of the tape recording at the United Nations triggered a renewed wave of anti-Soviet protests across the nation and throughout the world. A spontaneous boycott of Soviet vodka, including the popular Stolichnaya, spread from wholesale distributors to liquor stores to restaurants. At least eight states banned or curtailed the sale of Soviet liquor, and workers in Los Angeles harbor refused to unload a Soviet freighter carrying, among other things, Stolichnaya. A suburban protest erupted at the Glen Cove, Long Island, retreat of the Soviet diplomatic corps. Police officers eventually were forced to disperse the demonstrators, who, armed with baseball bats, sought to break in to the grounds of the thirty-six-acre estate. Tass complained about the "criminal bandit attack" on the estate, which was accorded diplomatic immunity, as is American embassy property in the Soviet Union. Canada, under the leadership of the Liberal premier Pierre Trudeau, pleased the White House by becoming the first ally to support the American call for a sixty-to-ninety-day suspension of landing and refueling privileges for Aeroflot. Demonstrations took place in Seoul, where an effigy of

Yuri Andropov was burned, and more than ten thousand protesters, many of them Koreans, took to the streets of Japan's two largest cities, Tokyo and Osaka. There were continued American and Japanese protests over alleged Soviet harrassment of the search-and-rescue teams still combing the Sea of Japan for signs of the two black boxes aboard Flight 007. The United States also protested the Soviet Union's refusal to permit U.S. vessels to expand the search into Soviet waters. Andrei Gromyko, en route to his rendezvous with George Shultz at the European Conference on Security and Cooperation in Madrid, was forced to cancel a planned day-long visit with French president François Mitterrand in Paris. No official reason was given by the French government, which initiated the cancellation, but none was needed.

Larry Speakes was still being asked by a few reporters about the validity of the intelligence and was continuing to insist that there was "irrefutable" documentation that could not be made public. After Reagan's speech and the theatrics at the United Nations, Speakes took a tougher stance at his daily press briefing on September 6: "For those who would seek to search for some Soviet mistake that would apologize and excuse them or mitigate their responsibility, I point out in the strongest terms that there is no excuse and never can be an excuse," he said. Other complaints, dealing with the accuracy of the translation of the Soviet pilot's remarks, similarly were swept aside. Dimitri K. Simes, a Moscow-born academic expert and former government consultant on Soviet affairs, telephoned friends in the State Department and White House to warn that the official translation released by Ambassador Kirkpatrick eventually would "embarrass" the government. "It was a one-way translation in which everything was out of context," Simes later recalled. It was clear to him that the administration's obvious intent was "to make as bad a case as it could." Simes, himself a sharp critic of the Soviet Union, felt that the administration was embarking on a dangerous crusade by completely ignoring any evidence indicating that the Soviet pilot had made a mistake. "I had problems not only with the translation, but also with the interpretation of Soviet behavior," he said. "From the first moment, I perceived that the Soviets thought it was a spy plane, and there is nothing more offensive than a good Russian put on the defensive. I thought we were precluding the possibility that the Soviets would come up with a reasonable explanation." Similarly, Charles William Maynes, a former assistant secretary of state in the Carter administration, was upset—as a reader of Russian—to find that the administration's translation did not jibe with his reading. He called a former colleague in Soviet Affairs in the State Department and asked the official, who was directly involved in the crisis, if he had read the original transcript in Russian. The official said he would take a look. "I never heard from him again," Maynes said, "and he's a good guy."

The administration may have persuaded the world that the Soviets had shot down an airliner after identifying it, but the real story began to emerge throughout the government by the end of the first week. Even the Defense Intelligence Agency concluded that Jim Pfautz and his intelligence staff had been right after all; the Soviet Air Defense Force undoubtedly had confused Flight 007 with the Cobra Ball mission off the Kamchatka Peninsula. Henry E. Catto, Jr., assistant secretary of defense for public affairs, was initially convinced that the Soviets had shot down the airliner in the full knowledge that it was not an American intelligence plane. After a briefing sometime during the first week, he recalled, "my final conclusion was that it was not total aggression. It was still unbelievable that they would do anything that dumb. The joy of total self-righteousness faded slowly." Similar turnabouts were taking place even at the White House. One aide who helped shape the president's public response in the first week of the crisis conceded that he "began to have doubts" about the accuracy of his information within four or five days of the shootdown. State Department officials similarly grew to have reservations about the initial accounts. One assistant secretary of state, who played a major public role in the American response to the shootdown, acknowledged that he eventually concluded that the Soviets "panicked" at the presence of Flight 007 above their territory; no such language was heard in the early days of the crisis. President Reagan has never given any public indication that he entertained any second thoughts about the initial intelligence, but one close associate has concluded that the president—like many others in his administration—"must have heard there were doubts on what the Soviets were doing."

The administration was locked into its position and nothing would change over the next months and years. One State Department official theorized that there were two reasons for those who knew better to stand by the early position. Most important, he said,

"There's an almost instinctive sense that you can't contradict the boss. Misspeaking is one thing, but to expect the White House or State Department to say what Air Force Intelligence was reporting is impossible. People would say you were precipitous" if you tried to question the judgment of the president and his advisers. The second reason was described by the official as the "Pandora's box syndrome." As he put it: "If you admit that the Soviets didn't know it was a 747—if you give any credence to any part of their story—there would be an irresistible conclusion" by some in the public and the press "that the Soviets are telling the truth" about America's role in sending Flight 007 over Kamchatka and Sakhalin.

Shultz's meeting on September 8 with Gromyko in Madrid became yet another public relations drama. Shultz came to the East-West foreign ministers' conference not to seek means of improving relations but to lobby for support for the United States' plan to isolate Soviet civil aviation, and to chastise Andrei Gromyko at their much-ballyhooed private meeting. No Soviet official, as the men around Shultz should have known, would stand still for what the press had been assured would be a tough dressing-down. The New York *Times* noted that the secretary of state was behaving "like a heavyweight contender trying to attract the press before a 15-round event." Newsmen and television crews were given extensive access at the American ambassador's residence as Shultz greeted Gromyko with unusual rudeness—no smile and no handshake. The reporters later were given exalted accounts, by Richard Burt and other aides, of the secretary of state's toughness. Gromyko was said at one point to have jumped up in anger over a Shultz comment and threatened to walk out. Shultz, who seemed not to be aware of the ambiguity of the evidence against the Soviets, jumped up in response and "glared at him," one eyewitness recalled, but both men stayed put and the meeting continued. Two years later, one of the Americans in the room would proudly insist in an interview that it was arguably the toughest meeting in the history of U.S.-Soviet affairs—as if toughness were a basic criterion of good diplomacy.

In his remarks the day before at the conference, Gromyko had summarized the official Soviet view on Flight 007: there had been no mistake by the Soviet Air Defense Force. Shultz was genuinely insulted at the lack of a Soviet apology for the shootdown; he seemed unable to link the Soviet response to his anti-Soviet lobbying in Madrid and to the eight days of relentless American attacks. Shultz later told newsmen that in his view, Gromyko had implied in his speech that "if anyone strays over them, they are ready to shoot them down again." Relations between the two superpowers, the New York *Times* reported from Madrid, "appear as bad as they have been in some time."

On September 9, the Soviets, battered by public opinion and protests worldwide, made what amounted to an unprecedented attempt to demonstrate that they had acted rationally in shooting down the airliner. Marshal Ogarkov and two senior Soviet officials, Georgi M. Kornienko, a first deputy foreign minister, and Leonid M. Zamyatin, head of the International Information Department of the Communist Party's Central Committee, held a two-hour news conference with foreign correspondents, televised live in the United States by the Cable News Network, in which they took tough questions from American reporters and promoted the Soviet argument that Flight 007 had to have been an intelligence plane. Ogarkov, defending his troops, insisted that the destruction of Flight 007 "was not an accident or an error." The Air Defense Force, he said, was "completely sure what we were dealing with here was a reconnaissance plane." The Soviet state commission had completed its inquiry, he added, and "It has been irrefutably proved that the intrusion of the plane of the South Korean airlines into Soviet airspace was a deliberate, thoroughly planned intelligence operation. It was directed from certain centers in the territory of the United States and Japan."

The shootdown had come full circle. The United States, making an allegation for which it had no evidence, had been insisting to newsmen that it had "irrefutable" and still-secret information to prove that the Soviets had identified the airliner and then shot it down. The Soviets, making an allegation for which it had no evidence, were insisting that Flight 007 had been on a preplanned intelligence mission. Both sides believed the worst of each other and were falsely claiming that they could prove it. Both believed that only their version of reality was the truth; dissenters—if there were counterparts to General James Pfautz in Moscow—were not heard by the public.

By the second week of the crisis, America had made up its mind, and the attitude toward the Soviet Union hardened to such a degree that there was little concern—or newspaper follow-up—after September 11, when the White House left it to the State Department to announce with embarrassment several revisions to the Japanese tape recording, as played at the United Nations. The pilot was quoted as saying, "I am now firing cannon bursts," the first evidence that the Soviet interceptor pilot may indeed have attempted to warn the airliner before shooting it down—as the Soviet Union, and the pilot, had publicly claimed.* It was explained that U.S. government linguistic experts had "continued to review the poor-quality transmission on the tape." There were few willing to question why the administration had not acknowledged such ambiguities earlier, and why the tape recording was made public with such certitude and fanfare at the U.N. Security Council. Civil war in Lebanon continued to flare, with obvious risks to the American marines there, and the White House press corps had moved on to other issues.

There was far more skepticism abroad about America's anti-Soviet crusade. The American-sponsored United Nations Security Council resolution of condemnation was vetoed, as expected, by the Soviet Union on September 12, but the United States had barely been able to get the necessary nine votes in support of presenting the resolution at all. It obtained them only after toning down the rhetoric of the initial

---

* The pilot appeared briefly on Soviet television on September 10 and insisted that he had sent repeated warning signals to the plane, including the firing of tracer shells and the flashing of lights, all of which were ignored. "If we could have landed him at the airport, we could have discovered everything behind this," the pilot, not identified by name, said.

draft and only after picking up the critical ninth vote from Malta at the last moment. Without that ninth vote, there would have been no need for the Soviet Union to cast its veto, and—given the enormous moral outrage being exhibited by the administration—that would have been a major embarrassment. In another international arena, the boycott of Soviet aviation began to falter by the middle of the month, despite initial support from many American allies in Europe, and most scheduled Aeroflot flights were eventually resumed after interruptions of two weeks or less. The Reagan administration did better in Montreal, where the thirty-three-member Council of the International Civil Aviation Organization, responding in part to enormous American pressure as well as to anger over the shootdown, voted overwhelmingly on September 16 for a resolution deploring the use of force against civil aviation and calling for an extensive investigation of the incident. In a tough speech before the vote, FAA administrator Helms stopped just short of saying that the Soviets had knowingly shot down the airliner: "This group of aviation experts knows well that the silhouette of the RC-135 is different from that of the Boeing 747. You must also share our conclusion that no military pilot using accepted intercept procedures could fail to recognize the Boeing 747 with its distinctive features."

By mid-September, the National Security Agency was finally beginning to tell the real story to Congress. A closed hearing of the Senate Foreign Relations Committee was informed that NSA analysts had concluded that the Soviet SU-15 pilot did not know his target was a civilian airliner. Most of the senators seemed to care little.* A few days later they would vote 95 to 0 in support of a resolution condemning the "cold-blooded barbarous attack" by the Soviet Union on Flight 007. Senator Charles H. Percy of Illinois, the Republican committee chairman, opened the top-secret briefing but quickly departed, leaving it in the hands of the lowest-ranking Republican, Senator Frank H. Murkowski, Republican of Alaska.† The most intense questioning came from two Democrats, Senators Paul S. Sarbanes of Maryland and Christopher J. Dodd of Connecticut. Not everybody got the

---

* During interviews, experienced NSA officials were scornful of what they see as Congress's refusal to do its homework and learn the complicated issues of communications intelligence. There were many pointed anecdotes. One senior official told of taking two young aides to a secret hearing before the Senate Intelligence Committee dealing with a budget request for new electronic eavesdropping equipment. During the hearing, Senator James A. McClure, a conservative Republican from Idaho, noted that the witnesses were knowledgeable about electronics and suddenly asked, "What TV set do you recommend?" Another intelligence officer recalled a highly classified briefing in West Berlin for Democratic senator John C. Stennis of Mississippi, chairman of the Armed Services Committee. Stennis was provided with a rundown on a newly installed satellite intelligence activity and then was politely asked whether he had any questions. The elderly senator hesitated a moment and then said, "Son, I just have one question—how do those things [satellites] stay up there anyhow?"

† In late September Murkowski chose to interject himself into a civil aviation matter by writing Secretary Elizabeth Dole of the Department of Transportation and requesting that Korean Air Lines be granted, "as a symbol of friendship and concern," direct passenger service rights between Anchorage and Seoul. The airline's service at Anchorage was limited at the time to technical stops for refueling. Mrs. Dole wrote the senator that while she

same story that week from NASA, however. General Lincoln Faurer, the NSA director, assured a New York *Times* reporter during a background interview that his agency "holds absolutely no intelligence whatsoever that in any way diminishes the story exactly as the U.S. government has described it."

The United States had won its worldwide propaganda victory over the Soviet Union, and many in the White House were eager to press the advantage. Included in that group were the president and William Clark, his NSC adviser. Clark ended weeks of silence by publicly deploring what he called "the sickening display of Soviet barbarism" in the shootdown. "The Soviet leadership has stated that it would commit another massacre if another civilian airliner entered its airspace, despite the outrage expressed by the entire civilized world," Clark told the annual convention of the Air Force Association on September 15. "They appear unfazed. They show no remorse, make no restitution, and threaten similar action in the future. No wonder U.S.-Soviet relations are not good." Clark's closest aides on the NSC acknowledged that they had simply not been informed of the early Air Force Intelligence analysis of Flight 007 and the deep dispute it created inside the intelligence community; one aide,

---

shared his concern over the tragedy, the shootdown "should not be seen, however, as a basis for granting the Korean Government commercial aviation opportunities. . . . Such action could establish a precedent which other friendly nations might expect us to follow in other cases—the unilateral grant of commercial opportunities as a token of friendship after a distressing incident."

who monitored much of the paper flow for Clark, found it unlikely that Clark could have been given such information without his knowledge. Two days after Clark's statement, Ronald Reagan, speaking with evangelistic fervor, told his radio audience that the Soviets "reserve for themselves the right to live by one set of rules, insisting everyone else live by another. They're supremely confident their crime and coverup will soon be forgotten and we'll all be back to business as usual." The shootdown, he added, had triggered "a fundamental and long-overdue reappraisal in countries all over the globe. The Soviet Union stands virtually alone against the world." Reagan fervently urged the American people to continue to harden their attitude toward the Soviets and to brace for constant struggle against godless Communism: "We can start preparing for what John F. Kennedy called a long twilight struggle. It won't be quick, it won't make headlines, and it sure won't be easy, but it's what we must do to keep America strong, keep it free, and yes, preserve the peace for our children and for our children's children. This is the most enduring lesson of the Korean Air Lines massacre."

The Soviets were listening. Andrei Gromyko canceled his annual visit to the United Nations, the first time in more than twenty years that he had missed the fall opening of the General Assembly, after being told that Governors Mario Cuomo of New York and Thomas Kean of New Jersey had taken it upon themselves to refuse routine permission for Gromyko's special civilian Aeroflot flight to land in the New York area. They explained that the arrival of the Soviet official was likely to trigger public demonstrations. The

State Department pointedly chose not to intercede, although the governors had clearly violated at least the spirit of a 1947 U.S. agreement with the United Nations forbidding any impediments to the transit of a representative of a U.N. member state. The Reagan administration eventually told Moscow that Gromyko would be permitted to land only in a "noncivilian" plane and at a noncommercial airport. When the Soviets protested at the United Nations, Charles Lichenstein, the U.S. delegate, astonished the other delegates by exclaiming that critics of America's function as U.N. hosts could take themselves and the United Nations elsewhere. "If in the judicious determination of the members of the United Nations they feel they were not welcome and treated with the hostly consideration that is their due," Lichenstein said, "the United States strongly encourages member states to seriously consider removing themselves and this organization from the soil of the United States. We will put no impediment in your way, and we will be at dockside bidding you a farewell as you set off into the sunset." Three days later, on September 22, President Reagan endorsed Lichenstein's comments and said he "had the hearty approval of most people in America." The message was loud and clear: anything anti-Soviet goes. The nation had applauded when the Reagan administration joined with the governors of New York and New Jersey to bar Gromyko from landing at a metropolitan airport. Even former Senator Walter F. Mondale, the leading candidate for the Democratic presidential nomination in 1984, supported the administration, calling the barring of the Soviet aircraft "a reasonable step." Mondale added that had he been president, he would have been tougher on the Soviets and insisted on some economic reprisals for the shoot-down.

The definitive Soviet response to the shoot-down and the escalating American rhetoric came from Premier Yuri Andropov, who broke his silence on the issue of Flight 007 in a statement released by Moscow on September 28. Andropov, later known to have been seriously ill that fall—he would die in February—was thought at the time to have returned to Moscow from an extended vacation. His statement attracted modest press notice at the time, but it represented the first authoritative evaluation of the Reagan administration's policies by the Soviet leadership. The Soviet premier essentially wrote off the possibility of doing business with Reagan. "If anyone had any illusions about the possibility of an evolution for the better in the policy of the present American administration," Andropov wrote, "recent events have dispelled them once and for all." In language that evoked the worst days of the Cold War in tone and toughness, Andropov seemed to equate the crisis over Flight 007 to the life and death of the state: "During the six and one-half decades of its existence, the Soviet state has successfully endured many trials, including the crucial one [World War II]. Those who encroached on the integrity of our state, its independence and our system found themselves on the garbage heap of history. It is high time that everybody to whom this applies understand that we shall be able to ensure the security of our country, the security of our friends and allies under any circumstances." The Reagan administration, he said, in "its imperial ambitions, goes so far that one begins to doubt whether Washington has any brakes at all preventing it from crossing the mark before which any sober-minded person must stop."

Andropov also endorsed the Soviet military's view of Flight 007 as a deliberate provocation masterminded by Ronald Reagan. He described the flight as "an example of extreme adventurism in politics. We have elucidated the factual aspect of the action in a thorough and authentic way," the premier said, referring to Marshal Ogarkov's news conference. "The guilt of its organizers, no matter how hard they might dodge and what false versions they might put forward, has been proved." Turning again to Reagan, Andropov said, "One must say bluntly it is an unattractive sight when, with a view to smearing the Soviet people, leaders of such a country as the United States resort to what almost amounts to obscenities alternating with hypocritical preaching about morality and humanism." As for the treatment of Gromyko at the United Nations, Andropov rhetorically questioned whether that body, "called upon to maintain peace and security, [could] remain in the country where outrageous militarist psychosis is being imposed and the good name of the organization insulted."

It was far more than name-calling. The shootdown and its vituperative aftermath had sunk U.S.-Soviet relations to the lowest point since the Berlin crisis and the missile crisis of the Kennedy administration. By early October, with each side hardening its position, the truth no longer mattered. On October 7, the New York *Times*, in a front-page story, provided the first indication that the intelligence community had collected data demonstrating that the Soviet fighter did not know he was attacking an airliner when he shot down Flight 007. Citing "informants," the *Times* said that most intelligence specialists "are now confident, as a result of the review, that the SU-15 fighter that fired the rockets . . . was below and behind the airliner, rather than parallel to it, as high-level officials in Washington at first believed." The experts concluded, the newspaper wrote, that the difficulties of identifying an airliner from below precluded any positive identification. The story triggered no discernible second thoughts from those members of the administration who knew that the *Times* had barely scratched the surface of what was known. Some reporters were told on an off-the-record and unofficial basis that the *Times* story was either "a fabrication or a lie" and that there were, in fact, some intelligence assessments concluding "that the Soviets must have known they were shooting down a civilian airliner." Officially, the administration responded by suggesting that the sole issue of the crisis was that the Soviets had shot down the aircraft without fully identifying it. "We never said that we had incontrovertible evidence that they knew it was a civilian airliner," State Department spokesman Alan Romberg insisted at a briefing. "We did have incontrovertible evidence and do that they purposely shot that airplane down." Romberg may not have known better, but some of his superiors who prepared him for the briefing assuredly did. But no official, not George Shultz, Lawrence Eagleburger, or Richard Burt, would jeopardize all that had been gained—in terms of damaging the Soviets in the eyes of the world and improving the status of the State Department with the president—by acknowledging that the administration initially had abused the intelligence gathered and then lacked the courage and integrity to set the record straight. The import of the *Times* story quickly disappeared, amid all of the misleading challenges by the Reagan administration and its spokesmen.

By early 1984, Robert McFarlane, the newly named national security adviser, could confidently assure a group of journalists during an off-the-record briefing in the White House that it would be wrong to describe the destruction of Flight 007 as "accidental." Asked if he thought the Soviet pilot knew what he was aiming at, McFarlane said yes, and added, according to an account in the Washington *Post:* "We believe that those levels of command and decision . . . who were involved were levels that at least we expect and believe must reflect a maturity and judgment that would foreclose this kind of thing."

14

An Official Inquiry

$\mathcal{S}$ince man first began to travel, navigation has depended on outside points of reference, such as the stars and the magnetic north pole or, more recently, radio beacons, to fix location and chart a course. The needs of space exploration changed all that and revolutionized commercial air travel. The National Aeronautics and Space Administration developed a new guidance device for its spacecraft—the Inertial Navigation System (INS)—that had immediate implications for commercial air traffic. The INS represents an enormous technological leap. It consists of a tiny platform inside the aircraft, stabilized by gyroscopes, that is constantly able to compute the airplane's position without reference to any outside point. Flying over the North Pole, with its severe magnetic distortion, thus poses no special problem and calls for no special navigation by the crew. The INS is programmed to always fly the most direct route between two points, known as a Great Circle track.* As further assurance that the aircraft remain on course, the INS constantly computes the effect of winds on the plane's preplanned Great Circle course and feeds that information seven times a second to the aircraft's automatic pilot. The complex system has been in widespread use on airliners, including the fleet of Boeing 747s owned by Korean Air Lines, since the late 1970s.

One of the basic questions facing the initial investigators of the shootdown of Flight 007—an ad hoc team of experts assembled by the International Civil Aviation Organization—was the operational status of the INS units aboard Flight 007. The ICAO investigation had been authorized as part of the resolution of condemnation that had been overwhelmingly approved by the ICAO Council—after intense U.S. lobbying—on September 16. The investigators were given only until mid-December to complete their inquiry, and they turned to INS malfunction or misprogramming as the most logical place to begin to seek an answer to the essential question posed by the shootdown: the failure of the seemingly competent Korean

---

* On a map, the shortest distance between two points seems to be a straight line, or a true compass course, such as due west or due east. But a map is nothing more than an attempt to depict a sphere—the earth—on a flat surface, and as such, it distorts distance. If you drew what seemed to be a straight line from Anchorage to Seoul on a map and flew those coordinates, you would be flying an arc and would travel more miles than necessary to get where you wanted to go. If, however, you took a string and stretched it on a globe from Anchorage to Seoul in a Great Circle route, it would appear as a curve if plotted on a map but navigationally it would be a straight line between the two points.

crew members to know they were lost. Sheer necessity was another reason for the ICAO team to turn to the INS: there was little else to work with. None of Flight 007's recorded communications with air traffic controllers in Anchorage and Tokyo seemed out of the ordinary, and no apparent clues were found in the preflight logs and documents on file at Anchorage.

Most Boeing 747s have three INS units in the cockpit, one each for the captain, copilot, and flight engineer. On most flights, as on Flight 007, the captain's INS actually controls the autopilot and thus navigates the aircraft; the other units are backup. The devices are designed to be separately programmed and to cross-check one another—making it extremely difficult to go astray.

And yet, as airline officials throughout the world describe it, the uncanny perfection of the INS has created a new generation of problems arising from the simple fact that flying an INS-equipped transoceanic jet airliner has become a mundane profession. There is little to do after takeoff and before landing except the periodic monitoring of instruments; complacency becomes almost inevitable. Pilots and the crew members of major international airlines have become experts in the seemingly simple business of staying awake and alert and not falling into the trap of flying by rote.

The industry has made no secret of the problem. In public testimony less than three weeks after Flight 007 was lost, for example, William D. Reynard, chairman of the FAA's Aviation Safety Reporting System, told a House Transportation subcommittee of the dangers inherent in the pilots' faith in what he called the "established reliance" on the INS. Over time, Reynard said, it has become clear to pilots and airlines management that the computerized navigation equipment in use today performs better and more reliably than human beings when it comes to the essential task of monitoring routine continuous activity. "This anticipation of correctness" on the part of pilots and crew members, Reynard added, "illustrates one of the paradoxes of modern technological development."*

The debate over what went wrong on Flight 007 has led many pilots and airline officials to argue that, even assuming that the airliner's INS had malfunctioned or was incorrectly programmed, there were many other systems that should have warned the crew members that they were off course. The most obvious of those was the aircraft's ground-mapping radar, which has a range of two hundred nautical miles and is displayed in front of both the pilot and the copilot. If Flight 007 had been on course, the radar would have shown nothing but water until the aircraft had flown beyond the Kamchatka Peninsula. Instead, Flight 007 directly overflew the land mass of Kamchatka for as

---

* After years of compiling a superb safety record, the airline industry suffered a series of disastrous crashes in 1985. There was widespread agreement that the marketplace pressures of deregulation had led to some cost-cutting in U.S. airline-maintenance procedures, and this presumably was responsible for some of the accidents. Other cases, however, clearly seem to involved some pilot error. By year's end, there had been twenty major commercial airliner crashes worldwide, involving the loss of more than 2,150 lives. Donald D. Engen, administrator of the FAA, told the Washington *Post*, "If I could answer the question of why, there wouldn't be accidents. It's very worrisome."

much as thirty minutes. Later, en route to Sakhalin Island, when the pilots should have been looking at the configuration of the northern Kurile Islands, there was nothing to see on radar, for the airliner was then over the vast Sea of Okhotsk. How could the crew have missed all that?

The fact is that many pilots simply do not rely on ground-mapping radar because—given the competence of the INS—they don't believe that it will tell them anything they need to know, and when it does depict conflicting data, they frequently choose to believe that it is malfunctioning. Many airliner pilots acknowledged during interviews that they placed limited reliance on the radar, but few were willing to be quoted. One exception is Harold H. Ewing, of Sumter, South Carolina, an airline captain who spent much of 1984 and 1985 independently investigating the flight path of the Korean airliner. Ewing has flown R-20 between Anchorage and the Far East repeatedly since 1980; in his view, a major function of ground-mapping radar on that route is "to tell you where the Kuriles are . . . to tell you if you're a little to the right [toward the Soviet Union]. You don't look down and see 100 percent ground cover and figure that it's Kamchatka—no way. You figure the radar's screwed up again, which it is half the time. If you're not okay, you just assume the radar's wrong." For many pilots, Ewing claims, ground-mapping radar serves as "a confidence check. It's not there to tell you of gross errors. If the radar depicts what you expect to see, you know everything is going well. But the obverse isn't true. If you fail to see what you expect to see, you don't know that anything is wrong. You just don't have that additional confirmation that everything is right." Another government aviation expert expressed the same thought in a somewhat different way. Pilots, he said, will utilize ground-mapping radar until it begins to depict something out of the ordinary. "Then they shut it down."

Such attitudes are not uncommon in the aviation industry. Every Federal Aviation Administration official or airline executive seems to have a favorite horror story about the haphazard attitudes in the cockpit stemming from the profound faith of airline crew members in their machinery. One FAA inspector told of a flight he took after the shootdown of Flight 007 on the national airline of a North African country. Entering the cockpit in midflight, he found all three crew members asleep at their duty positions, with their air navigation charts carefully taped to the cockpit windows to block the sun. Another oft-cited FAA story deals with the crash by an East European airliner into the side of a mountain. The cockpit voice recorder was recovered intact and showed that the pilot and a stewardess had been engaging in sex at the moment of impact.

A Washington attorney and former military pilot recalled a transatlantic trip he took on a prominent European carrier in the mid-1970s, shortly after the carrier completed the installation of INS on its fleet of 747s. The attorney had represented Litton Aero Products, one of the two major INS manufacturers, on various FAA proceedings dealing with the new navigation system. Curious about its actual use, he received permission shortly after takeoff to enter the cockpit.

He found the three crew members "playing cards on the navigator's table—about twelve feet from the window." He asked about the INS and was told by crew members that they were "saving it" and had not programmed it for the flight. Nor were they relying on any other internationally recognized navigation system, such as LORAN. Instead, the crew explained, the aircraft was flying on autopilot, with a heading supplied by the beacon of a commercial AM radio station in Nova Scotia. No allowance was being made for wind drift. At a certain point during the flight, the crew members explained, they would tune to another radio station in Barcelona, Spain, and fly toward it. They would make computations and adjustments later to ensure that they were on course. "I was really shocked," the attorney recalled.

Before the widespread installation of INS, navigational errors of thirty miles or more were recorded in roughly 1 percent of all flights. The INS changed all that: only twenty-one significant airliner navigational errors involving INS malfunction or pilot misprogramming were among the 22,429 incidents voluntarily reported to William Reynard's FAA Aviation Safety Reporting System over a five-year period ending in 1983.*

---

* Unpublished analyses by the International Civil Aviation Organization, which monitors all navigational deviations on a confidential basis, have confirmed the essential reliability of the FAA's voluntary study and have also shown that the vast majority of navigational errors are made by military and privately owned aircraft. In one six-month period ending in March 1985, for

The heart of the INS's mechanism is its ability to constantly measure what is known as the earthrate precession—one of the measurable motions of the earth as it turns on its axis. The rate of precession varies with latitude, and the INS is capable at any given latitude of determining what it should be. Once navigating, the INS not only computes its present position but senses any change in direction or speed; it therefore can easily navigate to any point on the earth with simple computations. The accuracy of the system depends on the accuracy of the navigational information supplied to it before takeoff. The copilot or flight engineer aboard a Boeing 747 is required by all airlines to enter the precise location of the aircraft into the three INS units separately as the aircraft is sitting on the ramp awaiting passengers; any discrepancy in the information in the units would immediately be sensed, and the INS's warning light would blink on. Once that threshold is successfully passed, the next step also calls for care. The copilot has to enter the flight plan into the system. This is done with the help of what are known as waypoints—a series of navigational stepping-stones (on R-20, the route between Anchorage and Seoul that Flight 007 would fly, each about forty-five minutes' flying time apart)—that serve as guideposts for the INS during flight. INS errors usually begin here, because the system can be "remote-

---

example, forty-eight navigational deviations of thirty miles or more were reported worldwide to ICAO; only five of those involved major international air carriers, while American military aircraft alone were responsible for nine significant deviations.

loaded": a crew member, after entering the more than one hundred digits—representing the aircraft's navigational points—into the captain's controlling INS, can select a remote-loading switch and automatically load the flight-plan waypoints into all three units. Remote loading is forbidden by many airlines, but pilots acknowledge that it goes on, largely because it saves a great deal of time in the busy moments before takeoff.

There are some limits to the INS. One drawback is that only nine waypoints can be loaded at any time. This means that on extremely long flights, the copilot must put additional waypoints into the INS while in flight to keep the aircraft on course. (On the flight over the North Pacific to Seoul, which requires seventeen waypoints, he must enter eight additional waypoints.) The present position of the aircraft while in flight is constantly maintained in the INS as waypoint zero. The pilot has the ability at all times to shift the INS from present position, or waypoint zero, to any other waypoint and fly directly there via a Great Circle route. Pilots operating on late-night flights in the United States often will be cleared shortly after takeoff directly to their destination, from Los Angeles to Kansas City, for example, or to a waypoint more than halfway to their destination. The pilot in such cases would simply direct the INS to fly from waypoint zero—present position—to the assigned waypoint, and the aircraft's autopilot would bypass the unneeded waypoints en route.

The INS has two display points at the pilot's knee that always depict which waypoint is being flown *from* and which waypoint the aircraft is flying *to*. This notion, that a waypoint is always being flown either *from* or *to*, is essential to understanding how the system works.* When the third waypoint is passed, for example, the pilot's display shows that the new *from* waypoint is waypoint three and the new *to* waypoint is waypoint four.

If the nine waypoints have been overflown and no further waypoints have been entered, the INS—after passing waypoint nine—will continue flying *from* waypoint nine *back* to waypoint one. The aircraft's autopilot will be directed to bank the aircraft around and return to its starting point.

What has been known, in fact, to have gone wrong on transoceanic flights is far more mundane. The INS knows only where it is, and where it's going *from* and where it's going *to*. It knows nothing beyond that. On many flights, the INS is updated when flying *from* the eighth *to* the ninth waypoints. Waypoints one through seven—which no longer have any navigational function—can be reprogrammed at this time. But if the copilot mistakenly enters the seven new waypoints too early in the flight, say between waypoints seven and eight, the INS—finding itself suddenly flying *to* waypoint eight *from* the new waypoint "seven" which is thousands of miles ahead—will conclude that something is wrong. Under such conditions, it is programmed to move forward to the next set of waypoints in the sequence. It will automatically shift

---

* A waypoint can never be empty. If the crew has somehow failed to enter navigational data into one, it will display all zeros—the intersection of the Greenwich meridian (0'0" longitude) and the equator (0'0" latitude), which is a point about one hundred miles off Equatorial Guinea on the African West Coast.

to a new course between waypoints eight and nine. The INS further will direct the autopilot to fly directly to the Great Circle track—the shortest distance between two points—defined by waypoints eight and nine. The aircraft, which had already been flying on the Great Circle track between waypoints seven and eight, must then move over to the new Great Circle route between waypoints eight and nine. On R-20 between Anchorage and Seoul, the new track would be just a few seconds—little more than a mile—to the north. Nonetheless, pilots in such situations have had their aircraft suddenly turn 90 degrees to fly to the new route—and, upon reaching that route, abruptly straighten out again to maintain it.

Commercial pilots are respectful of the complexity of the INS and, upon detecting in flight that the system has been programmed with inaccurate coordinates before takeoff, will often jettison fuel and return to the initial airport ramp, or to any airport with a known position, to start all over again. The system is just impossible to reprogram from scratch (as opposed to entering a revised set of waypoints) while in flight. Such costly and time-consuming interruptions had happened on Korean Air flights. An experienced accident investigator, William Hendricks of the National Transportation Safety Board, an independent federal safety agency, assisted by another expert, Frank S. Del Gandio of the FAA, quietly flew to Seoul a few days after Flight 007 was shot down, to assist Korean Air officials in their preliminary inquiry. The Americans learned from the airline that at least three prior flights had been aborted, with fuel jettisoned, in a series of pilot misprogrammings. The airline's management ir

Seoul responded to the aborted flights by placing its pilots on notice that there would be severe sanctions in case of future INS misprogramming. By the time they left Seoul, Del Gandio and Hendricks, who were later assigned to the ICAO's ad hoc investigatory team, had become convinced that the crew of Flight 007 had disregarded company rules—and common sense—by not comparing all of the INS coordinates before take-off with the entries in the original flight plan or, to avoid the possibility of typographical error, with the data in navigational charts. The two Americans said that the Koreans "didn't know what they were doing," according to an ICAO official.

The ICAO team, headed by M. Y. Wazirzada of Pakistan, did not publish the unflattering information about Korean Air's prior INS problems in its final report, in deference to what was described as a general reluctance inside ICAO to criticize publicly a member state's airline. ICAO officials said that it would be wrong and unfair to conclude that the Korean Air crew on duty that night was part of an overall pattern of incompetence and lackadaisical flying by the airline. "At that point, KAL was doing reasonably well," one senior ICAO official noted. "There were some horror stories being told, but you could find some in most airlines. It wasn't the best, but it wasn't the worst. Their crews were very well disciplined—perhaps too well."

In mid-November, operating in secrecy, ICAO assembled more than a dozen INS experts from industry and government at the Boeing Company's flight crew training facilities in Seattle, Washington, to try to simulate the last flight of the Korean airliner. The tests were conducted with the aid of engineers from Boeing, manufacturers of the 747, and from Litton Aero Products, whose INS may have malfunctioned or been misprogrammed. The ICAO effort was impeded by the refusal of the Soviets to supply any radar data. And the United States, which had monitored the Russian radar, refused to turn over its tracking data. Such information would have revealed Flight 007's precise flight path from Kamchatka on.

ICAO's report, although further hampered by severe time restraints and a reluctance to tell all it knew about Korean Air, was published in December 1983 and remains the most comprehensive—if flawed—official investigation to date on the shootdown. The report created five scenarios in an attempt to account for the navigational failure of Flight 007 and the aircraft's subsequent destruction over Sakhalin. Two of the scenarios seemed to approximate the errant flight path Flight 007 was believed to have followed en route to Sakhalin on the night of August 31–September 1.

One theory suggests that the crew of Flight 007 failed to engage the INS at all and flew to Sakhalin on a direct magnetic heading that would take the aircraft across the North Pacific. This error, known to have happened on at least five other INS-equipped flights since 1978, centers on a switch in the cockpit that enables the crew to go back and forth among three different navigational systems that can be linked to the automatic pilot. Turning the switch farthest to the left activates the INS, the aircraft's main flying mechanism and the system used most frequently on transoceanic flights. The next position is a magnetic-heading-mode switch, which allows the pilot to fly the aircraft on automatic pilot in a straight line in any compass heading he chooses. The third position enables the aircraft to respond to a radio beacon known as a VOR, for very-high-frequency omnidirectional radio range. A VOR consists of a scattered array of high-powered ground transmitters which emit thin radio beams known as radials. There were several times during the early stages of the final flight when the crew of Flight 007, if it had chosen to do so, could have tuned to a VOR—pilots call it capturing a radial—and discovered the navigational error.

In compiling the magnetic-heading scenario, the ICAO investigators noted that Flight 007's initial course that night was toward Cairn Mountain, Alaska, 175 miles to the southwest. To get there, the crew could have set the switch to the heading mode and flown on a course of 246 degrees. The pilot ordinarily would activate the INS upon verifying that the system was on track—perhaps after reaching Cairn Mountain, the flight's first waypoint and the site of a radio beacon, or perhaps after flying to the tiny Alaskan fishing village of Bethel, the second waypoint, twenty-five minutes away (Bethel is also the site of a VOR transmitter). The scenario says that instead of switching to INS the pilot mistakenly remained in the heading mode, continuing to fly to the southwest at a course of 246 degrees. That heading, the ICAO simulation showed, came close to duplicating the course of the flight but also placed the airliner at least eighty miles farther south than it was known to have flown. The discrepancy is evidence that Flight 007 did not end in catastrophe because the crew simply forgot to move a switch one position to the left—to the INS mode.

A more likely possibility, also given credibility by a simulation, was that the crew of the flight, in loading the aircraft's ground coordinates into the captain's INS, which actually controlled the flight, inadvertently put in one wrong digit. If the position had been inserted as W139 degrees instead of the correct W149 degrees, Flight 007's path would have been close to the one actually flown. Such misprogramming, called finger trouble by airline pilots, is known to have been the primary cause of at least four of the INS programming errors reported to the FAA's Aviation Safety Reporting System.

The unavoidable fact facing the ICAO investigators was that there were no witnesses to what actually happened aboard the Korean airliner. Furthermore, Flight 007's crash site had not been located and thus there was no possibility of recovering the plane's flight data and cockpit voice recorders—the so-called black boxes. Moreover, if the recorders had been found, there would be no assurance—assuming that the Korean crew members did not deliberately plan to go off course—that the recorded data would solve the basic problem of how the airliner ended up where it did. Another factor was political pressure: the inquiry was being closely watched by the United States and the Soviet Union, influential members of ICAO, and the international committee—given only a few months to prepare its study of the shootdown—was reluctant to find itself a pawn of the superpowers. In the final report, simply entitled *Destruction of Korean Air Lines*

Boeing 747 over Sea of Japan, the investigators emphasized facts. Enormous detail was presented about the specific navigational and radio equipment aboard the flight, as well as the full FAA transcripts of all pilot-to-air-controller exchanges. ICAO even compiled its own translation of the Japanese tape recording of the Soviet interceptor pilot, in an attempt to head off Soviet charges—which were filed nonetheless—that the transcripts had been altered by American intelligence to damage the Soviet case.

The report's scrupulous attention to detail was badly marred, however, by a few sentences at the conclusion in which the agency minimized the inconsistencies and maintained that either of its two main scenarios provided a flight path that was congruent with the known path of Flight 007: "It was possible to postulate that either the holding of a constant magnetic heading or an undetected error of 10 degrees east longitude . . . into one of the three INS units would have produced a track to the area of [KAL] 007's destruction that was also consistent with the radar track information" made public by the Soviet Union and Japan.

The ICAO report, in depicting the mishandling of a switch or a programming error as possible explanations for the errant flight, stressed that its scenarios "assumed a considerable degree of lack of alertness and attentiveness on the part of the entire flight crew, but not to a degree that was unknown in international civil aviation." The report attracted only cursory media attention in the United States and elsewhere—people had already made up their minds about the shootdown—but some who did study the findings found them unpersuasive. For example, ICAO's report candidly noted that one of the simulations had uncovered a major flaw in its 10-degree-error scenario: such an error in programming the captain's INS would have brought Flight 007 thirty-eight miles north of course at the time it was supposed to overfly Bethel. The airliner, as charted by radar, actually flew twelve miles north of Bethel. ICAO's critics argued that such a gross error should have been easily noticed by the crew of Flight 007—if the flight had proceeded as the scenario suggested.

ICAO's council, always leery of disputes among members, had agreed shortly after the initial submission of the report in December to have it reviewed by the organization's Air Navigation Commission, the in-house experts. That study, published in early February 1984, acknowledged that it was "unable to establish the exact cause for the significant deviation from track." The commission further reported that it could not "validate and endorse" the ICAO simulations "because any one of them contained some points which could not be explained satisfactorily." It also explicitly said what had not been said in the earlier report, that the "magnitude of the diversion cannot be explained, particularly as the aircraft was equipped with navigation equipment which should have enabled the crew to adhere to its track."

The findings of the commission encouraged those critics in the United States and elsewhere who were convinced that the Reagan administration was withholding information about the true mission of Flight 007. It also prompted a few of ICAO's aviation experts, as well as a few international pilots, to continue working on what had become a fascinating and haunting problem—why had KAL's INS system failed to warn the crew? Similar questions were being raised by the Soviet Union publicly and privately as part of its continuing campaign to fix blame for the shooting—and the loss of 269 lives—on the United States.

The Soviets remained convinced that there was evidence somewhere that would prove to the world that the airliner had been sent over their skies by the Reagan administration. In May 1984, shortly after beginning research on this book, I was granted permission to visit the Soviet Union and conduct interviews about the event. There was a long meeting with Marshal Nikolai Ogarkov and Deputy Foreign Minister Georgi Kornienko in an ornate conference room in central Moscow belonging to the Defense Ministry. After five days of interviews and briefings, I had been provided with no evidence to support the thesis— which Ogarkov and Kornienko seemed to believe— that Flight 007 was a deliberate provocation. I raised what seemed to be obvious questions. Why not simply tell the world, "We made a mistake and shot down the airliner in the belief that it was an American reconnaissance plane"? Why say that it had to be a spy plane when there obviously was no proof?

Kornienko informed me why I had been invited to Moscow: he and Ogarkov had agreed to my visa in the hope that they could persuade me, as a journalist, to investigate the CIA's role in the shootdown. Taken aback, but realizing that the two senior Soviet officials were serious, I asked Kornienko with a laugh whether he thought I was once again a New York *Times* reporter and he was trying to be my editor. His response came in English: "Your assignment is to find that it was an intruder." The deputy foreign minister added that the American public would never accept the shootdown as a rational act on the Soviets' part unless it could be proven that the overflight was deliberate. I could not decide which was more suprising: his faith in the American First Amendment or the explicit acknowledgment that his government, for all of its public finger-pointing, had no evidence of American involvement in the flight path of the Korean airliner. Marshal Ogarkov said: "We do not know all the intentions that preceded Flight 007. I'm sure that the day will come when we know the reasons why this mission was arranged."

The whole story of Flight 007 may never be told. Why and how had the Korean airliner gone so far off course? How had the most sophisticated navigational equipment failed to alert the crew? What did the Russians know? How did they confuse a commercial airliner with an American intelligence flight—one whose flight path they had routinely monitored for more than twenty years? Why did they fail to shoot it down right away? Some facts are known, however, and they make clear that the destruction of Flight 007 had its beginnings not in international intrigue but—as the ICAO investigators assumed—in the ordinary human failings of the Korean Air Line crew members who were responsible for the lives of hundreds of innocent airline passengers.

came in English. Any suggestion is to find that... Nor Jan initiated? The thing foreign observers added that the Russian public would never accept the shootdown as a rational act on the Soviet part unless ... produced he proven that the shoot-down was deliberate ... could not decide which was more appalling: the shot ... on the Korean First Instrument or the explicit acknowledgment that no equipment for all of its orbits ... He then pointed out that no evidence of American involvement in the flight path of the plane ... the ... Marshal Ogarkov said "... do not know whose instructions this plane had. Flight 007 ... and even if it is a spy craft, when was again, the reasons why these ... was aroused."

The whole story of Flight 007 may never be told. Why did and how had the Korean airliner strayed so far off course? How had the most sophisticated navigational equipment failed to alert the crew to their location? If the same knew, how did they not just continue on ... lian with an American intelligence-gathering mission on flight path, but not ... and monitor themselves and then ... twice in two ... would they fail to show up on various ...? Same facts are known: how over and above make what their desires ... of flight not had in ... things not in ... of flight being ... help the ICAO investigators assumed ... in the ultimate conclusions ... of the Korean Air Line crew members who were ... sponsible for the lives of hundreds of unsuspecting passengers.

BOOK IV

The
Flight

BOOK IV

The
Flight

15

To Kamchatka

The captain of Korean Air Flight 007 on the night of August 31–September 1, 1983, was Chun Byung-in, forty-five years old, who had been flying for KAL since 1972, after ten years of service in the Korean Air Force. He was highly regarded for his safety record and had been chosen as a backup pilot on three of South Korean president Chun Doo Hwan's state visits. Captain Chun had flown the North Pacific route between Anchorage and Seoul eighty-three times, including twenty-seven flights along the specific route—R-20—that Flight 007 had been assigned that night by the Anchorage air traffic control center. Captain Chun's copilot, Son Dong-Hwin, forty-seven years old, also had extensive experience in the North Pacific, having flown between Asia and Anchorage fifty-two times in his four years with KAL while logging nearly 3,500 hours in a Boeing 747. He had flown R-20 only seventeen days earlier, one of thirty such trips he had made. The flight engineer, Kim Eui Dong, thirty-two years old, had traveled North Pacific routes forty-four times, including three trips in the prior year. This was to be his first trip along R-20. Captain Chun and his colleagues were fresh and well rested; another crew had flown the first leg of flight 007 from New York City to Anchorage without incident.

There was little reason for the experienced crew to look forward to its assignment. Piloting a modern jetliner, as the crew understood, was far less glamorous than is popularly perceived. Nearly all of the significant navigation would be done by the aircraft's inertial navigation system, which controlled the autopilot. The INS, with its amazing accuracy in point-to-point navigation, took much of the work out of flying—as well as much of the fun. Flight 007 would take about eight hours and cover 4,100 miles, most of it over water, most of it in darkness. Even the fact that the flight plan called for the airliner, with its 240 passengers and 29 crew members, to fly to within fewer than fifty miles of the Soviet Union was routine.

The over-water route between Anchorage and Asia is especially tedious, according to Dennis Wilham, the FAA's Asian representative. "The thing about this particular route in these days is—it's so boring, so damn boring. The only thing that's happening is the [Kurile] Islands going by," said Wilham, whose FAA assignment in Tokyo includes periodic checking of American crew members who fly the North Pacific routes.

Even the flight plan for Captain Chun's trip across the ocean that night was drawn up in advance—by computer—detailing the speed and altitude of the airliner en route to Seoul. Many pilots routinely follow such prepackaged plans; others do not and, after checking weather and other flight conditions, will modify and adjust the plan. Captain Chun made his own decisions about his flight altitude. The computerized plan called for the airliner to climb to an altitude of 33,000 feet after about two hours at 31,000 feet, and to 35,000 feet after about four hours. Each climb was to be made after the aircraft had burned off enough fuel to lighten it and enable it to fly more efficiently at the higher altitude. Yet the airliner did not request permission to climb to 33,000 feet until more than three hours had passed. A copy of the computerized flight plan was printed in the appendix to the December 1983 ICAO report, and it showed jottings—obviously made by Captain Chun and left on file at Korean Air's flight operations office at Anchorage—indicating that the captain had spent the few minutes before takeoff revising the flight plan. He apparently was seeking ways of making the flight more efficient—and saving fuel by so doing—and elected, according to his notations on the flight plan, to delay the aircraft's climb to 33,000 feet. Captain Chun had analyzed the data and concluded that it would be more fuel-efficient to delay both climbs until more fuel had been burned off. His effort to modify and improve the flight plan impressed Harold Ewing: Captain Chun seemed to be "a guy going the extra mile. The guy was looking for ways to be more efficient. He was looking under all the rocks."

Captain Chun's last-minute revision to the flight plan may have led him and his crew to rush through the other, more routine, preflight checks. For instance, there is evidence that the captain made a monumental error in computing the aircraft's weight and balance—

the most important factor, as any pilot can attest, in determining takeoff speed and distance. Other documents reproduced in the appendix to the ICAO report showed that before departure Chun had signed a flight-release sheet listing the on-board fuel at 253,700 pounds. A few moments later he signed a weight-and-balance manifest listing the fuel at 263,700 pounds. Under some circumstances, an additional 10,000 pounds can mean the difference between a successful takeoff and a crash. For example, if the captain was carrying 10,000 pounds (or five tons) more fuel than he realized, and if the aircraft was already fully loaded upon takeoff—as many airliners are, but not Flight 007 that night—the miscalculation could have led to an aborted takeoff or a disaster. "The point is not the safety of that particular takeoff," noted Harold Ewing,* "but the fact that they didn't do it right. It's not hard to get it right, but they did not. It's a mistake—a big mistake."

In theory, a captain and his crew strive not only to work together but to reinforce each other and make it more difficult for significant mistakes to take place—

---

* Ewing forced ICAO to look again at the discrepancy, which was found at the time of the initial investigation but attributed then to Captain Chun's desire, not uncommon on North Pacific flights, to add more fuel at the last moment as a hedge against stronger-than-expected head winds. ICAO and officials of Korean Air reopened the issue more than a year later and confirmed, by checking fuel deliveries to the aircraft, that Flight 007 did, in fact, take off with 253,700 pounds of fuel and that the captain and his colleagues indeed had wrongly computed weight and balance. The importance of weight and balance was reaffirmed early in 1986 when the Canadian Aviation Safety Board reported that the crew of the chartered Arrow

such as the error in computing the amount of fuel aboard. In practice, the personal dynamics in the cockpit often make it more difficult to correct errors—even potentially deadly ones.

The captain, invariably senior in experience and prestige, is king of the flight deck; copilots and flight engineers are reluctant to challenge his judgment and have been known to remain silent even when confronted with catastrophe. Not surprisingly, the captain's dominance is most pronounced among airlines in Asia, where elders and superiors are traditionally highly respected. Yet deference to a captain's orders, even when clearly dangerous, can also be found among Western airline crews. The cases most often cited include a March 1977 runway collision of two 747s in the Canary Islands. The crash was triggered by a KLM captain who, despite a warning by his copilot, started to take off without clearance from the control tower. "Wait a minute, we do not have a clearance," the copilot said, according to the cockpit recorder. The captain paused as the copilot radioed the tower. He received no takeoff clearance, only

---

Air jetliner that crashed the previous December in Newfoundland, killing all 256 aboard, had miscalculated its weight by at least 12,000 pounds by underestimating the baggage weight. The aircraft's official weight-and-balance manifest listed the weight at 330,000 pounds, 25,000 pounds short of the airliner's capacity. The error in the manifest, plus the accumulated weight of ice on the wings, could have been responsible for the crash, investigators said in a preliminary report. Most of those killed were American GIs returning to their home base in Kentucky after five months of U.N. peacekeeping duty in the Middle East. Arrow Air petitioned for reorganization under the Bankruptcy Act two months after the crash.

navigation instructions. As the copilot was repeating those instructions to the captain, the captain suddenly exclaimed, in Dutch, "We're going, check thrust." The 747 then slammed into a taxiing Pan Am 747, killing 577 people in the world's worst airline disaster. Similarly, in December 1974, a Trans World Airlines jet crashed into a mountain near Dulles Airport outside Washington, D.C., when the captain decided that the air traffic controller had cleared the plane for initial approach altitude, a predetermined height for approaching the runway. His copilot disagreed. A brief discussion ended with the captain abruptly cutting off his copilot and saying: "When he [the air controller] clears you, [expletive deleted], that means you can go to your . . . initial approach altitude." The captain was wrong.

The INS has not eliminated such behavior, nor could it have prevented disasters such as the Canary Islands collision. But it has made it easier for crews with good working relationships to discover and rectify navigational mistakes. Of the twenty-one instances of significant INS malfunction and misprogramming referred to the Aviation Safety Reporting System before 1983, only one resulted in an incorrect flight path of 250 miles or more. And none of the aircraft, prior to Flight 007, crashed or intruded into hostile airspace. Investigators have determined that most of the errors were caught by crew members within moments, precisely as the system's manufacturers intended them to be. INS relies on a very primitive premise to catch programming mistakes: redundancy. The three INS units aboard the airliner are designed to verify that each has been supplied with the same information.

. . .

   How could such a carefully designed system
go so wrong? Harold Ewing, who has been flying
since he was sixteen and by 1985 was a virtual com-
muter between Alaska and the Far East on Boeing 747s
over the North Pacific, remained perplexed by the
many unanswered questions of Flight 007 and finally,
late in 1984, decided to do something about them. He
reviewed the ICAO data and then took a further step
on his own flights; he began entering the waypoints of
the various scenarios into one of the backup inertial
navigation systems in his Boeing 747. He was disturbed, he recalled, by the public's perception that the
INS could not have been misprogrammed because of
the system's redundancy checks. He knew better:
"The INS is fraught with danger. It's not foolproof."
After a year of on-the-job testing, Ewing was convinced that he had learned some of the answers to the
saga of Flight 007 and said as much in an unsolicited
report that he forwarded to ICAO's Air Navigation
Commission. A senior ICAO official, speaking privately in early 1986, described Ewing's account as the
"most studios and comprehensive to date." More important, those at ICAO who still research the mystery
of Flight 007 have incorporated many of Ewing's
findings in their own informal scenario, which is constantly being updated.
   What follows is a scenario, as devised by Ewing and
elaborated upon by ICAO, that explains Flight 007 in
terms of what is known and what has not yet been
revealed. The scenario is consistent with information
obtained and kept secret by American intelligence

agencies—not known to Ewing or anyone at ICAO, but told to me during my research—about the exact flight path of the airliner just prior to the shootdown. It begins just as the original ICAO scenarios did, with pilot error.

Korean Air Line records show that the first crew member to enter the cockpit that morning was Flight Engineer Kim Eui Dong. It was thus his responsibility not only to activate the INS but also to enter the aircraft's present position separately into each unit. This was one of the few periods that the INS, with its built-in gyroscopes and its ability to function as an internal navigational point of reference, would be vulnerable to error. Kim Eui Dong began with the captain's unit, which would control the autopilot during the flight, and it was at this point that he made the fatal finger error: entering the runway ramp position as W139 degrees longitude instead of W149 degrees, which meant that as far as the aircraft's controlling INS was concerned, Flight 007 was now located three hundred nautical miles to the east—the mileage of a 10-degree error at the latitude at Anchorage.* (Ewing's

---

* Inertial Navigation Systems have an inherent ability, since they constantly measure the speed of the earth's rotation, to detect even small errors in latitude. Officials of Litton Aero Products, manufacturers of the INS units aboard Flight 007, acknowledge that there is a significant limitation to the system they produce: it is sensitive, even when not in operation, to changes in latitude, the angular distance north or south from the equator, but is not designed to pick up changes in longitude during the initial programming.

scenario is consistent at this point with one ICAO scenario.) Once the computer running the captain's INS accepted the information, the engineer immediately switched the INS display to "desired track/status"—a step in determining the flight-readiness of the INS. The position coordinates no longer were displayed. Kim then put the correct coordinates into the copilot's INS and immediately got a warning—an amber light that said something was wrong. The computer in the copilot's INS had noted the difference between the W149 degrees correctly entered in its system and the W139 degrees in the captain's. Human nature then took over. The warning came while Kim was loading coordinates into the number-two INS. Therefore, he assumed—as many crew members would—that his problem was in INS number two. It couldn't be number one; that INS was loaded and ready to go. "It can happen so easily it makes your blood run cold," noted Ewing. The coordinates of the copilot's INS were digitally displayed for easy reading—as they had been on the captain's INS—and Engineer Kim checked the data that he had entered in the second INS against his worksheets. He saw that they were the same so he "cleared" the machine by merely pressing a button on the INS. The flight engineer resolved the problem by getting rid of it, by turning off the warning light and leaving the error intact.*

---

* Clearing the system would have been much more difficult on the INS manufactured by Delco Electronics, the major competitor to Litton Aero Products. Pilots describe the Delco product as being manufactured with more flexible computer software that

There was a pattern behind his action: pilots find that the INS's sensitivity to changes in latitude, even to shifts or movements while a plane is parked at the airport ramp, often makes the computer reject as inaccurate the coordinates for present position when, in fact, they are correct. A shift of only a few feet will make the INS go tilt. In such cases, the pilots—faced with a choice of either clearing the system or reprogramming it—invariably push the clear button.*

Kim now turned to the third INS, the one he was to monitor, and again entered the correct coordinates.

---

makes it harder to misprogram. Even after being cleared, for example, a Delco INS would continue to compare internally initial ramp-position data and issue warnings. The model of Litton INS aboard the Korean airliner did not have such a feature, according to the ICAO report. Special software for the Litton INS is available, according to ICAO officials, but had not been installed on the units in service on Korean Air Lines.

* Pilots have long expressed concern about the increasing penchant of aircraft crews to consider system warnings, such as that given by the INS to Flight Engineer Kim, as something to act on or ignore according to circumstances. The underlying problem is the fact that there are various categories of warnings. Some, such as the alarms that go off when an aircraft's landing gear has not been lowered, are treated with great seriousness and cannot be cleared by the pilot no matter what the circumstances. Other warnings function only to point out potential or real problems that have to be solved—perhaps with later troubleshooting. Some INS warnings, which are cancelable merely by clearing the machine, are obviously considered by some pilots as signs of minor problems that can be taken care of later. An implicit formula thus emerges: any problem that cannot be canceled is serious; one that is cancelable is minor.

There was no complaint from the number-three INS, because the INS's warning system, once canceled, was programmed to no longer react to any further discrepancy among the INS units. Now all three inertial navigation systems "agreed," although the captain's machine, which was going to fly the plane, was programmed incorrectly.

By the time the pilot and copilot joined the flight engineer in the cockpit, about a half hour later, the INS was ready to accept navigational information. The pilot was supposed to double-check the coordinates as put in by the flight engineer, but, as FAA and ICAO officials acknowledge, such checking is not always done.

The next step was the insertion of the first nine waypoints for the flight from Anchorage to Seoul. This was usually done prudently. Some U.S.-owned airlines insist that their crews list the aircraft's ramp position at the Anchorage airport or the VOR at Anchorage, six miles away, as the first waypoint in their flight plan. The goal is to provide immediate verification, after takeoff, of the aircraft's present position, and also to verify the distance to the first INS waypoint. The Anchorage VOR was out of commission on August 31 for routine maintenance, a fact that had little impact on the planning for Flight 007 since many international pilots routinely use Cairn Mountain, 175 miles to the southwest, as the first waypoint, as does Ewing's scenario. Cairn Mountain and Bethel, the first two waypoints, have ground-based navigational aids that can be used to verify the accuracy of the INS

programming.* Once Flight 007 overflew Bethel, the
final waypoint on the Alaskan mainland, verification
would be much more difficult. For the next 2,500
miles, Flight 007 would be flying over a series of artifi-
cially created waypoints in the North Pacific. These
waypoints, each about 300 miles apart, have been given
a series of colorful, albeit meaningless, names—
NABIE, NUKKS, NEEVA, NINNO, NIPPI,
NYTIM, NOKKA, and so forth. The crew members
of Flight 007, like all crews of flights toward Tokyo
from Anchorage, were able to program their INS computers only through NOKKA, the ninth waypoint.
Thus, before passing the ninth waypoint, NOKKA,
Copilot Son Dong-Hwin would have had to insert at
least one new waypoint to prevent the flight from
turning back, and he would probably have inserted
seven new waypoints to carry the flight to a VOR
beacon located outside of Seoul. All of this was standard practice.

Flight 007 taxied to the runway. Its takeoff a minute
or so after 10:00 P.M. Tokyo time from runway 32, the
runway facing 320 degrees to the northwest, was uneventful. Less than two minutes later, as the airliner
began to turn toward its previously assigned heading,
the Anchorage control tower routinely told the aircraft to "proceed direct Bethel when able." This is a
shortcut. The FAA's Anchorage tower could have
kept Flight 007 on an airway between Anchorage and

---

* In its December 1983 report, ICAO inadvertently confused matters by listing the VOR at Anchorage as Flight 007's first waypoint without any evidence that it was.

Bethel known as J-501. Instead, the tower told the crew members of 007 that they did not need to complete their swing to the south, to J-501, but could navigate a more direct Anchorage–Bethel southwest route, in essence, eliminate a dogleg to save time and perhaps some fuel. (At this point, according to the scenario, Captain Chun switched to the INS mode without initially confirming that he was on course.) The airliner now should have been on a direct path for Bethel, flying from waypoint zero—present position—to waypoint two. Korean Air Line flight rules forbid coupling the INS to the autopilot without a VOR fix, but with the Anchorage VOR out of commission, the Flight 007 crew, as most crews would do under the circumstances, committed a technical violation of the rule book in its handling of the INS. The VOR at Bethel would not be in range for at least another fifteen to twenty minutes. And furthermore, there is no reason to believe that the copilot's insertion of the waypoints, with its scores of separate entries, was independently double-checked by the captain, as is also prescribed by the airline's flight rules.*

The crew members, Ewing's scenario continues, should have been confronted with a clue that something was wrong with the flight plan—the displayed

---

* The author, while visiting in the cockpit of an American carrier before an R-20 flight from Anchorage to Tokyo in October 1985, watched carefully as the copilot inserted the waypoints into all three inertial navigation systems with no immediate cross-checking from other crew members, who were busy talking to passengers. The possibility exists that cross-checking was done later, perhaps—as is said to be common—when the aircraft was taxiing for takeoff.

distance to Bethel in Captain Chun's INS would not be 350 miles or so but closer to 650 miles, the actual mileage plus the 300 miles added by the 10-degree error in programming.

Harold Ewing's goal was to take the INS misprogramming thesis, which he found credible, and rework it to see if it could be made to fit what he knew the actual flight path to have been. His basic theory was that the captain of Flight 007, always interested—as his earlier modification of the flight plan showed—in flying efficiently and saving fuel, did much more than merely couple the INS system to the autopilot upon being freed by the control tower to "proceed direct Bethel." Ewing's hypothesis about Captain Chun's next step is one that Ewing and his supporters in ICAO acknowledge to be speculative but believe to be compatible with what happened: just minutes after takeoff, the captain chose to enter a new second waypoint into his INS only, one bypassing Bethel. In other words, although he was cleared to go directly to Bethel, he never went there. If he had set out to overfly Bethel, Ewing believes, it would have been difficult for him not to notice that his distance to go there, as displayed by the INS, was greater than it should be—and even if he somehow missed that contradiction, he would have realized when he came abeam of the VOR of Bethel that he was 38 miles north of it. But he did not learn that he missed Bethel, in Ewing's scenario, because he never wanted to go there anyway. The captain's new second waypoint was a navigational point 190 nautical miles to the southwest of Bethel; he chose it because it seemed to be a more direct line from his present position near Anchorage to a point on R-20 between Bethel and the third waypoint, NABIE, 658 miles from Anchorage. Flight 007's new route not only would save time and fuel but would not deviate significantly from the original flight plan as filed in Anchorage; any major deviation in the first twenty-five minutes of flight, when the airliner still was in radar contact with Anchorage, would be noticed and possibly generate reports.*

Even if the captain had followed his new flight plan, it would not explain the actual route Flight 007 took, because the airliner did not go to the new waypoint. Ewing's scenario says that Captain Chun made another programming mistake. Chun correctly entered into his INS the coordinates for the latitude of the new waypoint but failed to change the original INS longitude coordinates for Bethel in the computer. (Latitude is always entered before longitude when a new waypoint is being programmed.) In this scenario, the longitudinal coordinates had already been shifted 10 degrees by the flight engineer's initial programming error. Flight 007 was now en route to the unknown— flying toward a new "hybrid" waypoint, as Ewing calls it. Ewing acknowledged that his scenario calls for a leap of faith at this point but he notes that Captain Chun could have been interrupted while inserting the

---

* The new flight path would actually produce only a slight saving in terms of flying time, Ewing discovered after running simulations on a computer. At first glance at the flight charts, however, the saving appears to be much greater. "All in all," Ewing concluded in the analysis he presented to ICAO, "this would seem a simple and harmless fuel-saving trick, consistent with KAL's reputation."

new waypoint and not have returned to the task of entering the longitudinal coordinates. Another possibility is simply that the INS unit refused to accept the longitude component; such rejection of coordinates had happened before.*

Thus, when Flight 007 flew abeam of the first waypoint at Cairn Mountain, the copilot's and flight engineer's INSs routinely shifted and showed that the aircraft was flying *to* waypoint two (Bethel) *from* waypoint one (Cairn Mountain). The captain's INS recorded no shift; as reprogrammed, it was, so he thought, flying the plane directly from waypoint zero (present position) to waypoint two, 190 miles southwest of Bethel.

Ewing's scenario provides a flight model that is consistent with the known flight path; it provides specific theories about the poor performance of the crew; and it posits, he said, "only a tragic lack of attention to detail while engaged in an unauthorized operation which, had the disaster not occurred, would have been considered a minor violation at most."

The key to Ewing's thesis is cockpit behavior. In the first weeks after the shootdown of Flight 007, ICAO investigators were given access to many pilots and officials of Korean Air, including the crew of Ko-

---

* Pilots have come to learn that INS units will at some point simply refuse to accept longitudinal or latitudinal coordinates, no matter how carefully entered. In most cases, the INS simply maintains the previous coordinates, but the system has also been known to register the new position as all zeroes. Such malfunctions seem to take place more often when the units are remote-loaded.

rean Flight 015. The investigators became convinced that the most significant event in the cockpit took place well before Flight 007 reached its cruising altitude of 31,000 feet, and perhaps soon after the passenger seat-belt sign was taken off at 10,000 feet. Captain Chun, having established the aircraft on what he believed was the flight path he wanted, left the routine monitoring and reporting of waypoints to his crew members. It was time to do what was required of him as a senior Korean Air officer; he moved back into the passenger section to greet the various dignitaries on board, including Congressman Larry McDonald. There were also three off-duty Korean Air Line captains and three other nonworking crew members in the first-class cabin, all being ferried to Seoul for new flight assignments. ICAO officials believe that the captain spent much of the next five hours chatting away. He was not heard from again on the aircraft's radio, not even by the crew of the Korean Air Flight 015, which was flying from Anchorage to Tokyo, and whose crew would spend some time in the early morning relaying position reports from Flight 007, now out of normal communication range, to the Anchorage traffic control center. The two Korean airliners, initially minutes apart but flying ever farther away from each other, were able to talk back and forth with ease throughout the night, however, and held at least eight, and perhaps as many as ten, conversations, none of which were recorded. It was the usual chitchat, so the crew members of Flight 015 later told ICAO investigators, with discussions of future assignments, rest facilities in Anchorage, where to eat, and, of course, the boredom of flying all night over water. These conversations would

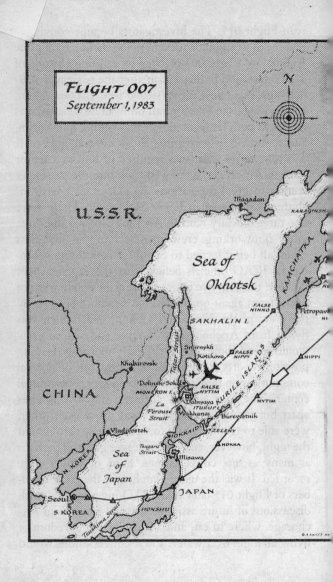

FLIGHT 007
September 1, 1983

N

U.S.S.R.

Magadan

KARAGINSK

Sea of
Okhotsk

KAMCHATKA

FALSE
NINNO

Petropavl
NI

SAKHALIN I.

Smirnykh
Kotikovo

FALSE
NIPPI

NIPPI

Khabarovsk

Dolinsk-Sokol
MONERON I.

FALSE
NYTIM

CHINA

La
Perouse
Strait

Dalnyaya
Wakkanai
ITURUP

Burevestnik

NYTIM

Vladivostok

Tsugaru
Strait

HOKKAIDO

ZELENY

ANOKKA

Misawa

Sea
of
Japan

JAPAN

N. KOREA

Seoul

S. KOREA

HONSHU

Tartar Strait

KURILE ISLANDS

Tsushima Strait

© A. Karl / 7 Ae

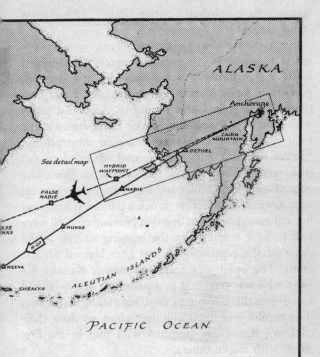

ALASKA

Anchorage

CAIRN
MOUNTAIN

BETHEL

See detail map

HYBRID
WAYPOINT

FALSE
NABIE

NABIE

NUKKS

R-20

NEEVA

ALEUTIAN ISLANDS

SHEMYA

PACIFIC OCEAN

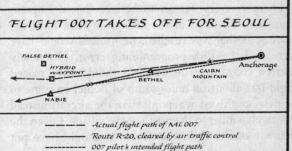

FLIGHT 007 TAKES OFF FOR SEOUL

FALSE BETHEL

HYBRID
WAYPOINT

BETHEL

CAIRN
MOUNTAIN

Anchorage

NABIE

- - - - - - - Actual flight path of KAL 007
——————— Route R-20, cleared by air traffic control
– · – · – · – 007 pilot's intended flight path

certainly have involved Captain Chun if he had been in the cockpit.

Even if they had doubts, the crew would have found it difficult to challenge the captain's jury-rigged flight path. Junior officers just did not second-guess the pilot on Korean Air, particularly one as prestigious as Captain Chun Byung-in. American pilots who have served with Korean Air Force crews in the military find the crew's acquiescence unsurprising. "Those Korean copilots and second officers don't say boo," one American said. "They just sit there like vegetables." The copilot and flight engineer of an errant Korean Air 747 that struck a parked vehicle and burned upon landing at Seoul in November 1980 were said to have remained in the burning aircraft at the order of the captain, who was later blamed for the crash. The order was heard by another Korean Air pilot who was traveling as a passenger and who had raced into the cockpit to urge his colleagues to flee. The copilot and flight engineer chose to share their captain's shame and perished with him in the fire, along with eleven others.

There is every reason to believe that if Captain Chun had remained in the cockpit at least until the VOR at Bethel was reached, he himself would have uncovered the INS programming error. His newly inserted coordinates in his INS should have placed Flight 007 about six miles south of Bethel en route to the new southwest waypoint two; the aircraft instead flew twelve miles to the north of the village. Given the accuracy of the INS, the deviation should have put him on notice that something was wrong. (The copilot's and flight engineer's INS units, once abeam

Bethel, would have routinely noted its passing by shift-ing *from* waypoint two, Bethel, *to* the third waypoint, NABIE. The captain's INS, with its initial 10-degree programming error, was still flying *from* waypoint zero *to* waypoint two when Bethel was bypassed.)

At any point after reprogramming his INS outside of Anchorage, the captain—if he had been in the cock-pit—theoretically could have noticed a discrepancy be-tween the distance to go to what he thought was his new waypoint two—on R-20, about 190 miles south-west of Bethel—and the distance to go as actually dis-played by his INS, which, unbeknownst to any of the crew, was navigating to the new "hybrid" waypoint far to the north. The distance from Anchorage to what the captain thought was his new waypoint was 528 miles; the actual distance to the "hybrid" waypoint was 637 miles, a discrepancy of 109 miles. The cap-tain's reprogramming of waypoint two masked the magnitude of the initial 10-degree programming error. If the captain had chosen to fly directly to any other waypoint—NABIE, for instance—the displayed dis-tance to go from Anchorage would have been wrong by approximately 300 miles because of the 10-degree error (and, more important, Flight 007 would have passed more than twenty-five miles south of Bethel, far enough off course to have been observed on radar by FAA tower officials in Anchorage). Creating the "hy-brid" waypoint reduced the discrepancy by two-thirds at the point during the flight when the navigational error could most easily have been detected.

Other airline pilots have made preflight program-ming errors similar to Flight Engineer Kim's, but they were quickly detected in most cases because the crew saw that there was a discrepancy between the distance to go to the first waypoint as shown on their flight plan or navigation chart and the displayed distance to go to the first waypoint on the INS. The captain of Flight 007, by picking a new waypoint and then misprogramming it or failing to observe that the INS had rejected it, significantly diminished the amount of discrepancy. More important, his new waypoint was not printed on his flight plan, and his navigation charts had no distance information to that point. The captain could not readily compare the distance to go on his flight plan with the distance to go as displayed by his INS; he had lost his ability to cross-check distance—the ability that had saved previous flights.

Any alertness on the part of the crew would have been made all but useless by the captain's personal detour. The original flight plan called for the airliner to reach the third waypoint at NABIE ninety minutes after takeoff, and the flight—which flew 109 miles, or thirteen minutes, out of its way because of the 10-degree programming error, as masked—would have arrived at the new "hybrid" waypoint to the northwest of Bethel in ninety-three minutes. The crew could have concluded early in the flight that the captain had simply programmed his INS directly to NABIE, that is, from waypoint zero to waypoint three, in the first moments after takeoff from Anchorage. The discrepancy of 109 miles would have meant little to the crew members, who would have known that the captain had changed waypoints, but not much else. Moreover, neither the copilot nor the flight engineer would dare ask for an explanation nor question what the captain did. But they would know that they were twelve miles north of Bethel when they filed their routine position and altitude report to Anchorage Air Route Traffic Control Center.* It should also be noted that by the time 007 passed north of Bethel it was well out of radar range of the Anchorage air route traffic control center, which was nonetheless continuing to monitor 007 by radio.† The copilot's report from Bethel was routine; there was no reason for anyone in Anchorage to assume other than that all was well with the flight. In Harold Ewing's view, Captain Chun's decision to abrogate his flight plan was the crucial factor that made it impossible for his crew to discover the 10-degree error. "From a professional standpoint," Ewing said, "you can forgive putting in a wrong coordinate and not catching it—but not a willful decision to deviate from a flight plan. He's not going to his preplanned position, so his first officer couldn't check it. If indeed that's what he did, Chun threw away all of his cross-checks."

---

* The language used by the copilot in making his report was cryptic, as such reports invariably are: the officer merely said "Report Bethel," and proceeded to give altitude and estimate time of arrival at NABIE, Flight 007's next waypoint.

† Flight 007's off-course position at Bethel was picked up by the unmanned Air Force military radar at King Salmon, Alaska. The military facility had no FAA reporting responsibility at the time, and its information, although routinely forwarded by remote control to the traffic control center at Anchorage, was not utilized because, according to the ICAO report, "it was not certified for use." There is little likelihood, even if the data had been made known to the air controllers, that a twelve-mile deviation at Bethel would have been considered significant enough to justify alerting the crew of Flight 007.

There was still another INS discrepancy that the captain, had he been in the cockpit the moment the "hybrid" waypoint was overflown, would have found hard to miss. The distance from the captain's intended new waypoint two southwest of Bethel to the third waypoint at NABIE should have been displayed as 122 miles, as reprogrammed into the captain's INS. The captain assumed that his plane would fly from his new waypoint to the real NABIE; in fact, according to the scenario, it was en route for more than 300 miles from the "hybrid" waypoint to what Harold Ewing and ICAO officials call a "false NABIE"—a position far north of the third waypoint but considered by Captain Chun's INS to be NABIE. Because of the initial 10-degree programming error, Flight 007 was now abeam of NABIE; that is, at the same longitude but much farther north. The INS computers are programmed to sense the passage of a waypoint even if the airliner is hundreds of miles to the north or south of it. Flight 007's second and third INS units, used by the copilot and the flight engineer, sensed at that moment that the waypoint they were abeam of was NABIE and moved up to the next set of waypoints, from NABIE to NUKKS, the fourth waypoint in the North Pacific. Meanwhile, the captain's INS still was proceeding—so its computer thought—from the new waypoint two west of Bethel to the "false NABIE," its third waypoint. Flight 007's inertial navigation system was now in total disarray, with the aircraft far off course and two of its three INS units in disagreement with the third.

In other words, the captain's INS, which was navigating the aircraft, was one waypoint behind the other two INSs in the cockpit.

At this point, reassuringly, the actual distance from the "hybrid" waypoint to the "false NABIE," to which the captain's INS was directing the airliner, was 303 miles, very close to the 296 miles shown on navigation charts as the distance from NABIE to NUKKS, the next waypoint. According to the Ewing scenario, many doubts on the part of the crew members would have been assuaged: they knew they had passed a waypoint just about the time the flight plan called for the airliner to pass NABIE, and, if they had bothered to look, they would have seen that the distance to go displayed on all three INS units was very close to what the flight plan depicted as the distance to go to NUKKS. If the captain had been in the cockpit at the moment the airliner flew abeam NABIE he would undoubtedly have realized something was wrong. After all, he had chosen his new waypoint to save time and fuel and now his aircraft had gotten abeam of NABIE before he had reached his corner-cutting waypoint.

As far as air traffic officials at Anchorage could determine, Copilot Son was routinely at work during this early phase of the flight, although some of his reports were relayed through KAL 015, a common-enough occurrence since, as the ICAO investigation noted, "communication difficulties frequently arose" in many parts of the North Pacific. The copilot's reports consisted of little more than routine messages telling Anchorage that the flight had reached a waypoint, estimating when it would reach the next reporting point, and giving fuel, weather, and altitude information. The INS was essential to those reports, too. At each waypoint, all three systems would flash a light to alert the crew that a waypoint had been reached. On other flights, with more complicated routes, the INS would automatically make any required turn at that moment. But R-20 was a continuum of evenly spaced waypoints needing only minor course adjustments. This quirk of geography may be another reason that the crew members missed the essential fact that the aircraft was off course.

There was another quirk of geography in Ewing's scenario that came into play after Flight 007 left the Alaskan mainland. The initial 300-miles (10-degree) error in programming the captain's INS was roughly the same distance, give or take a few minutes of flying time, as between the waypoints along R-20 across much of the North Pacific. From that point on, geography would ease any lingering concern—if there was any—shared by the copilot and flight engineer. All three INS computers would flash signals indicating that a waypoint had been passed at the same time—or close to the same time. There would be no way for even the most alert crew member to realize that the INS was going haywire.

Nor was it likely that the other ongoing discrepancy would be caught. The copilot's and flight engineer's INS computers would continue to count waypoints in a sequence different from that of the captain's. Harold Ewing is not troubled by the scenario's implication that today's pilots would be capable of such sloppy cockpit performance. "No pilot I've talked to had ever actually checked, on any flight, whether or not all of the INSs were displaying the same waypoint selection, or ever thought it was necessary to do so," he said. "I am absolutely comfortable with the idea that this situation could have existed throughout the flight without being detected: it is a completely passive factor. There is nothing to call attention to it—and it is an item which there is no requirement or procedure to check, and which is in fact never checked."

When the aircraft flew abeam of the fourth waypoint at NUKKS, Captain Chun's misprogrammed INS showed that it was over the third waypoint, NABIE. The other two INS units correctly noted the passing of the fourth waypoint and were programmed to move to the fifth waypoint at NEEVA. The captain's INS continued to guide the airliner far to the north of R-20, toward the Kamchatka Peninsula and the flight path of an American RC-135 intelligence plane, the Cobra Ball.

16

Cobra Ball II

Cobra Ball, en route home to Shemya after yet another unsuccessful mission, faded from Soviet radar coverage roughly ten minutes after 1:00 A.M. Tokyo time. At that moment according to Ewing, Flight 007, nearly 1,400 miles from Anchorage and 150 miles off course, was overflying what its crew thought was waypoint NEEVA, the fifth waypoint, which the captain's INS recorded as waypoint four, NUKKS. Flight 007 was now flying through the same area off Kamchatka that Cobra Ball had patrolled.

Precisely what happened inside the Soviet Air Defense Force will probably never be known, even if the Soviet military takes the unprecedented step of making available its internal reports on the incident. Many American intelligence officials believe that the Soviet General Staff, headed by Marshal Nikolai Ogarkov, had problems in the days following the shootdown in getting at the story—and still may not know all the facts. The marshal, in his news conference in Moscow nine days after the shootdown, reported that Soviet radar first noticed what was assumed to be an American reconnaissance plane at 12:51 A.M. Tokyo time. In his account, the aircraft was tracked as it rendezvoused nine minutes later with a second American reconnaissance plane, one that had been operating for hours off the coast of Kamchatka on what had been assumed to be another American intelligence mission. Ogarkov claimed that the two aircraft, in what Soviet analysts took to be a prearranged meeting, flew alongside each other for ten minutes, at roughly the same height and speed. The reconnaissance plane that had been on patrol for hours suddenly broke away to return to Shemya, while the other reconnaissance craft apparently headed southwest straight toward Petropavlovsk, the most important installation on Kamchatka, where as many as thirty missile-firing submarines, half the Soviet fleet, were stationed.

At this point, Ogarkov told the press, "[T]he conclusion was made at Soviet antiaircraft command posts: an intelligence aircraft is approaching the Soviet Union's airspace. The suggestion arises: how can this be a question of a mistake in this case? It is perfectly evident that this aircraft's flight was being controlled, I would say precisely controlled. And therefore this flight was premeditated."

A very different explanation for the Soviet error in identification, however, was provided by Marshal Piotr S. Kirsanov, former Air Force commander in the Far East, during an interview with the author at a military air base near Moscow in May 1984. The marshal, who had left the Far East the previous August, said that his Air Defense experts had witnessed many rendezvous of American RC-135s in the international waters off Karaginskiy Island. "We know that the 135s fly together for refueling purposes. In this particular case, our specialists thought it was just refueling." Once one of the planes began to fly toward the Soviet mainland, Kirsanov said, it was "firmly fixed" as an RC-135. Moreover, before taking any direct action against the plane, the Air Defense Force commander at Kamchatka asked the local air traffic control, which monitors civilian air traffic, whether it knew of any unscheduled or unaccounted for military or civilian airplanes in the area. "It was late at night," Kirsanov said, "when it was unlikely to be any military exercises going on." After being told no, the Air Defense commander claimed, he then attempted to contact the plane on emergency frequencies, with no success.* Four Soviet interceptors, Kirsanov said, were scrambled as soon as the aircraft—still identified as an RC-135—crossed the border, but they got into the air too late to force down the intruder or destroy it.

----

* The Soviet MiG-23 and SU-15 interceptors involved in the chase and destruction of Flight 007 did not attempt to communicate by voice with the airliner, even on the internationally recognized emergency frequencies, which suggested to many American analysts that the Soviets did not install appropriate equipment aboard their fighters because of the possibility of defection (the pilots presumably would have been able to contact foreign air traffic controllers and arrange for safe passage). Soviet officials vigorously disputed those reports and took the author, during a visit to the Soviet Union in 1984, to an airfield outside Moscow to see an SU-15 interceptor equipped with the necessary gear for international communication. It remains a fact that even American interceptors would not have been able

Ogarkov and Kirsanov were wrong about Flight 007 and Cobra Ball flying parallel over Kamchatka and either have chosen not to tell the whole story or were lied to by subordinates. American technicians searched through thousands of feet of NSA recordings and files to re-create, to the extent possible, much of the Soviet radar tracking of both Cobra Ball and Flight 007, over Kamchatka that morning, and no such side-by-side flying was found. Nor was there any refueling operation in the area. Instead, the American intelligence community, while disagreeing about some details, has categorically concluded that the regional Air Defense commander at Kamchatka merely watched as what he assumed was an American reconnaissance plane approached the border a few minutes after 1:30 A.M. Tokyo time. The Soviet commander was convinced, despite the target aircraft's unusually high altitude and speed, that the plane was a Cobra Ball mission and would do what similar flights had done for years: fly looping figure eights in international airspace. At its farthest point from the coast, a Cobra Ball mission,

---

to communicate with the Korean airliner. According to a December 30, 1983, research study published by the Air Force's Foreign Technology Division, American tactical fighters, "having limited weight and volume allowances," are equipped with transceivers capable only of monitoring ultrahigh frequencies (UHF). Since most airliners, including those of Korean Air, carry radio equipment for communication only in high-frequency (HF) or very-high-frequency (VHF) bands, "the probability of finding common frequency band," the Air Force report noted, "is low." U.S. interceptors are in fact often unable to communicate with American commercial airliners that inadvertently fly over restricted areas inside the continental United States.

while waiting for a Soviet missile test, could finish a loop more than two hundred miles off the coast, beyond the reach of Soviet radar; at its closest point, the Cobra Ball could fly to within fifty or even fewer miles of the mainland, just outside the Soviet Coastal Buffer Zone, before turning away, and do so without causing a Soviet interceptor scramble. It was not until 1:37 A.M. that the four Soviet interceptors were scrambled, a delay that most American analysts believe was due not to prudence—as Marshal Kirsanov suggested—but to a mistaken assumption on the part of the regional commander. Panic must have broken out among the Air Defense officers in Kamchatka when Flight 007 did not turn away, as American reconnaissance aircraft always did, but instead raced—flying at a speed of more than eight miles a minute—southwest for twenty-five minutes or more past the offshore buffer zone, across the Kamchatka Peninsula and into the Sea of Okhotsk, heading on a direct course for Sakhalin Island and points beyond. The NSA later monitored messages showing that the Soviet interceptors had been given incorrect coordinates by the Air Defense radar facility at Talinskaya Bukhta (Bay), a few miles northeast of Petropavlovsk. Even if the pilots had been scrambled more quickly, they would never have found their target in time to take any action against it.

Once again, the crew members of the Korean airliner seemed to have no inkling of what was going on below. At 1:23 A.M. Tokyo time, as the aircraft was nearing the Kamchatka mainland, Copilot Son tried to clear up his radio transmission problems. He established contact again with the international flight service station at Anchorage and asked for a check of his assigned frequency. Communication was difficult; ICAO would later report that Anchorage could barely hear him. None of this could have been especially troubling to Flight 007. Its crew members knew that they could still communicate to Anchorage through their sister ship if necessary; and, assuming that the flight was minutes away from NINNO, the sixth waypoint, and well on the way to waypoint NIPPI, the crew also knew that soon control of the flight would be transferred to the aviation authorities at Tokyo, who would be responsible for the final leg. Once beyond NIPPI, Copilot Son would have to enter new waypoints into the INS to take the flight all the way to Seoul. There was nothing in the copilot's early-morning reports indicating any stress or concern.

There had to have been acute fear at the Soviet Air Defense headquarters on Kamchatka. What if the 1978 fiasco, in which a Korean airliner believed to be a military spy plane had been allowed to penetrate Soviet airspace over Murmansk, was repeated? Many of those involved, as the men at Kamchatka knew, had been demoted or transferred. Careers were on the line once again. By the time the Soviets were able to get their interceptors scrambled and over Kamchatka, the fighters could do nothing but watch and track the airliner as it moved into international air space over the Sea of Okhotsk. The next penetration of Soviet airspace would be at Sakhalin Island, 500 miles to the south across the Sea of Okhotsk.

Incredibly, there is no evidence that the Soviet Air Defense units at Kamchatka shared what information they had either with their superiors in the district command post at Khabarovsk, on the Soviet mainland 750 miles to the southwest, or with the heavily fortified military outposts at Sakhalin. One theory is that the Air Defense Force officials at Kamchatka delayed making their reports in the hope that the American reconnaissance plane would realize its mistake (if it was one), or end its mission (if it was one), and fly unmolested out of the area through the Sea of Okhotsk. If that happened, the less said or reported the better. No command would be eager to volunteer details of its incompetence.

The American intelligence agencies would be intrigued for many months after the shootdown by the issue of just what happened to the Soviet Air Defense Force. There was widespread agreement that Soviet radar technology and procedures were suspect. The Soviet Air Defense Force was known to have repeatedly made identification errors in the past and had in fact mistakenly authorized the destruction of Soviet passenger airliners, with heavy loss of life.

The Air Force's Electronic Security Command, working through its floor stations at Misawa, Anchorage, and Honolulu, conducted exhaustive after-action reviews in an effort to understand what had gone wrong inside the Soviet Air Defense Force. In the Air Force view, the Soviet radar operators may well have been utilizing a standard tracking technique—known as dead reckoning—that had the unforeseen effect in the early-morning hours of complicating what would have been a difficult-enough procedure of sorting passerby from foe. These analysts believe that the Soviet radar technicians confused the radar track of Flight 007 with that of the Cobra Ball, and assumed from that point on that they were dealing only with another special reconnaissance plane. One Air Force officer, who reviewed the Soviet radar data, speculates, "As the Cobra Ball is going out [of the Soviet radar zone], one of the Soviet Air Defense trackers looks like he's practice-tracking"—that is, using dead reckoning in an effort to guess where the American reconnaissance plane would reenter if it decided to return into the range of Soviet radar. "He's doing a nominal route— working some practice plots to signify that the RC-135 [Cobra Ball] is coming back into the system." The Soviet operators knew that Cobra Ball often circled in and out of radar range while waiting for a Soviet test missile to come within camera range. On this night, however, the American officer added, as the far-off-course Flight 007 actually moved into the Soviet radar zone for the first time, the Soviet operator erased his nominal track for the Cobra Ball and replaced it with Flight 007, assigning the airliner (as American intelligence analysts believe he must, under Soviet standard operating procedure) a separate track designation,*

---

* There are similar procedures in the Air Force radar monitoring stations. One former Air Force radar operator explained that after a Soviet aircraft being tracked made a sharp turn, "you lost him on radar" for a few moments. "He presented a different aspect, and you lost him. What the operator does then is dead reckoning—plot his path where you assume he's going to be." Under Air Force guidelines, operators mark "d.r." on their logs to indicate exactly when they lost actual radar contact and began to dead-reckon. Soviet technicians, as well as American, are also compelled—after losing a track for a set amount of time—to

but convinced that he was still tracking the same reconnaissance aircraft. "To the Soviets," the officer said, "it could be the Cobra Ball. It's a strange series of coincidences." Two track numbers thus were assigned by the Air Defense men, but they were tracking the same plane, an RC-135.

A different analysis of the Soviet reaction was arrived at by the National Security Agency and presented in secret briefings to the Senate and House intelligence committees within two weeks of the shootdown. The NSA revealed that the Soviet radar operators did indeed report to higher commands, as Ogarkov claimed at his news conference, that they were monitoring two aircraft tracks over the Kamchatka Peninsula. The NSA told Congress that the Soviets tracked one of the aircraft—the Cobra Ball flight—as it flew back to Shemya. What the Soviets did about the second aircraft, Flight 007, which they also continued to monitor, the NSA said, was to make a leap of faith and simply assume it also was an American reconnaissance plane.

Congress was not told that the Soviet leap of faith, if that's what it was, as outlined by the NSA, was not quite as irrational as it might seem. For years, the United States has been routinely flying separate Rivet

---

assign it a new identification number once it reappears on radar. There is some belief that the Soviet operators also must put the aircraft through a reidentification process, checking height and speed. All of these procedures, if followed, would have made little difference; as far as the Soviet radar technicians were concerned, they were convinced they were tracking an intruder.

Joint reconnaissance missions around the southern tip of Kamchatka and into the Sea of Okhotsk, a protected deployment area for the Soviet's missile submarines. The goal of such missions, as of those in Western Europe, is to monitor Soviet communications and Air Defense activities. The Rivet Joint flights, which operate out of Eielson Air Force Base near Fairbanks, Alaska, approach Kamchatka from the northeast—much as Flight 007 did—and then, if not assigned to patrol in the Sea of Okhotsk, slide down the coast toward Sakhalin Island. Because there are more Soviet communications and more air traffic to monitor during the day, the vast majority of intelligence flights take place then. But not all. "We go in there in odd hours every month or month and a half or so," one former Rivet Joint crew member recalled, "just to make sure that they aren't running exercises. A lot of times it's dead, but it's dead because of us. And sometimes we'd just walk into an exercise." On those few occasions when Cobra Ball and Rivet Joint operated simultaneously off Kamchatka, they were totally independent of each other—each with a different mission. Yet both would be monitored by Soviet Air Defense forces.

A senior Air Force intelligence officer speculated that the Soviet Air Defense Force would have faced a difficult decision that night, assuming that they had identified the Cobra Ball flight and watched it turn back toward Shemya, only to be replaced by what they assumed was another American military aircraft. "The radar operators are young troops, inexperienced," the officer said. "There is at least one senior man on duty who has seen—or known of it through word of mouth—an R-J [Rivet Joint] and a Cobra Ball mission operating together. He provides the credibility and says, 'Hey, three months ago there was a joint mission.' They were never told of the possibility that it was a civilian plane."

The small area of dispute between the NSA and the Electronic Security Command over the origin of the Soviet mistake—whether it occurred because of dead reckoning or not—has one common thread: that the Soviet Air Defense Force was convinced that it was dealing with an American reconnaissance plane, one whose flight path—whether it was a Cobra Ball or a Rivet Joint Mission—they knew all too well. It was this certitude, American intelligence officials agree, that led to the Soviet decision not to challenge the aircraft as it first began to drift closer and closer to the Soviet mainland. There was little reason for the Soviet Air Defense officials to become alarmed: the old days of American cross-border penetrations had ended in the early 1960s, with the advent of satellite intelligence.* The American reconnais-

---

* In 1970, the Defense Department formally ended the already dwindling practice of sending American military aircraft deliberately into Soviet territory in order to provoke reaction. All reconnaissance missions also were to be closely monitored while in flight. The new and highly secret guidelines were the product of an extensive study directed by Dr. Gerald P. Dinneen, an intelligence specialist and NSA consultant, and originated in the April 14, 1969, destruction of a Navy EC-121 reconnaissance plane off the coast of North Korea with a loss of thirty-one lives. The Dinneen study raised a number of questions about the need for such operations, whose risk seemed to far outweigh any possible intelligence gain. The study, it should be noted, apparently did not extend to the Navy's secret submarine operations inside the territorial waters of the Soviet Union, which are known to continue today.

sance plane, they were convinced, would turn aside.

Out of all this emerges one consensus: the newly reorganized Soviet military command-and-control system operated by rote early that morning and failed to respond to an unusual situation, thus deeply embarrassing its top leadership. The panic and confusion among the various command elements, compounded by anxiety over future promotions, made it difficult for those officers (and there were some) who argued for common sense, careful identification, and caution, to prevail. Instead, the system fell apart—as it had over Murmansk in 1978.

The Soviet failure would get much worse once Flight 007 reached Sakhalin.

17

Shootdown

The Sea of Okhotsk was not the place for a commercial passenger plane that had lost its way. The little-known sea is the home waters for the Soviet Union's naval presence in the Far East. It is strategic water, closely tied to Soviet perceptions of its responsibility and strength as a superpower: a refuge for ballistic missile submarines, which are capable—from the inland sea—of striking targets in the United States with submarine-launched ballistic missiles (SLBMs). The importance of the sea as a sanctuary has been enhanced by the increasing skill of the United States and Japan in monitoring and tracking the Soviet submarine fleet in open waters. In response, the Soviets have prudently withdrawn some of their strategic submarines from patrols in the North Pacific and Sea of Japan and ordered them to operate closer to home, in the Sea of Okhotsk, where they are more protected.

The Soviets claim the sea as part of the sovereign territory of the USSR and insist that foreign vessels seeking access obtain prior approval. Some in the U.S. Navy have advocated sending destroyers on patrol there to establish rights of transit as part of the Navy's "forward strategy," but the Reagan administration has instead chosen to operate covertly and not to challenge openly the Soviet's use of the sea as an operational sanctuary for its submarine fleet. The area has become a focal point for American intelligence activities. Rivet Joint RC-135 missions routinely overfly it, as does the Navy's P-3 antisubmarine aircraft, whose assignment is to keep track of the Soviet underwater activity. America's most sophisticated, high-altitude intelligence planes, the U-2 Black Widows and SR-71 Blackbirds, also overfly the sea. Below the surface, specially rigged American submarines track Soviet submarines and monitor Soviet underwater communications and electronics.

At 1:58 A.M. Tokyo time, Flight 007 left Soviet airspace above Kamchatka and flew into international airspace over the Sea of Okhotsk; its crew members were unaware that a group of Soviet fighters had previously failed by minutes to intercept the aircraft. There was still opportunity, if the crew members somehow could discover their plight, for the airliner to turn to the east and avoid entering Soviet airspace again. At 2:08 A.M., the crew thought NIPPI, the seventh waypoint, was being overflown. Another routine position-and-weather report was due. Flight 007 should have been a little more than 1,800 nautical miles from Anchorage, and if it had been flying along R-20, communication should have been easy. Once again, it was difficult for the off-course airliner to raise Anchor-

age, but the copilot, Son Dong-Hwin, unruffled by
what he must have assumed was a routine communications glitch, filed the report instead to Tokyo air traffic
control. His next report would not have to be filed for
eighty minutes, at 3:26 A.M., as he approached what he
thought was NOKKA, the ninth waypoint. Sometime
before then, however, Copilot Son would need to
enter new waypoints into the INS to navigate the
flight to Seoul.

In its classified briefings to Congress, the National
Security Agency noted the Soviets at Sakhalin first
picked up Flight 007 at 2:44 A.M.; the Korean airliner
was detected by the radar site at Burevestnik Air Field,
on Iturup Island in the Kuriles, and by at least two
radar sites on Sakhalin, including the main facility at
Yuzhno-Sakhalinsk. Flight 007 was then about 225
miles northeast of Sakhalin, still over the Sea of Okhotsk and closing in at the rate of eight miles a minute.
The radar operators on Iturup and Sakhalin had an
obvious advantage over their colleagues on Kamchatka: they knew that what they were looking at was
unusual. American reconnaissance planes routinely
flew on an east-west track as they sought to move
deeper into the Sea of Okhotsk. They had never been
known to fly in a direct southwest heading, as was
Flight 007, into radar range of Sakhalin. An intruder
on a flight path never seen before was heading right at
them.

At least one Soviet interceptor was airborne
by 2:56 A.M. The pilot's initial comment—checking a
heading with his ground controller—may even have
been overheard by an operator at Project CLEF; the

aircraft also activated the highly sensitive Japanese recording system at Wakkanai. For the next thirty minutes Japanese and American intelligence collected evidence of the impending destruction of Flight 007. Four aircraft, three SU-15s and a MiG-23, were monitored during the chase; two other MiGs, following Soviet procedure, flew at a much lower altitude and in radio silence, ready if needed. It took nine minutes for one of the SU-15s to begin tracking his target on radar and, missiles at the ready, to confirm that he and the intruder were on the same heading.

It is not clear how much the Soviet command system knew and when it learned what it did. The regional officials on Kamchatka, as well as those on Sakhalin, were obliged to report all significant radar data to the military district headquarters at Khabarovsk, 250 miles southwest of Sakhalin on the Soviet mainland. Under the recent reorganization of Soviet forces, the district commander at Khabarovsk had been put in direct control of both the Soviet Air Force and the Air Defense units. His deputy for Air Defense had been abruptly woken up by a duty officer and told that the regional Air Defense forces at Sakhalin had gone on alert. He was also informed about the scramble at Kamchatka and the failure of the Air Defense Force there to make a positive identification of the intruder. But when was Khabarovsk told about the events of Kamchatka? Some NSA officials believe that this information, so crucial to subsequent events, was not relayed by Kamchatka until after the first alerts from the radar sites on Sakhalin. The commanders at Kamchatka had simply hoped that the intruder, once out of their radar coverage, would disappear. The deputy commander for Air Defense at Khabarovsk had to decide what to do without the reassurance of knowing just what was heading his way. It would be inexcusable to destroy an innocent aircraft but far worse not to shoot and find that an American intelligence plane had successfully overflown Mother Russia. The deputy commander's thoughts must have turned to the 1978 incident over Murmansk and the fact that some of his Air Defense colleagues had been relieved of their posts and their careers had been ruined for allowing an unidentified airliner to penetrate the coast.

In the cockpit of the Korean airliner, it was still yawn-and-stretch time. There was a final desultory conversation between Copilot Son and the men piloting the sister ship supposedly ten minutes behind on R-20. Crew members of Korean Air Flight 015 later told ICAO investigators that they initiated the chitchat at around three in the morning, when there were still three hours left to fly. "It's quiet," a Flight 015 crew member remembered saying. Son Dong-Hwin agreed, replying with equal banality that it was the strange time between night and day. "The sun will come up soon," he was quoted as saying. There was still no indication of Captain Chun Byung-in's presence in the cockpit.

It was at this point, too, according to Harold Ewing's scenario, that Son Dong-Hwin decided to reprogram the aircraft's three inertial navigation systems. His INS was showing that Flight 007 was en route from waypoint eight, NYTIM, to waypoint nine, NOKKA. The copilot knew that he could not replace waypoints eight and nine with new ones while he was still between them, but that he could reprogram the seven already passed. He was concerned at this stage only with his INS, Flight 007's backup unit, for once he had entered the seven new waypoints, he would do what he did at the Anchorage airport and had done on scores of previous flights—remote-load the new waypoints from his INS into the captain's and the flight engineer's systems. The new waypoints would navigate Flight 007 to the Seoul airport.

No crew member could imagine how fouled-up things were. As the airliner approached Sakhalin, the captain's INS was flying from what it thought was the seventh waypoint, NIPPI, to NYTIM, the eighth—and not from the eighth to the ninth waypoint, as the other two INS units said. It was now a few minutes after three in the morning, and Flight 007 was approaching the coast of Sakhalin. The copilot, having finished the tedious task of entering the new waypoints into his INS, remote-loaded them into the other two units. The captain's INS was confronted with a new waypoint "seven"—the VOR navigational facility a few miles outside of Seoul. Captain Chun's INS was suddenly flying *to* its next waypoint *from* a destination more than fifteen hundred miles ahead. The new information was beyond toleration and the INS was programmed in such cases to jump ahead automatically to the next set of waypoints—in this case from waypoint NYTIM to waypoint NOKKA—and to fly between those points via the Great Circle route. Flight 007 abruptly began to turn right, to the northwest, as it searched out its new route. The shift in course put the aircraft on a flight path between two major air bases, Dolinsk-Sokol in southern Sakhalin, where a regiment of SU-15s was stationed, and Smirnykh in the center of Sakhalin, home of a MiG-23 regiment. The senior Soviet Air Defense Force officials at Sakhalin obviously concluded that the aircraft's turn had been deliberate, an attempt to avoid directly overflying the extensive antiaircraft missile installations that protected both air bases. Copilot Son was caught unawares by the turn, which began just after he remote-loaded the INS. It took him at least forty-five seconds, according to the scenario devised by Harold Ewing, to observe what was going on—and react. Still, there was no cause for alarm. Such mistakes in reprogramming happened often enough and were invariably recognized for what they were. The pilot would either punch the INS forward to the next set of waypoints, immediately forcing the plane to fly to the next waypoint, or take the wheel himself to guide the aircraft gently to a return to course, taking care not to disturb sleeping passengers.

Harold Ewing's scenario—highly speculative as it may be—melds perfectly with the Korean Air flight-path information collected by American intelligence. The Air Force's Electronic Security Command in Japan monitored at least three radar sites as Soviet operators tracked Flight 007 early that morning through a last-minute change in course. The Soviet Union, in its public statements and subsequently published maps and charts, depicted Flight 007 as making a sharp turn of more than 50 degrees to the right just before reaching Sakhalin, then turning back toward its original heading until its destruction at 3:26 A.M. The Electronic Security Command's monitoring of the Soviet radar tracking produced a flight path that was more consistent with Ewing's scenario; it showed a far more gradual turn—"more of a jog, really," as one intelligence analyst put it. "Not a dramatic curve," said another. The American data were compiled from more than one intelligence installation and are believed to depict the airliner's flight path more accurately than the chart re-created by the Soviets, simply because the Soviet General Staff was forced to rely on the personal recollections of its radar operators. The Soviets did not have recorded data on the airliner's last minutes of flight, as did the NSA.*

---

* The United States, while refusing to turn over its tracking data to ICAO, nevertheless made public a chart of the airliner's flight path during its presentation at the United Nations on September 6, 1983. The U.S. chart, prepared by the NSA, depicted no course changes at all over Sakhalin; Flight 007 simply flew on a steady compass heading of 240 degrees. Similarly, radar trackings made public by the Japanese Self-Defense Forces showed no course change, but did show what seemed to be a swerve just as Flight 007 approached Sakhalin. State Department officials explain the discrepancy between the Soviet and American radar plottings as the result of a phenomenon known as the slant-range effect, common to all two-dimensional radars such as those used by the Soviets on Sakhalin Island. Such radars can display only range and bearing, and not altitude, and thus an aircraft passing directly overhead will be displayed as though it moved temporarily from one side or the other of its actual course, with the extent of deviation equaling its altitude. The arguments are correct in theory but ignore the fact—apparently not known even to many in the State Department—that field stations of the Electronic Security Command monitored at least three Soviet radar sites tracking Flight 007 that morning and thus were able to compute

The Soviet interceptor pilots assigned to Sakhalin were old hands; they had scrambled hundreds of times in exercises or to check out the RC-135 Rivet Joint missions as they passed Sakhalin en route to the Sea of Okhotsk. One of the SU-15 pilots calmly reported at 3:06 A.M., twenty minutes before the shootdown, that he was "flying behind" the intruder about eighty miles from the coast. The interceptor pilot could not see the airliner but understood from his ground controller that his target plane was turning to the right. He found it hard to believe, apparently because the Soviet mainland lay to the right—it seemed to be the last direction in which an enemy plane would attempt to flee. "Repeat the course," he asked his controller. "To the left, probably? Not to the right." Sixteen seconds later, the SU-15—apparently after a direct order from his ground controller—also turned to the right. At this point, the pilot had to have been aware that this mission was different. Whatever doubts the pilot may have had (he later claimed publicly to have had none) disappeared once the intruder aircraft began what seemed

---

its path accurately. The site at Burevestnik on Iturup Island, which filed one of the first snap-ons about Flight 007, is southeast of Sakhalin; at no time was it underneath or even near the Korean airliner's flight path. Members of the Electronic Security Command who were directly involved that morning insist that—slant-range effect to the contrary notwithstanding—Flight 007 did turn before reaching Sakhalin. They further argue that the Soviet pilot's intercepted remarks demonstrate that he and his ground controllers were tracking what seemed to be a change in the course of the intruder. The dispute is another example of the difficulty of dealing with raw intelligence; even a seemingly incontrovertible radar plotting can have ambiguities that need extensive analysis and refining.

to be its evasive turn.* Within the next sixty seconds, according to the Ewing scenario, the crew aboard Flight 007 resolved its INS problems and began guiding the airliner back on track, unintentionally heading once again for Vladivostok. At 3:09, the SU-15 pilot confirmed what seemed obviously to be a radar report from his ground controllers: "Yes, it has turned. . . . The target is eighty degrees to my left." Over the next four minutes, the SU-15 pilot, following standard Soviet interception techniques, sought to maneuver his plane closer to the target, in what seemed to be an attempt to make a visual identification. At 3:12 he reported that he could "see it visually [apparently the aircraft's running-lights] and on radar." A minute later, the pilot announced to his ground controller that he was ready to fire if so ordered: "I see it. I'm locked on to the target."

For the first time since Flight 007 was observed on

---

* Marshal Ogarkov later claimed that the maneuvers of Flight 007 over Sakhalin eliminated any residual doubt inside the Air Defense command as to its purpose. "The actions of the aircraft here became outrageous," he told newsmen during his September 9 press conference in Moscow. "[I]t began to change simultaneously the direction, altitude, and speed of flight, obviously trying to evade the Soviet Air Defense planes. It was extremely characteristic that at 6:02 Sakhalin time [3:02 A.M. Tokyo time] the intruder aircraft . . . sharply changed its course and circumvented the positions of our Air Defense missile units, passing over important military facilities in the southern part of Sakhalin Island. There remained no doubt that a reconnaissance aircraft was in the air." The Soviet belief that the 747 was trying to evade a Mach 2 SU-15 on its tail is considered ridiculous by military and civilian pilots. "It's like trying to get away from a souped-up police car while driving a Greyhound bus," said one 747 pilot. "It's hopeless—just can't be done."

radar outside of Kamchatka two and one-half hours earlier, a Soviet military aircraft was in position to take action against it. The SU-15 pilot was waiting for further instruction—prepared, of course, to pull the trigger if asked. But the pilot had spent thirteen years chasing down real and suspected intruders off the coast of Sakhalin and undoubtedly had announced many times to ground controllers that he was locked on to the target and was ready to fire without being ordered to do so. He could not have been surprised that somebody down below was being exceedingly cautious.

Ten seconds after announcing that he was locked on to the target, the pilot was ordered to make another attempt, by electronic means, to identify the intruder or, at the least, to ensure that the target was not a Soviet military aircraft. The SU-15 was capable of making contact with Soviet planes by activating an electronic interrogator, which is standard equipment on most Soviet military aircraft. The device is known in aviation as IFF, for identification, friend or foe. If Flight 007 had been a Soviet cargo plane, for example, its transponder would automatically have responded to the SU-15's IFF interrogation, thus ending any doubt as to its identity. The transponders on American and other nations' military aircraft are not capable of responding to Soviet interrogation.

American intelligence officials consider the controller's call for an IFF interrogation as a break with usual Soviet procedure for intercepting American reconnaissance aircraft. The fact that it was used is another indication that the Soviets were uncertain of the identity of the intruder aircraft and were assuring themselves it was not one of their own.*

Fourteen seconds after the SU-15 pilot reported no IFF response, he was telling ground control that his weapons system was "switched on." Flight 007 had now returned to its original course. The SU-15, poised to fire if ordered, was in position and traveling fast enough, so its pilot told the ground controllers: "I have [enough] speed. I don't need to turn on my afterburner."

It was now 3:15 A.M. The crew of Flight 007, still oblivious of the armed Soviet interceptors trailing behind, continued to proceed routinely. Copilot Son radioed Tokyo for permission to climb from 33,000 to 35,000 feet, the second delayed fuel-saving maneuver that Captain Chun had worked out before takeoff.

A minute later, according to the chronology pre-

---

* All commercial airlines that fly the North Pacific routes near the Soviet Union are equipped with transponders that can be interrogated and immediately identified as civilian by ground-based equipment known as Secondary Surveillance Radar (SSR), which is in widespread use in military and civilian installations around the world, including the Soviet Union. Transponders, when interrogated, flash a green light in the cockpit of a Boeing 747. Pilots who have flown R-20, Harold Ewing among them, recall being occasionally interrogated while in flight along the coast of the Soviet Union. There is no evidence that any of the Soviet radar facilities on Kamchatka, Sakhalin, or the Kurile Islands did, in fact, interrogate Flight 007 and receive a response indicating that the aircraft was civilian. Such a response, as in the case of the 1978 Korean Air shootdown over Murmansk, would not necessarily have prevented the Soviet Air Defense officials from telling themselves that they were dealing with a military intruder.

sented to the ICAO investigation by the Soviet Union, Flight 007 directly overflew the east coast of Sakhalin. The Soviet Air Defense officers had only a few minutes to decide what to do.

With the intruder aircraft not much more than ten minutes from the southwest corner of Sakhalin and international airspace, the SU-15 pilot was apparently ordered by his ground controllers to try to signal the intruder and force him to land. There were some clouds and storm centers in the area and it was difficult to see. Normal interception procedure called for enormous caution, including approaching an intruder only with cover, that is, with at least a second interceptor flying above and to the left of the first, providing protection in case of hostile fire. But the Soviet scramble over Sakhalin continued to be chaotic and poorly coordinated. None of the SU-15's colleagues was in position to help. He would have to act by himself.

At some point earlier in the drama in the sky above Sakhalin, the deputy for air defense at district headquarters at Khabarovsk decided that he could not shoot down an intruder without higher authority, even if it had been identified as an American military plane. There would be severe repercussions. He attempted to contact Marshal Alexandr I. Koldunov, in Moscow, commander in chief of the Soviet Air Defense Force and a deputy minister of defense. It was after ten at night in Moscow. A special unit of the NSA that is targeted on transmissions to and from Soviet satellites later learned the specifics of the call through a combination of luck and skill—mostly luck.

Incredibly, as the NSA learned, the Soviet reorganization had left the deputy commander for air defense at Khabarovsk with no secure satellite voice link of his own to Moscow; in order to forward an urgent verbal message that needed encoding, he had to send an aide to another building—"across the street," as one NSA analyst described it—to Air Force headquarters, where he could arrange to talk in secret with the Soviet General Staff by using a prearranged call sign that activates the encoding system. The Soviet system is a model of simplicity. The two military units that need to communicate—in this case, Khabarovsk and Moscow—establish what amounts to an ordinary microwave telephone link, via the Soviet Raduga satellite. Such communications are easily intercepted by NSA's floor stations and satellites, as the Soviets know. At a designated moment, the two officers activate a sophisticated encoding system (given a two-syllable code name by the NSA) and carry on their conversation. The Americans monitoring the call, or, as is more likely, listening later to a tape recording of the call as captured by satellite, are suddenly confronted with a form of encrypted speech that sounds like a buzz saw.

As it turned out, the Raduga satelite was in a decaying orbit at precisely the time the men in Khabarovsk and Moscow needed to talk over the scrambler.* The

---

* Missed connections are routine in satellite communications, because the ability to make contact often depends on the satellite's point of orbit. The U.S. Air Force, for example, relies on unmanned installations for the remote collection of intelligence in many parts of the world, and their reporting system utilizes an RCA satellite link. Some American SIGINT officials, told of the failure of the Raduga satellite, complained that the RCA system's satellites always seemed to be at an out-of-contact point in mo-

aide was desperate; nothing like this had happened before in the command. He tried the call sign at least three times before giving up and carrying on his conversation with Moscow in the clear, that is, directly in Russian and unscrambled. The message was straightforward, one analyst remembered: "He obviously was under pressure to get a decision [from Moscow]. He wasn't going to shoot down an American aircraft without getting some authorization from higher headquarters. He knows he has a bogey"—an American military intruder.

The deputy commander's message got through to a duty officer at the Air Defense headquarters in Moscow, who—as would happen in America—promptly put the aide on hold. At this point, the direct NSA intercept trail dwindles, for the duty officer, when he returned a moment later to the conversation, did manage to activate the encoding system. "The cipher signal snapped on," one NSA official said, "and some long-precedence [high-priority] message was sent" from Moscow to Khabarovsk. The NSA officials would not say anything further about the message.

Thus, it is not known whether Marshal Koldunov or any of his personal deputies on the Air Defense Force staff in Moscow directly ordered the destruction of the intruder. There are some in the NSA who believe that the order to shoot may have originated instead from an

---

ments of crisis. It should be noted that the mere fact that the deputy commander at Khabarovsk chose to communicate via scrambler, and not by slower means, such as Morse code or teletype, was a clue to the importance of the message and helped the NSA isolate that conversation for speedy analysis.

officer identified as Colonel General Semenovsky, who was the duty officer that morning at the Air Defense Force's command bunker and operations center located at Kalinin, just north of Moscow, and who may have been alerted to the call from Khabarovsk.

What is known is that within minutes an urgent encoded message was sent from the deputy commander's office in Khabarovsk to the command center at Dolinsk-Sokol in Sakhalin and, according to an NSA official, "that's when the order to shoot came down." The message relayed by Khabarovsk to the regional Air Defense headquarters at Sakhalin was not categorical but pointedly reminded the officers in the field of the Soviet rules of engagement. The officers were told once again that they must make a visual identification of the intruder before shooting it down. The message from Khabarovsk (and perhaps Kalinin) also reviewed the question of which field commanders were authorized to give an order to fire; in military terms, the commander wanted to make sure his subordinates understood who was "cleared to shoot."

A senior American intelligence officer vividly recalled his reaction well after the shootdown of Flight 007, upon being shown a copy of the deputy commander's intercepted and decoded message to Sakhalin: "When I read it, I thought: 'Those assholes violated their own rules of engagement.'"

By 3:17, the pilot of the SU-15 was continuing to pursue Flight 007 over Sakhalin with his weapons system still turned on. He was contacted by a fellow interceptor, one of the MiG-23s, who relayed a question from a ground controller: "Do you see the target or not?" The message from the deputy commander at Khabarovsk apparently had gotten through. The SU-15 pilot asked "Who's calling?" and then requested that the message be repeated. Ninety seconds passed before the SU-15 pilot reported once again that he could see the aircraft's flashing navigation lights. Merely seeing the navigation lights, of course, was not good enough. Thirty seconds later, at 3:19, he announced: "I am closing on the target. . . . I have enough time." (It was during the last stages of the chase, according to one of the NSA's after-action transcripts, that the pilot reported he could not see the target. It could not be learned at what point in the final chase the remark, which apparently was not initially decipherable by NSA linguists, had been made.)

Some American analysts believe that at 3:20 the Soviet interceptor was ordered by his local commanders to make a final attempt to signal the intruder with cannon fire and, if unsuccessful, to shoot down the aircraft. "Oh, my God!," or "*Yolki palki*," the pilot exclaimed. He had spent thirteen years tracking and intercepting American intelligence planes as an Air Defense Force officer in the Far East, thirteen years of chasing but never destroying. Perhaps before the order came the Soviet pilot had been preparing himself for yet another order to break off contact.* There was an

---

* Normal procedure called for a Soviet pilot to check out each Rivet Joint flight visually as it skirted the coast of Sakhalin in American aviation parlance, the Soviets "tap" the RC-135s. Air Force pilots who have flown RC-135s report that the pilot of a Soviet SU-15 or MiG-23, upon approach to the reconnaissance plane, invariably is ordered by his ground controller to "maintain one-mile separation." In many cases, however, the Soviets

inevitable camaraderie and respect for competence among the professional military aviators. The American officers piloting the RC-135 Rivet Joint or Cobra Ball missions often exchanged communications with the Soviets as the interceptor pilots flew by—usually just nods and smiles, but occasionally a *Playboy* magazine centerfold was held up for Soviet approval.

In the next sixty seconds, the SU-15 drew much closer to the intruder and, following instructions from his ground controllers, fired four bursts of cannon fire—120 shells in all, the Soviets later claimed—in a last-ditch attempt to attract the intruder's attention. At the time, according to later American analysis, the SU-15 was at least 3,000 feet below the intruder—a relative position he maintained throughout the chase. Military men agree that the shells, initially bright red, would have burned out before coming close to the airliner and thus would have been extremely difficult, if not impossible, for the Korean crew members to see—even if they had been alert.

There is no evidence that they were. A moment earlier, just as the Soviet interceptor pilot was exclaiming "Oh, my God!" over his new orders, Tokyo radio had granted Flight 007 permission to climb to 35,000 feet. The Boeing 747 probably was climbing, with its

---

instead swing to within forty feet of the left wing of the four-engine intelligence plane and hang there for at least twenty minutes before breaking away. The Soviet interceptor pilots even developed individual signatures for breaking off such contacts; one Air Force general approvingly told of a MiG pilot who would depart only after flying directly under the RC-135 and zooming off in front.

nose pointed up, as the Soviet tracers flew by far below.

As it began its climb, the huge airliner started to lose speed. The Soviet pilot had flown to within little more than one mile of the airliner to fire the cannons—the closest he had yet come to the airliner—and watched as the intruder, seemingly in response, began to climb. By 3:22 he angrily complained to his ground controllers that the intruder's sudden slowdown had forced his high-speed craft to bolt past his target and he had missed an opportunity to fire. He slowed down and began to fall back. The tension was acute. "It should have been earlier," he lamented, referring to the delay in issuing the shoot-to-kill order. "How can I chase it? I'm already abeam of the target"—that is, parallel with the airliner although still 3,000 or so feet below it. At 3:23, Copilot Son, ever dutiful, reported to Tokyo that the airliner had reached 35,000 feet. While Son was talking, the SU-15 pilot continued to fall back and by 3:25 once again was behind the intruder. "I am closing on the target, am in lock-on," he reported. There were no more course changes and the pilot had little more to say to his ground controller. The mission was in his hands now.

There was no hesitancy in the Soviet command system at this point, with the intruder only minutes from international waters. NSA intercepts showed that the Air Defense Force's most deadly antiaircraft weapon, the SAM-5 surface-to-air missile, was placed on alert at the last moment at Dal'nyaya, site of an extensive antiaircraft battery on the southern tip of Sakhalin. Nothing further was monitored about that morning's demand from the deputy commander at Khabarovsk that the interceptor actually see the intruder before firing. Someone on Sakhalin took the rules into his own hands, and later paid with his job.

The end came swiftly. Between 3:26 and 3:27 the Soviet interceptor fired two air-to-air AA-3 ANAB missiles. Flight 007 was struck and the SU-15 pilot reported, "The target is destroyed." One missile probably devastated the airliner's engines on the left wing; the subsequent explosion and fire undoubtedly damaged the fuselage. A second missile could have struck the rear of the aircraft, blowing out a bulkhead and immediately depressurizing the passenger cabin. There was startled confusion in the cockpit as the missile struck and the crew members sought to understand what had happened; they literally didn't know what had hit them. No Mayday calls were made; instead, forty seconds after the impact, Flight 007 radioed Tokyo air traffic control a message in English, only a few words of which were intelligible: ". . . rapid compressions . . ." (decompression?) and ". . . descending to one zero thousand"—the standard emergency level of 10,000 feet at which passengers can breathe depressurized air. Even at that moment, there was nothing to suggest that they realized that they had been struck by hostile fire. Ironically, given their lack of attention to so many basics during the flight, Co-pilot Son or whoever was at the helm was credited by an American member of the ICAO investigation team with having performed professionally once under attack. The pilot, perhaps not realizing the extent of damage, instinctively sought to make a turn and pull the aircraft away from and parallel to what he thought was the R-20 commercial flight track. "He did right," the investigator said. It didn't matter. Japanese radar trackings from Wakkanai suggest that the Boeing 747, still partially under the pilot's control, made an emergency descent over the next eight minutes to about sixteen thousand feet. At that altitude the pilot may have tried to slow down the rate of descent, but the aircraft, by now depleted of hydraulic fluid, gyrated increasingly out of control for four more searing minutes. As the aircraft went into its final uncontrollable roll—perhaps it was on its back—and barely overflew the terrified Japanese fishermen in the Sea of Japan, the pilot, who may have throttled back on the remaining intact engines in an effort to slow down, had no choice but to use engine power in a last-ditch effort to regain enough control to avoid the inevitable. It was too late. The fishermen could hear the suddenly racing engines and see fire break out—their first actual sight of the airliner. Flight 007 was visible once again as it crashed near Soviet territorial waters. It was at that moment that those who had survived the fall were killed.

The Soviet view of the chase, published later in *Red Star*, a Soviet Army newspaper, cast all of Flight 007's last-minute maneuvering as irrefutable proof of its intelligence mission. In an interview, the SU-15 pilot described the captain of the "intruder aircraft" as "an expert at his work. Do you know how he maneuvered when he saw me? He threw his craft about, changing course, altitude, and speed. He saw me very clearly and knew what to do under the circumstances." The Soviet pilot, who was not identified, told of his years of chasing RC-135s in the area and added: "This is what happens: as soon as you catch up with one, he pulls this trick—lowers his flaps and loses speed rapidly. Why? So that I, flying at high speed, will overshoot him. Meanwhile, I take time and space to turn around and get back on this tail. In those few minutes the RC-135 figures on being able to avoid observation and pursuit. I already know all these tricks by heart. You won't catch me falling for them. It may well be that the South Korean colonel at the controls of the spy aircraft had no idea that all the American tricks were so well known to me and that I had my own methods to counter them."

Within a few weeks, the shootdown of Flight 007 had become, for most Americans, an example of the intrinsic difference between the Soviet society and their's: the Soviets had done what no American fighting force would do—they had deliberately shot down an innocent airliner whose mistake had been to get lost over their borders, and they had publicly professed to be proud of it. Any lingering doubts about not having been told the full story were swept away by anger and horror at the Soviet wrongdoing.

Few Americans—even in the White House—were informed that by the end of September the Soviet General Staff, also angered and dismayed by the shootdown, began a sweeping reorganization of the Air Defense Force in the Far East, just five years after having completed a major review. Two senior officers on duty at Sakhalin at the time of the shootdown were relieved of command and presumably demoted. The deputy commander for air defense at Khabarovsk, who had insisted at the last minute that the pursued aircraft be visually identified, was promoted—the only senior Soviet officer to emerge untainted from the crisis. The Soviet reaction did not stop with personnel changes: Marshal Ogarkov and his colleagues on the Soviet General Staff ordered a restructuring of the Air Defense Force at Sakhalin, Kamchatka, and the Kurile Islands, including a revision of the rules of engagement. By early October, the Air Force's Rivet Joint missions were escorted by as many as four Soviet interceptors, closely directed by ground controllers. The smiles and waves were gone, as well as the displays of centerfolds. "They were serious now," one senior Air Force officer said. "They recognized that they had fucked up."

The aftermath proved to be an intelligence bonanza for the NSA, as the Soviets, obviously suspecting the worst from the Reagan administration, activated a series of special command communication links. "They were shocked and surprised. They didn't know what was happening," one NSA official said, referring to the wave of anti-Soviet statements from Washington. "Outfits we didn't know existed suddenly popped up. They went through their checklists and started activating every special link they had." The United States kept track as the Soviet General Staff took to the air in airborne command posts and military men began chatting to each other on special circuits and frequencies. There was an opportunity to monitor and study little-used communications links between Moscow and the Far East, and between Khabarovsk and Sakhalin.

Two weeks after the crisis, CIA director Casey,

with approval from the president, circulated a memorandum to the State Department, Pentagon, and White House warning against any further discussion of intelligence or assessments regarding the shootdown. Too much detail about American "sources and methods" had been revealed, Casey argued. General Faurer, in obvious agreement, told a September 15 dinner meeting of the National Military Intelligence Association that "you have read and heard more about my business in the past two weeks than I would desire. . . . it's now time to circle the wagons and stop talking. The story has been told accurately and to push further will not provide valuable clarification, but rather will unnecessarily put at risk further intelligence support to our national security."

The Reagan administration had successfully shielded its propagandizing of the shootdown behind solemn talk of national security and the protection of "sources and methods." But there were many officers in communications intelligence who understood what has systematically been hidden from the public and the Congress—the fact that the most sensitive foreign intercepts are as open to abuses, manipulation, and interservice disputes as are the annual intelligence estimates of Soviet missile strength.

At the time of his speech to the Military Intelligence Association, for example, General Faurer—as a senior Air Force officer—was in a smarmy and unprofessional battle with the Navy over access to intelligence from the Sea of Japan, the search area for Flight 007's flight recorders. The Navy NSA component at Misawa, known as Naval Security Group Activity (NSGA), was seen by the Air Force men who ran

Misawa and who worked under General Faurer at Fort Meade as being reluctant to share vital intelligence information about the search-and-rescue operation; instead, it was believed, the NSGA at Misawa was relaying its most important data directly to the Pacific Fleet headquarters and, through that command, to the office of the chief of naval operations in Washington. General Faurer responded in kind. The 6920th at Misawa had intercepted a series of sensitive General Staff messages in which the local Soviet commanders discussed the rules of engagement in case of a crisis during the search-and-rescue operations. It was essential information for the Navy commanders running the rescue operation, but, according to officials directly involved, General Faurer refused to release the intercepts to the Navy. "He was sharing it in Washington but not with the three- and four-star operational commanders in the Pacific Fleet," one Navy communications intelligence officer angrily recalled. "It was the kind of information commanders needed." Two weeks after the shootdown, Faurer rejected a personal request for the data from a ranking member of the staff of Admiral Foley, commander in chief of the Pacific Fleet. After that, the Navy did what it thought it had to do—and somehow managed unofficially to retrieve the highly classified information from NSA headquarters. It was a corrupt incident in an intelligence system that has been held to be above the battle.

American rhetoric did not lead to the loss of innocent lives, and the poor performance of the American intelligence community and the White House cannot diminish the international significance of the Soviet mistake over Sakhalin. Nonetheless, there is much for Americans to learn from the incident and its aftermath. The exaggerations and distortions of what was known about the destruction of Flight 007 demonstrate that there is no intelligence agency in the United States government that can be counted on to challenge the views of the president and his senior advisers. A tragic and brutal Soviet mistake—never acknowledged by Moscow—was escalated into a tinderbox issue on the basis of misunderstood and distorted intelligence, while the NSA, which knew better, chose not to tell others in the government what they didn't want to hear.

BOOK V

Aftermath

18

The Next Time

The hunt by American and Japanese Navy ships for the Korean airliner's flight data and cockpit voice recorders officially ended in late October 1983, after more than six weeks of often tense patrolling and confrontation with the Soviet destroyers that were always nearby. The Soviets refused to permit American or Japanese vessels to search any suspected crash areas inside Soviet waters, and they did their best to disrupt the American and Japanese search in international waters. One effective Soviet destroyer tactic was to steam toward and drive off the Japanese fishing vessels that had been recruited to mark the boundaries of the U.S.-Japanese search areas. The main search site for the United States throughout the crisis, however, was not inside Soviet territory but at least thirty miles southeast of Sakhalin Island, where the Navy had located some underwater "pinging." The airliner's flight recorders were designed to emit such signals for up to thirty days in case of disaster, and

345

American and Japanese vessels spent weeks in fruitless sweeping and dragging on the ocean floor.

The search for the black boxes was over by the time an American Navy officer discovered the small group of Japanese fishermen who, while hauling in octopus near Soviet waters north of Moneron Island, had witnessed the nearby crash of the airliner. American officials subsequently concluded that the Soviets may have dropped a false pinger in the waters east of the island in an effort to drive the American and Japanese search away from the actual crash site. Moscow did briefly permit a team of American and Japanese military and civilian officials to come ashore Sakhalin Island late in September and again in December at Nevelsk, a fishing village on the west coast, to retrieve clothing and other debris picked up from Flight 007. The visits caused some diplomatic pain, however, because the Soviets refused to permit entry to any representatives of the Republic of South Korean, and the Seoul government was extremely distressed—although in private—that the United States decided to go to Nevelsk without even asking for any Korean representation.

The destruction of the airliner and its immediate aftermath reaffirmed the Soviet Union's and the United States' essential distrust of each other and ended any hope of an immediate solution to the expanding nuclear arms race. Late November 1983 saw the failure of the European peace campaign as the West German parliament voted to accept 108 medium-range Pershing II missiles for deployment and the Reagan administration immediately began shipping missile components. The Soviets, as expected, broke off the strategic arms reduction negotiations in Geneva, accusing Washington of "wrecking" the talks and describing the Germans as "nuclear maniacs." Soviet premier Andropov, who would be dead in three months, issued a statement vowing to retaliate for the Pershings by increasing the number of Soviet submarine-based missiles targeted at the United States.

There were many inside the Reagan administration and in sensitive positions in allied governments who soon discovered that misunderstood and then suppressed communications intelligence had been invoked to expand the crisis, but only one spoke out—Prime Minister Pierre Trudeau of Canada. There had been ten Canadians aboard Flight 007, and the White House had been pleased and surprised in early September when Trudeau's liberal government in Canada became the first to join in what Washington hoped would be worldwide sanctions against Aeroflot. Canada, however, is a full partner with the National Security Agency in the collection and sharing of allied communications intelligence,* and within a week of the shootdown, the Canadian intelligence community began circulating its assessment of the incident, concluding that the Soviets had made a tragic mistake. During a political visit in late September to Sault Ste.

---

* Canada's Communications Security Establishment (CSE), Ottawa's equivalent to the NSA, was in fact responsible for writing the final after-action report on the 1978 Soviet shootdown of the Korean airliner in the Kola Peninsula. The CSE is responsible under the SIGINT Combined Operating List (SCOL) for that region of the Soviet Union, and cooperation is close.

Marie, Ontario, Trudeau declared that it was "a sad occasion" that "this kind of accident can happen," and warned that if the "other side" can mistake a commercial 747 for a military craft, the Western powers have to take steps to ensure that more serious accidents don't occur. Two weeks later, on October 4, during a bitter debate in the Canadian House of Commons over his comments, Trudeau again said: "I do not believe that the people in the Kremlin deliberately murdered or killed some two hundred or three hundred passengers in the Korean airliner. I do not believe that. I believe it was a tragic accident, an accident of war."

Trudeau, who resigned as prime minister in early 1984 to practice law in Montreal, acknowledged in a later conversation that he had based his statements, both in Ontario and in the House of Commons, on highly classified communications intelligence—something he chose not to say at the time. "It was obvious to me very early in the game," Trudeau said, "that the Reagan people were trying to create another bone of contention with the Soviets when they didn't have a leg to stand on." He was dismayed, in turn, by the Soviets' denial of responsibility and their refusal to apologize, action that only heightened the anti-Soviet feelings throughout the world. "The Americans knew that it was an accident," Trudeau said, "and the Soviets knew that the plane was not sent by the Americans. The two superpowers were talking past each other."

Trudeau subsequently decided to initiate his personal "peace campaign"—an unprecedented around-the-world sweep later that fall in which the prime minister, insisting that something must be done to reduce international tensions, met with twenty-three heads of state within a month and argued that all world leaders had an obligation to urge the superpowers to begin dealing with each other in a more meaningful way. "The event that tipped the scale was KAL," Trudeau explained later. "I said, 'Well, put your doubts aside' and decided it was time to act." He was awarded the 1984 Albert Einstein Peace Prize for his efforts, although his peace initiative went nowhere.

Major General Jim Pfautz, who had done as much as he could inside the system to tell the real story, remained on active duty as director of Air Force Intelligence until mid-1985, when he retired. He remained controversial to the end and was passed over for promotion to director of the Defense Intelligence Agency—and another star—after telling Secretary of Defense Caspar Weinberger that once in the job he would immediately move to clean house inside the DIA's civilian bureaucracy. His effort to get out the full story of the destruction of Flight 007 left its mark, too; there were many general officers in the military who—in fairness or not—cited Pfautz's ambition and his unwillingness to share intelligence as arguments against further promotion.

Pfautz, in a later interview, remained dismayed about George Shultz's and Ronald Reagan's handling of the shootdown: "We did the best job we could in a very short time, and then we turned it over to the policymakers—and they disgusted me. It was very, very clumsily handled." What the Soviets did over Sakhalin Island "was a single isolated act and if a single isolated event can warp our reactions in such a way, then we'd better get a new act or new people. It's all up for grabs," Pfautz added, "unless we have people in Washington who will weigh in during crises and give them [the Soviets] the benefit of the doubt where it exists. We can't go to the brink every time.

"I feel there's hope for mankind if at a time of crisis we can say, 'Hey, we think they've screwed up.' If you can hold the rhetoric until we get all the facts in, the other guy might say, 'Hey, maybe they're not so bad after all.' I've always felt that we react spastically to the Soviets without getting all the facts. Some day we'll not make it."

In the United States and the Soviet Union, the original beliefs solidified and hardened to such a degree that there was no room for correction or reasoned analysis. For months after the shootdown, the CIA reported on the possible blight to the career of Marshal Alexander Koldunov, who was in charge of the Soviet Air Defense Force on the night it performed so badly. And yet, in April 1984, Koldunov was permitted to publish an article in *Pravda* praising the Air Defense Force for its "high level of readiness." He was promoted to chief marshal of aviation six months later. Marshal Nikolai Ogarkov also seemed to come through unscathed. In September 1984, one year after the shootdown (and four months after the author interviewed him in Moscow), Ogarkov was abruptly removed as chief of the Soviet General Staff. There was speculation that his ouster was related to the military's handling of the Korean Air shootdown, but few facts were available. In June 1985, Ogarkov returned to public life with the publication of a new book on strategic issues. Some U.S. officials insist that Ogarkov was not really demoted, but was reassigned as commander of the Western theater, the Soviet Union's most important combat command. The issue was still unclear for many intelligence officials as of mid-1986; the United States simply did not know what was going on at the top level of the Soviet military.

President Reagan continued to be avidly supported by Americans for his handling of the shootdown and went on to an overwhelming reelection victory over Walter Mondale in 1984. George Shultz, buttressed by his showing in the crisis, became much more influential in Reagan's second term and began to speak out more openly, and more vividly, about what he saw as the Soviet threat. William Casey continued as CIA director in the second term and remained committed to covert and overt challenge to the Soviet Union, which he viewed—despite intelligence to the contrary—as playing a major role in support of the Sandinista government of Nicaragua. William Clark, never comfortable with what he viewed as Nancy Reagan's hostility to him, suddenly resigned as national security adviser in October 1983 and was replaced, after a bitter fight between hard-liners and pragmatists in the Reagan administration, with Robert McFarlane, viewed as a moderate. Richard Burt's hard-line performances, on television and elsewhere, during the Korean Air crisis did not earn him the position he coveted in the second Reagan term—as national security adviser in the White House—and he was named ambassador to West Germany in 1985. Larry Eagleburger resigned that year and joined his former mentor, Henry Kissinger, in business.

As for General Lincoln Faurer, he retired as NSA

director and as a lieutenant general a few months earlier than scheduled in 1985, without being awarded a
final promotion and a fourth star, which most of his
predecessors in the NSA job had won. Faurer's problems were not based on his performance at the NSA,
however, but on what his peers in the government
perceived as an unbecoming arrogance and temper.
His retirement had been hastened by a budget dispute
with a senior Defense Department official, a dispute
based on pique as much as anything else. It was only
his subordinates in the Air Force and the Electronic
Security Command who faulted his action—or lack of
it—during the Korean Air crisis. Where was he when
the State Department and White House made public
and then distorted the NSA intelligence? Why hadn't
he spoken out?

As NSA director, Faurer was charged with protecting America's communications secrets. In theory he
had the right and the obligation to resist George
Shultz's declassification of the Japanese intercepts on
the first day of the shootdown. To have done so, in
fact, would have been in keeping with his reputation.
The general, however, played an active role, with William Casey, in making the material public. He was on
the team that morning. Faurer, unquestionably an
honorable man, was convinced his assessment of the
intelligence was correct. Nonetheless, it is a fact that
if he had concluded otherwise, he would have risked
his standing inside the administration.

In an interview in mid-1985, after he left government service, Faurer reiterated that the initial communications intelligence clearly showed that the
Soviet pilot should have been able to identify the air-

craft as a civilian airliner. He and his two senior managers at NSA, Dick Lord and Bob Rich, made a "corporate decision" that the political good of releasing the intelligence outweighed the long-term harm. "We knew we'd have to pay a penalty for going public"—in terms of future access to Soviet communications in the Sakhalin area—the general said. But the argument for going public was compelling: "It was such an unbelievable act that I don't believe the public would have believed even Ronald Reagan saying that the Soviets had shot down a plane without some proof." He knew there was a different view of the shootdown at Air Force Intelligence, but Major General James Pfautz's opinion on the incident "did not make a great deal of difference." What happened over Sakhalin, Faurer added, was "essentially a SIGINT show"—the intercepts alone told as much of the story as the government needed to know. Pfautz's theory that the Soviets had confused Flight 007 with the Cobra Ball mission that night "never occurred to us because there was absolutely no connection." One of his first acts, said Faurer, who earned his first star as a brigadier general while serving as commander at Shemya, was to make certain that the Cobra Ball had parked at its hangar there before the shootdown. It had done so, and thus, Faurer added, there was no need for George Shultz to make any mention of the RC-135 reconnaissance flight at his news conference.

His view two years later remained the same as on the morning of September 1, the general said: "The Soviets could have IDed it"—Flight 007—and did not. "Therefore, why take them off the hook? Why bend over backwards to say they didn't know—when they could have known?"

The question was rhetorical but many of Faurer's former subordinates in the NSA and Air Force Intelligence could have supplied a good answer, if given the chance: the goal of intelligence is to report what took place and why. What the Soviets should have done is far less important than what they did and why.

Each side found support for its action concerning Flight 007. The Reagan administration viewed the shootdown and the Soviet refusal to accept responsibility for it as proof of the regime's essential brutality and indifference to human rights—and also as justification for the United States' hard-line policies. The Soviets continued to insist that the incident had been provoked by the United States and then manipulated at the United Nations and elsewhere to slander their nation. They saw the American leaders as dishonorable men who could be counted on to manipulate the truth in a crisis.

The Soviets did not know that George Shultz, William Casey, and Ronald Reagan had initially rushed to judgment over Flight 007 in what amounted to good faith—their strong hostility to Communism had led them to misread the intelligence and then, much more ominously, to look the other way when better information became available. Those who ran the American government did not want to learn that the Soviets had honestly been confused and panic-stricken about the enemy intruder, and so they continued to believe what they wanted. They found it easy to agree that the American public could not be told the full story of the shootdown, not only because it was highly classified but also because it would raise doubts about all the United States had said about its lack of involvement in the errant flight of the Korean airliner. The full story, perhaps, would also diminish the American anger toward the Soviet government. That anger would be an obvious political asset in the 1984 elections. Twelve months after the shootdown but only two months before the election, a mid-level State Department official was upbraided by the White House after volunteering, during a background press briefing, his personal opinion that the Soviet pilot did believe he was shooting down an American intelligence plane. The line between what had happened and what had not became blurred with time; what stood out after one year and continues to stand out today is a generally accepted belief that the Soviets, in their brutal fashion, deliberately shot down the Korean airliner.

The Flight 007 incident demonstrates the importance of honest intelligence in a world where the concept of deterrence is predicated on the assumption that the men with their fingers on the trigger have accurate information. Those in Washington who chose to increase international tension, and their counterparts in Moscow who responded in kind, were acting in ignorance of the facts and the realities. Flight 007 was a full-fledged crisis made far more dangerous by the extent of misunderstanding and anti-Soviet feeling it engendered. And yet, for all of the outcry and misunderstanding, deliberate and otherwise, the shootdown did not increase international tensions to the flash point. The world, as Jim Pfautz suggested, may not be so lucky the next time.

Notes

As of June 1986, five books had been published in the United States on the destruction of Flight 007, all of them basically syntheses of the information available in newspapers and magazines. The most useful work was *Black Box*, by Alexander Dallin (University of California, 1985), which is extensively annotated and benefits from Dallin's expertise as a Soviet scholar. Dallin somehow concludes, however, on the basis of no evidence, that "with the passage of time" the argument that the flight of the airliner was "engineered by the United States . . . looms stronger than before." Surprisingly useful was *The KAL 007 Massacre*, by Franz A. Kadell (Western Goals Foundation, 1985). Western Goals was set up by Representative Larry McDonald in 1979 to propagandize about the evils of Communism. Kadell, a West German journalist, while insistently critical of the American press for refusing to always believe and report the worst about the Soviet Union, did not conclude—as many in Western Goals believed—that the real target of the Soviets in the shootdown was McDonald. He also compiled a valuable day-by-day chronology of the crisis, focusing on the public protests over the shootdown around the world. The other works, *Shootdown: Flight 007 and the American Connection*, by R. W. Johnson (Viking, 1986); *KAL Flight 007: The Hidden Story*, by Oliver Clubb (The Permanent Press, 1985), and *Day of the Cobra*, by Jeffrey St. John (Thomas Nelson, 1984), seemed to rely extensively on the available day-to-day newspaper clips, with Johnson and Clubb arguing in essence that Flight 007 was on an espionage mission for the Reagan administration and St. John suggesting, among other things, that the Soviets may have deliberately lured Flight 007 off course in order to shoot it down. None of the authors made any discernible effort to interview the involved American or Japanese military and civilian officials; in general, they took each newspaper account at face value—if it agreed with or added to their own particular thesis.

An excellent general source for the history and organization of the National Security Agency, through the late 1970s, is *The Puzzle Palace*, by James Bamford (Houghton Mifflin, 1982). Bamford provides a much-valued overview of the satellite and technical-intelligence programs of the NSA. Also very useful on imaging and signals intelligence is *The U.S. Intelligence Community* (Ballinger, 1985), by Jeffrey T. Richelson.

The author relied on the day-to-day dispatches on Flight 007 in the New York *Times* and the Washington *Post* for the chronology of events following the shootdown; only articles of special interest are cited herein. It should be emphasized that the identification of sources in these notes is far from complete. Those who did talk on the record, and agreed to be identified as doing so, provided only a small portion of the information in this book. Most of the material was provided during interviews with men and women who processed or analyzed the communications intelligence stemming from the shootdown of Flight 007. Of course they cannot be named. Other officials who served in the White House, State Department, and Pentagon agreed to be interviewed on the condition that they not be named.

1. The First Shootdown

Little comprehensive reporting was done on the 1978 shootdown. One exception was "Shot Down Over Russia!," by

Anthony Paul, in the *Reader's Digest*, November 1978, beginning at page 138. A description of the KH-11 and other photographic satellites can be found in *The Ties That Bind*, by Jeffrey Richelson and Desmond Ball (Allen & Unwin, 1985), at page 97 et seq. See also "The Keyhole Satellite Program," by Richelson, in the *Journal of Strategic Studies*, June 1984, beginning at page 121. Richelson and Ball describe Norway's role in American intelligence collection in *The Ties That Bind*. Much of their information came from *Intelligence Installations in Norway: Their Number, Location, Function and Legality*, by Owen Wilkes and Nilse Petter Gleditsch (PRIO of Oslo, Norway, 1979). The role of American RC-135 reconnaissance aircraft has been widely documented. For background on the strategic need for such flights as seen by the Air Force, see *S.I.O.P.*, by Peter Pringle and William Arkin (Norton, 1983), beginning at page 65. See also "U.S. Airborne ELINT System, Part 3: The Boeing RC-135 Family," by Martin Streetly, in *Jane's Defense Weekly*, March 16, 1985, page 460. Official statistics on the number of U.S. military aircraft that were shot down or reported missing while on flights over or near the Soviet Union can be found, beginning on pages S121283 of the *Congressional Record* for September 14, 1983. The 1968 forced landing of the Seaboard World Airways aircraft on Soviet territory was given extensive coverage in the New York *Times* for the first four days of July 1968. Brzezinski's faux pas (footnote) was reported in the New York *Times;* see "Brzezinski Remark Stirs Fear of Security Breach," by Bernard Weinraub, April 26, 1978, page 3. His remark enraged NSA officials, who felt that the national security adviser had breached security merely to score a short-range propaganda point against the Soviets—a goal not considered worth the risk. "He rubbed their noses in it," one former senior NSA official, still angry, told the author in a 1985 interview. Both Alexander Dallin, at page 81 in *Black Box*, and Andrew Cockburn, at page 227 of *The Threat* (Random House, 1983), his study of the Soviet military, report correctly, although very briefly, on the extent of confusion inside the Soviet Air Defense during the 1978 shootdown.

2. A Fleet Exercise

The Reagan administration's decision to seek a change in the internal policies of the Soviet Union was initially reported by Robert C. Toth in the Los Angeles *Times*, March 16, 1983, "Economic Squeeze of Soviets Ordered." Military expert William Arkin is one of the few to discuss the Navy's forward strategy in terms of arms control: see "Raising the Stakes in the Pacific," by Arkin and David Chappell, in *World Policy Journal*, Summer 1985, page 481. Also see "Provocations at Sea," by Arkin, in the November 1985 *Bulletin of the Atomic Scientists*, page 6. The general atmosphere of the region is discussed in "Tensions in the North Pacific," by Walden Bello and Peter Hayes, in the *Nation* magazine, October 1, 1983, page 274. The overall question of the command and control of nuclear forces is discussed in two excellent books, *Strategic Command and Control*, by Bruce G. Blair (Brookings Institution, 1985), and *The Command and Control of Nuclear Weapons*, by Paul Bracken (Yale University Press, 1983). The cited testimony of Admiral James Watkins can be found at pages 3890 and 3893 of hearings into "Sea Power and Force Projection" before the Senate Armed Services Committee, March 14, 1984. For another view, see "At Sea," by Michael R. Gordon, in the *National Journal*, July 6, 1985, page 1599. The Soviet demarche to the American government was provided to the author by Georgi Kornienko, deputy foreign minister, during a meeting in Moscow in May 1984. It was subsequently confirmed by American embassy officials in Moscow and senior officials in Washington. For a brief history of the Soviet-Japanese debate over the Kurile see *Soviet Power*, by Jonathan Steele (Simon & Schuster, 1983), page 154 et seq. The testimony on the Soviet buildup in the Far East (footnote) was initially cited by Arkin and Chappell. Oleg Sokolov and Thomas Simons were interviewed in Washington.

3. "They Had a Right to Live"

A wealth of detail about preflight briefing and maintenance of Korean Air Flight 007 can be found in *Destruction of Korean Air Lines Boeing 747 over Sea of Japan, 31 August 1983: Report of ICAO Fact-Finding Investigation*, published December 2, 1983, by the International Civil Aviation Authority. The ICAO report is catalogued by ICAO as Document C-WP/7764. For more on John Oldham, Mrs. Rebecca Scruton, and the others, see "Purpose and Chance Put Victims on Flight 007," by Barton Gellman and Peter Perl, Washington *Post*, September 2, 1983, page 1, and "U.S. Toll at 52, Widening Circle of Grief, Chance," by Howard Kurtz and Mary Battiata, Washington *Post*, September 3, 1983, page 1. Franz Kadell's study of Flight 007 is especially detailed on the victims aboard the airliner as well as the reaction among conservatives, including Senator Jesse Helms, in the United States.

4. Cobra Ball I

For a physical description of Shemya, see "Geology of the Near Islands, Alaska," by Olcott Gates, Howard A. Powers, and Ray E. Wilcox, in the *Geological Survey Bulletin, 1028-U* (U.S. Government Printing Office, 1971), beginning at page 710. For an account of the lassitude of duty during World War II in the Aleutians, read *Williwaw*, Gore Vidal's first published novel (E. P. Dutton, 1946, reprinted by Ballantine, 1978). "Williwaw" is the Indian word for the prevailing winds of the Aleutians. Far more upbeat is "That Island Base," by Major R. J. Hayes, in *Airman* magazine, January 1984. A basic source of information about current conditions for the military men stationed at Shemya was the *Hard Rock Times*, the weekly newspaper of Shemya Air Force Base. Copies of the newspaper were made available under the Freedom of Information Act. Much detail on the operations of the RC-135s at Shemya was provided in a regulation entitled "Operations Aircrew and Staff Procedures," dated September 30, 1983, and promulgated by the Headquarters Sixth

Strategic Wing (SAC), Eielson Air Force Base, Alaska. The regulation was made available under the Freedom of Information Act. Edwin Williamson was interviewed at his photography store in Natick, Massachusetts; his mistaken belief that there still were intelligence functions at Shemya in 1983 was initially reported in "The Last Flight of KAL 007," by James Bamford, Washington *Post* magazine, January 8, 1984, beginning at page 4. A very confused and misleading account of the capabilities of the RC-135 flights is "Recon Plane Has Powers Washington Concealing," by T. Edward Eskelson and Tom Bernard, who served aboard RC-135s during the Vietnam War, published on September 19, 1983, in the Cleveland *Plain-Dealer*. The Eskelson-Bernard article, initially written for the Denver *Post*, suggested that the Cobra Ball flight was capable of monitoring the Soviet scramble over Kamchatka as well as ground communications of the Air Defense Force. It was reprinted in dozens of American and European newspapers and was heavily relied upon by those who believed that the United States could have warned Flight 007 of its peril well before the shootdown. The operations of DEFSMAC were described in *The Puzzle Palace*; documents on the activity also were made available under the Freedom of Information Act. The loss of the two forward listening posts in Iran was widely reported in the United States; see, for example, "U.S. Abandons Base in Iran Near Soviet," by Richard Burt, New York *Times*, March 1, 1979, page 1. For a glimpse of the perceived intelligence loss, see "U.S. Aides Say Loss of Iran Sites Cuts Data on Soviet Missile Tests," by Bernard Weinraub, New York *Times*, April 25, 1979.

5. First Signals

For a profile of the Air Forces Electronic Security Command, see "The Electronic Security Command," by Hal Gershanoff, *Journal of Electronic Defense*, April 1983. Much basic information on the organization and day-to-day operations of the Electronic Security Command was obtained under the Freedom of Information Act. Most important was the top-secret "History of the 6920th Electronic Security Group" for July 1 through December 31, 1983, written by Sergeant Michael J. Joyner, and a similar "History" from January 1, 1984, to June 30, 1984, written by Joyner and Staff Sergeant David S. Sublett. The 6920th also submitted an extensive year-end review and evaluation to NSA headquarters for 1983; that document also was supplied in declassified form under the Freedom of Information Act. Misawa's weekly base newspaper, *Northern Light,* was immensely useful, not only in providing data about current operations but also for its history of the region and the 6920th. Another excellent unclassified source was "Misawa AB," an unofficial pamphlet published privately off-base that is distributed to all new arrivals at Misawa. A telephone directory for the 6920th as of the fall of 1983 was made available through the Freedom of Information Act.

The history and locale of Misawa are special; the base itself, on the northeastern tip of the main Japanese island of Honshu, seems more appropriate for a college campus than for a military facility. The weather, 360 miles north of Tokyo, is idyllic, with crisp falls and snowy winters; numerous ski areas are within a short car-ride. A huge lake lies just to the southwest and provides boating, fishing, and swimming in the spring and summer. The area's woods and pastures prompted Japanese breeders as far back as the thirteenth century to set up horse farms; by the nineteenth century there were an estimated 700 such farms in the immediate area. Misawa, not unnaturally, became the cavalry training center for the Japanese Imperial Army and remained unchanged in that mission until 1938, when a primitive airstrip was cut from the woods as a bomber base. The initial assignment was to defend northern Japan during the war with China and, if necessary, to launch attacks on the United States and the Soviet Union. The Japanese Naval Air Corps took over the base in 1942 as a training-and-research facility; in 1944, with the war against the United States and its allies going poorly, Misawa became a training site for the kamikaze suicide pilots who inflicted so much damage to allied forces in the last year of the war. In August 1945, just a few days before the end of the World War II, American B-29 bombers struck and heavily damaged the base.

Americans first occupied Misawa the next month and began rebuilding; by the end of 1946, control of the facility was handed over to the U.S. Army's 49th Fighter Group. The base has remained in American hands since, and by the mid-1980s, amid the increased U.S.-USSR tensions in the Far East, it was undergoing a construction boom. In 1985, a squadron of the Air Force's most advanced fighter plane, the F-16, was deployed at Misawa, the first time in fourteen years that American fighter planes were stationed in Honshu. The air base's isolation in northern Japan and its location—across the Sea of Japan from North Korea, China, and the Soviet Union—made its designation as an electronic-intelligence site inevitable. The first detachment set up camp in 1954 with tents, prefabricated buildings, and an operations center covering 5,000 square feet. By 1985 the complex's 100,000-square-foot operations center was considered vastly inadequate.

Even low-status assignments at the 6920th can have implications and importance. For example, the NSA has in the past invested enormous resources in monitoring weather reports from the Soviet Union and China. Both nations, according to former NSA officials, were reluctant to broadcast reliable weather reports—they simply didn't want the rest of the world to know. The NSA monitored all civilian and military weather broadcasts because such data were considered an important barometer of pending military exercises and also a possible strategic indicator: the broadcast of a strange weather forecast could be the first signal of a surprise military attack. One major Soviet rocket-force facility for years constantly broadcast high-altitude wind-and-icing reports, data that could affect the in-flight performance of an intercontinental ballistic missile. The first five characters of those reports were in code and referred to the location in the world to which the weather forecast pertained. The NSA learned that the messages were usually bogus; the base was simply broadcasting phony weather information twenty-four hours a day. The station continued to be monitored nonetheless, because it was known to have missiles targeted on the United States under its control; if the weather information it was broadcasting, bogus or not, turned out to be for a location in the United States, it would be reported as a critical event to NSA.

Similarly, some all-night radio stations in key areas of the Soviet Union have been constantly monitored by NSA personnel for years—and may still be—for no other reason than to provide a baseline for bomb-damage assessments. The disappearance of a radio signal after a nuclear strike would be evidence that the weapon had been effective. (Such monitoring will be obsolete by 1988, when a new U.S. satellite system, the Nuclear Detection System, is scheduled to become fully operational. The satellites are reportedly capable of fixing the location of a nuclear burst—to within 100 meters—at any point in the world.) Some of the twenty-four-hour stations would also provide a navigation waypoint for U.S. strategic bombers in case they were ordered to attack nuclear targets inside the USSR.

The amount of data collected on a daily basis by the 6920th ESC and other field stations throughout the world is staggering, and the National Security Agency has a mechanism for organizing and disseminating information. Known as TEXTA, an acronym for technical abstracts of traffic analysis, it is considered the bible of communications intelligence. In essence, TEXTA is the main data bank and cataloguing procedure maintained by the signals intelligence community at every facility in the world. It is in force, too, for those nations—Britain, Canada, Australia, and New Zealand—that collect and share communications intelligence as partners with the National Security Agency. Other allied nations with whom the United States maintains collaborative arrangements for the collection and processing of communications intelligence, such as Japan, Taiwan, South Korea, West Germany, Norway, and the Philippines, also use TEXTA.

As explained by former NSA officials, TEXTA is primarily an accounting device in which all intercepted communications are given what is known as a case notation, composed of four letters and five numbers. The first two letters of the case notation determine which country is involved; Cuba is CU, for example, and China is CH. (The Soviet Union, because of its enormous size and the enormous volume of material collected, has been given only one letter under TEXTA—R, to enable the case notation system to catalogue the data efficiently.) The third letter usually denotes the organization or branch of military service that is being intercepted, and the final letter depicts which specific geographic district is involved. In Soviet intercepts, the fourth letter usually depicts the technical means of communication that is intercepted; whether, for example, Morse code or telephone. The numbers in a typical TEXTA sequence are meant to tell which type of communications link is involved: that is, whether it is a main secure line between two Soviet Air Force bases, or a less consequential link between a remote headquarters and a surface-to-air missile battery. Every military and civilian facility in the world has been provided with a classified guidebook to the case notation system, and an experienced NSA operator can tell within seconds which country, organization, location, and echelon of headquarters he or she is dealing with. RACS 00201 would mean, to an experienced operator, that he or she is dealing with an intercepted voice transmission, from a secondary communications link, between Soviet tactical Air Force bases at Tbilisi, the capital of Georgia, and Batumi, a city just above the Turkish border on the Black Sea. Batumi used to be former Soviet premier Nikita Khrushchev's favorite resort and was an area heavily monitored at one time by the NSA.

TEXTA obviously provides the framework that helps the NSA function, but it is far from the most important document in the SIGINT community. Most NSA officials would agree that a bulky black-bound set of volumes known as TECHINs, for technical instructions, are the core of the American ability to collect information successfully. TE-CHINs are very detailed documents that describe how the NSA's code-breaking machines work and how an NSA intercept facility operates. The American government has never publicly said so, but it is well-known inside the intelligence community that much of the TEXTA and many TE-CHINs have fallen into the hands of the Soviet Union. The documents were aboard the USS *Pueblo*, a spy ship on patrol for the Naval Security Group, when it was seized in January 1968 by the North Koreans. For reasons not made clear, the *Pueblo* was carrying—to the NSA's subsequent horror—as noted in a footnote in the text, highly classified documents, including many TECHINs, that had little to do with its reconnaissance mission. "We'd just gotten too sloppy," one Naval Security Group officer recalled, adding that the spy ship also had "the entire corpus of NSA material on Soviet satellites." After the seizure of the *Pueblo*, and an internal review, the NSA sharply reduced the number of documents that could be made available to field sites. The full extent of the loss to national security did not emerge in the subsequent court-martial proceedings and congressional investigations. Before the seizure, for example, the Naval Security Group had been able to deduce not only when the Soviet fleet would change communications call signs but what the new call signs would be. "Before the first of the month [when Soviet signals were routinely switched], we could predict what the new Soviet system would be," one involved officer recalled. "We were way ahead. We knew where they were and when. The *Pueblo* gave away this enormous advantage."

6. Project CLEF

Project CLEF was listed by name in the index to the 6920th ESC's annual history and assessment that was presented to NSA headquarters as part of the annual competition for best NSA field station. The top-secret document was declassified and released to the author in 1985 by the Electronic Security Command.

7. Two CRITICs

The 6920th's first CRITIC received by the State Department's Operations Center was logged in at 7:10 P.M. Washington time, according to a declassified Situation Report

("No. 1") of the Department's Informal Working Group on KAL Incident, which was made available to the author. A good chronology of early-morning events in Japan can be found in "KAL Aircraft Incident and SDF [Self-Defense Forces]," by Yoshitaro Masuo, published in Japanese in the May 1985 issue of *Sekai*. Masuo is a member of the Association for Clearing Up the Truth of the KAL Aircraft Incident; a translation of his article was made available by the State Department. See also the previously cited Bamford article in the Washington *Post* magazine, "The Last Flight of KAL 007." General Lincoln Faurer was interviewed in suburban Washington.

8. First Analysis

General James Pfautz was interviewed at his home in suburban Virginia. It should be noted that he was interviewed after men who had served under him had provided the author with an account of his staff's action that night. Pfautz agreed to discuss the politics of the situation, not the specifics, and, unlike other officers and enlisted men, was willing to be quoted on his opinions. For one of the most recent of the many articles and analyses of the failure of the current military intelligence system, see "The Pentagon's Intelligence Mess," by former CIA director Stansfield Turner, Washington *Post* Sunday "Outlook" section, January 12, 1986, page C-1.

9. The Announcement

For *Time* magazine's criticisms of Shultz, see "Disappearing Act at Foggy Bottom," August 8, 1983, page 28. William Clark was on the cover of the magazine that week. The *Time* article on him, entitled "The Man with the President's Ear," begins at page 30. The New York *Times* Magazine published its cover piece, entitled "The Influence of William Clark," by Steven R. Weisman, on August 14. Shultz's threat to return to California was made public in the August 22, 1983, edition of *Newsweek* magazine, "Shultz: No More Mr. Nice

Guy?" For analyses of Shultz's dwindling status, see "Shultz Finds He's No Longer Immune to Criticism," by Bernard Gwertzman, New York *Times*, June 7, 1983; "Shultz's First Year," by James Reston, New York *Times*, August 3, 1983; "Shultz No Longer Perceived as Driving Force in Foreign Policy," by John M. Goshko and Michael Getler, Washington *Post*, August 15, 1983, and "Shultz—on the Spot Again," by Henry Trewhitt, Baltimore *Sun*, August 21, 1983. The continued State Department contacts with the Soviets were initially reported by Leslie H. Gelb in the New York *Times*, June 30, 1983, "Expanding Contacts with Soviet: Shultz and Dobrynin Make a Start." For excellent background on the Pershing II issue and the Reagan administration's stance on arms control, see *Deadly Gambits*, by Strobe Talbott (Knopf, 1984); Burt's quote about "getting them in" can be found on page 187. CBS and NBC provided transcripts of the various broadcasts, scheduled and unscheduled, in the first days of the crisis, and ABC's *Nightline* also supplied transcripts of its relevant shows.

10. "We Ate Their Sandwich"

General Jerome O'Malley was commander of the Air Force Tactical Air Command when he was killed. See the Washington *Post*, April 23, 1985, for his obituary. General John Vessey was interviewed by telephone in his retirement home in Garrison, Minnesota.

11. The President

For the news conferences and briefings, the day-to-day coverage of the Washington *Post*, the New York *Times*, and major television networks was relied upon, as were the official White House and State Department transcripts. Soviet documents were provided by officials in Moscow as well as by the CIA's Foreign Broadcast Information Service (FBIS), which publishes official translations daily and distributes them widely to government offices, libraries, and journalists. Dozens of magazine and newspaper articles emerged in the first months after the crisis outlining what amounted to a conspiracy theory about the shootdown. The articles usually suggested that the Korean airliner had deliberately gone off course and, in a few cases, also implied that the White House had to have been behind the incident. See "K.A.L. 007: What the U.S. Knew and When We Knew It," by David Pearson, *The Nation*, August 18–25, 1984; "K.A.L. 007: Unanswered Questions," also by Pearson, *The Nation*, August 17–24, 1985; "The unQuiet Grave of Flight 007," by Walt Crowley, *LA Weekly*, October 3–9, 1984; see also "Safe on Sakhalin," *LA Weekly*, October 26–November 1, 1984; "Was KAL 007 a Spy?," by Jim Motovalli, Hartford *Advocate*, October 24, 1984; "What Really Happened to KE007," by Duncan Campbell, *New Statesman*, April 26, 1985; and "Reassessing the Sakhalin Incident," by PQ Mann, *Defense Attaché* No. 3 (May–June), 1984. The *Defense Attaché* article, whose author was never identified (PQ Mann was a pseudonym), posited a complicated theory involving American intelligence coordination with the overflights of an American-manned space shuttle flight. It received wide publicity. The magazine was sued by Korean Air Lines and formally retracted its account in a British court on November 19, 1984. A critique of the original article, "Sakhalin: Sense and Nonsense," by James Oberg, was published in *Defense Attaché* No. 1 (January–February), 1985. There were many in the CIA and the Pentagon who were convinced that some of the articles, including those mentioned herein, had been underwritten by the Soviet Union as part of a disinformation plot. A subsequent investigation turned up no evidence to support the view, which was said to be shared by William Casey, the CIA director. The most extensive rebuttal of the various charges and accusations stemming from Flight 007 came in an analysis entitled "Tragedy of Errors," by Thomas Maertens, a State Department foreign service officer, published in the *Foreign Service Journal* of September 1985, beginning at page 24. Maerten's views, which are known to be shared by many government officials, were officially described as his own, and not those of the U.S. government, which nonetheless reviewed the article prior to publication. The suggestion that antiaircraft missiles be shipped to Afghanistan (footnote) is reported in "Casey Strengthens Roles Under 'Reagan Doctrine,'" by Patrick E. Tyler and David B. Ottaway, Washington *Post*, March 3, 1986. Lee Atwater was interviewed at his offices in suburban Virginia. Stuart Spencer was interviewed at a Washington hotel. Tommy Toles was interviewed in Washington, as was Frederic Smith. Michael Deaver was interviewed in Washington, as was Kenneth Duberstein. Charles Lichenstein was interviewed by telephone. W. Scott Thompson was interviewed in Washington. Ronald Reagan's decision-making process has baffled many; for one of the better attempts to come to grips with it, see "The Mind of the President," by Leslie H. Gelb, in the New York *Times* Sunday magazine for October 6, 1985. Gelb makes the point that Reagan, as in the Flight 007 crisis, relies on his instinct and intuition more than on empirical data.

12. A Good Ally

For an overview of the defense issues between Japan and the United States, see "Japanese Defense Policy: Issues for the United States," by Larry A. Niksch, Congressional Research Service, the Library of Congress, December 15, 1984. Masaharu Gotoda was interviewed in Tokyo. Dennis Wilham was interviewed in Tokyo. For details on the GIs receiving token departure gifts when the Seaboard World Airways DC-8 was forced down in 1968, see "Pilot of Freed Jet Denies He Flew in Soviet Airspace," by Robert Trumbull, New York *Times*, July 4, 1968. Jangnai Sohn was interviewed in Washington. Vice Minister Shinji Yazaki was interviewed in Tokyo, as was Ambassador Mike Mansfield.

13. Defending the Faith

Michael Getler's worrisome—to the White House—article in the Washington *Post* was headlined "Analysts Suspect Mis-Identification Led to the Attack," and appeared on page 1 on Saturday, September 3, 1983. Leslie Janka was interviewed in Washington. Stephen Meyer was interviewed at his office in Cambridge, Massachusetts. For more on the ambivalent poll, see "Poll Finds Country Confused on Jet Downing," by Adam Clymer, New York *Times*, September 16, 1983, page 1. Bentley Elliott was interviewed by telephone at his White House office. Anthony Dolan was interviewed in Washington. NSDD 102, as declassified, was provided to the author under the Freedom of Information Act. Nikolai Ogarkov was interviewed at Defense Ministry offices in Moscow. For a commentary on "*Yolki palki*," see an unpublished paper by Michael K. Launer and Marilyn J. Young of the Florida State University at Tallahassee. The paper is subtitled "Who Said What on the Night of September 1, 1983?" Robert Kiernan was interviewed by telephone in Chicago. Dimitri Simes was interviewed at his offices at the Carnegie Endowment for International Peace in Washington; Charles Maynes, also at the Carnegie Endowment, was interviewed by telephone there. Henry Catto was interviewed in Washington. For an account of Shultz's gamesmanship at Madrid, see ". . . and Shultz Jousts with Gromyko," by Bernard Gwertzman, New York *Times*, September 13, 1983. The full 21-page transcript of the Moscow news conference of Ogarkov, Kornienko, and Zamyatin was published by the Foreign Broadcast Information Service on September 12, 1983, beginning at page DD-10 of the USSR International Affairs section. The State Department's acknowledgment that the government's initial translation of the SU-15 interceptor pilot's remarks had been faulty was fully covered by the press; see "A New U.S. Transcript Indicates Soviet Pilot Fired 'Cannon Bursts,'" by Bernard Gwertzman, New York *Times*, September 12, 1983. Senator Frank Murkowski's letter to the Department of Transportation about landing rights for Korean Air Lines and Mrs. Elizabeth Dole's response were released under the Freedom of Information Act. William Clark's renewed attack on the Soviets over Flight 007 led to some caustic headlines; see "Yes, It Is the 'Evil Empire,'" Washington *Post* "Outlook," September 18, 1983, page C-5. Andropov's harsh September 28 speech caused only a mild stir in Washington; see "White

House Restrained in Reacting to Andropov," by Bernard Gwertzman, New York *Times*, September 30, 1983. For the importance of the Andropov statement, see *Détente and Confrontation*, by Raymond L. Garthoff (Brookings Institution, 1985), pages 1015–18. The New York *Times* story hinting at a more complicated intelligence picture was "U.S. Experts Say Soviet Didn't See Jet Was Civilian," by David Shribman, October 7, 1983. For the government's response, see "Officials Deny Report KAL Attack an Error," by Ted Agres, Washington *Times*, October 13, 1983, and "Second Opinion," *Time* magazine, October 17, 1983, page 25. The essayist William Pfaff was one of the few to grasp the significance of the American manipulation of the intelligence about Flight 007; see "How U.S. Distorted Jet Crisis," Los Angeles *Times*, November 1, 1983, page 1-E.

14. An Official Inquiry

The Inertial Navigation System and its link to the errant flight path of the Korean airliner has been exhaustively studied, with those who believe that the U.S. government had some role in the incident arguing that it would be impossible for the INS aboard Flight 007 to fail as thoroughly as it did without myriad and all-but-impossible-to-ignore warnings. This view is argued heatedly by, among others, David Pearson in his *Nation* magazine articles. See a two-part series, beginning May 20, 1984, by Murray Sayle, "Flightpath to Disaster," in the London Sunday *Times* for another point of view. Sayle's articles were subsequently published in slightly different form on April 25, 1985, in the *New York Review of Books*, "KE007: A Conspiracy of Circumstance." For David Pearson's rejoinder and Sayle's answer to that, see "The Fate of KE007: An Exchange," in the *New York Review of Books* for September 26, 1985. It was this debate that helped attract Harold Ewing to the issue. Ewing was interviewed both in Washington and by telephone at his home in Sumter, South Carolina.

William Reynard's testimony came at a hearing on September 19, 1983, into "Aircraft Navigation Technology and

Errors" before the House Subcommittee on Transportation, Aviation, and Materials. The analysis of airline safety (footnote) came from "Airline Safety Record in a Nose Dive," by Douglas Feaver, Washington *Post*, September 14, 1983. For more on airline safety, see another Feaver dispatch, "Flaws Cited in Technology on Korean Jet," Washington *Post*, September 11, 1983. For a typical press account of the December ICAO study, see "ICAO Report Dismisses Soviet Charges," by James Ott, *Aviation Week & Space Technology*, December 19, 1983. ICAO's Air Navigation Commission's report was entitled *Final Report of Investigation as Required by Council Resolution of 16 September 1983*, and published as document C-WP/7809 on February 2, 1984.

15. To Kamchatka

Detail on the background and experience of the crew members of Korean Flight 007 came from the December 1983 ICAO report cited earlier. For more on the error in Arrow Air's weight-and-balance manifest (footnote), see "Error on Arrow Jet's Weight," New York *Times*, February 15, 1986. The 1977 Canary Islands 747 crash and the 1974 crash near Dulles Airport were cited by Douglas Feaver in his September 11, 1983, dispatch in the Washington *Post*. Harold Ewing's initial written analysis of Flight 007's INS trouble, as presented to officials of ICAO's Air Navigation Commission, was entitled "An Analysis and Scenario of Probable Cause of the Course Deviation Incident FLT KE007." It was undated. The November 1980 Korean Air Lines crash was covered only briefly by the American press: see "Jet Crashes on Landing at Seoul: 8 of 226 Aboard Are Believed Dead," by Henry Scott Stokes, New York *Times*, November 20, 1983, page A-14. Information about the suicide of the crew was kept from the press but became known to Harold Ewing and to others inside the airliner industry. ICAO's initial report included a full transcript of all transmissions from Flight 007 to Anchorage and Tokyo, as monitored by FAA facilities, as well as an independent translation of the Soviet interceptor pilot's comments.

16. Cobra Ball II

Marshal Kirsanov was interviewed for more than five hours, including over lunch, at a Soviet military installation outside Moscow. The Air Force research paper mentioned in a footnote was entitled "Compatibility of Soviet and Western Airborne Communication Transceivers" and was published December 30, 1983, by the Air Force's Foreign Technology Division as document FTD-2660P-127/38-83.

17. Shootdown

See the previously cited Arkin-Chappell paper in the *World Policy Journal* for more on the Sea of Okhotsk and its strategic importance. An accurate account of the Soviet purge was filed by Dusko Doder, the senior Moscow correspondent of the Washington *Post* (who had been out of Moscow during most of September) for publication on October 6, 1983; "Soviets Said to Remove Air Officers." Doder also revealed in the dispatch, with no details, that there had been direct telephone contact between the Soviet Far East command and "top military officials in Moscow." His information was the closest any journalist would come to the truth. A good account of the development of the scrambler, as well as fascinating history of the early days of communications intelligence, can be found in *Alan Turing: The Enigma*, by Andrew Hodges (Simon & Schuster Touchstone, 1984). General Lincoln Faurer's protest about too much publicity was reported in the September 20, 1983, edition of *Aerospace Daily*: "Intelligence Community Has Said Enough About KAL 007: NSA Chief."

18. The Next Time

The hunt by the American and Japanese navies for the black boxes, and the Soviet interference with the search, were extensively covered in the daily press. Pierre Trudeau's troublesome speech in Ontario was reported by *The Sault Star* on September 26, 1983: "Peace Requires Patience—PM."

Trudeau's remarks in the House of Commons can be found on page 27720 of the *Commons Debates* for October 4, 1983. The prime minister's peace campaign was the subject of a cover story in *Maclean's* magazine for December 5, 1983, "Trudeau's Peace Crusade," by Robert Miller. Trudeau was interviewed by telephone at his law offices in Montreal. Ogarkov's demise—and seeming revival—has been the subject of intense study by American intelligence agencies as they try to estimate its significance. See "Ousted Soviet Chief of Staff Returns to Scene as Author," by Dusko Doder, Washington *Post*, June 10, 1985.

Acknowledgments

Robert Loomis, my editor at Random House, and Howard Kaminsky, Publisher and Chief Executive Officer of Random House Trade Department, consistently encouraged me, financially and otherwise, to write this book. Bob Loomis, as usual, was caring and intelligent in his editing of the manuscript.

This book also was immensely aided by a number of men who cannot be named, former members of the American intelligence community who took time to read the manuscript carefully and make recommendations as to accuracy and interpretation. Their goal was to ensure that the process works better in the inevitable next crisis.

William M. Arkin, an expert on military affairs, and his staff—Julie Morrissey, Kathleen Clark, David Chappell, and Richard Fieldhouse—at the Arms Race and Nuclear Weapons Research Project in Washington worked closely with me in shaping my requests for documents under the Freedom of Information Act. Arkin also provided many helpful suggestions and recommendations during the research and writing of this book. Additional research was handled expertly by Andrew Nussbaum.

Finally, my agent, Sterling Lord, was as steady and dependable as his backhand.

—Seymour M. Hersh
Washington, D.C.
May 1986

Index

379

About the Author

SEYMOUR M. HERSH was born in Chicago in 1937 and graduated from the University of Chicago. He began his newspaper career as a police reporter for the City News Bureau in Chicago. After Army service, he was hired by United Press International in Pierre, South Dakota. In 1963 he joined the Associated Press in Chicago and in 1965 went to Washington for the AP to cover the Pentagon. He served as press secretary and speech writer for Senator Eugene J. McCarthy in the famed "Children's Crusade"—the 1968 New Hampshire Democratic primary campaign against Lyndon Johnson. In 1969, as a free-lance journalist, Mr. Hersh wrote the first account of the My Lai massacre, distributing five newspaper stories on the atrocity through Dispatch News Service. He joined the New York *Times* in 1972 and worked out of both Washington and New York until his resignation in 1979 to begin *The Price of Power.* In early 1983 he joined the *Atlantic* magazine as National Correspondent.

Mr. Hersh has won more than a dozen major journalism prizes. For his account of the My Lai massacre he earned the 1970 Pulitzer Prize for International Reporting, the George Polk Award, the Sigma Delta Chi Distinguished Service Award, and a second Polk Award in 1974. The next year he won the Drew Pearson Award, the John Peter Zenger Freedom of the Press Award, the Sidney Hillman Foundation Award, and a third Polk Award for his stories on the CIA and Chile and on CIA domestic spying. In 1981 he received a second Sigma Delta Chi Award and his fourth Polk Award for two articles in the New York *Times Magazine* on the involvement of former CIA agents in arms sales to Libya. He is also the recipient of the National Book Critics Circle Award and the Los Angeles *Times* Book Award for *The Price of Power: Kissinger in the Nixon White House.*

Mr. Hersh's previous books are *Chemical and Biological Warfare: America's Hidden Arsenal; My Lai 4: A Report on the Massacre and Its Aftermath; Cover-up: The Army's Secret Investigation of the Massacre of My Lai;* and *The Price of Power: Kissinger in the Nixon White House.* His articles have appeared in *The New Yorker, Saturday Review,* the *New York Review of Books,* and the *New Republic.* He lives in Washington with his wife and three children.